BRADDOCK'S BIG RACE GUIDE

BRADDOCK'S BIG RACE GUIDE

PETER BRADDOCK

Longman

Longman Scientific & Technical,
Longman Group UK Limited,
Longman House, Burnt Mill, Harlow,
Essex CM20 2JE, England
and Associated Companies throughout the world.

First published 1989

British Library Cataloguing in Publication Data

Braddock, Peter, *1930–*
    Braddock's big race guide.
    1. England. Racehorses. Racing. Races
    I. Title
    798.4′00942
    ISBN 0-582-03186-9

Set in 10/11pt Linotron Bembo

Printed and Bound in Great Britain
at the Bath Press, Avon

CONTENTS

CONTENTS

PHOTOGRAPHY

Photographs on pages 5, 8, 20, 24, 27, 38, 42, 49, 61, 64, 73, 76, 79, 82, 105, 107, 116, 121, 124, 126, 130, 136, 139, 143, 146, 151, 155, 160, 181, 188, 192, 194, 199, 211, 216, 219, 223, 227 and front cover by **Ed Byrne.**

Photographs on pages 15, 17, 45, 52, 55, 58, 67, 70, 85, 99, 102, 111, 168, 174, 203 and back cover by **Alec Russell.**

SPONSORSHIP

Sponsorship of individual races has benefited racing in many ways, not least in the huge rise in available prize money for competitors.

However, sponsorship does change over the years, and in this survey of the past fifteen years of racing it has not been practicable to make reference to the changing details of sponsorship, except where a sponsor's name, by custom and practice, has become an integral part of the name of a particular race.

In due acknowledgement to these benefactors of racing we list here the sponsorships of the major races covered in this book, as known at the time of going to press.

PATTERN RACES

Trust House Forte Mile	Sandown	April
General Accident 1000 Guineas	Newmarket	April/May
General Accident Jockey Club Stakes	Newmarket	April/May
General Accident 2000 Guineas	Newmarket	April/May
Mecca Dante Stakes	York	May
Crowthers Yorkshire Cup	York	May
Juddmonte Lockinge Stakes	Newbury	May
Sears Temple Stakes	Sandown	May
Ever Ready Derby	Epsom	June
Hanson Coronation Cup	Epsom	June
Gold Seal Oaks	Epsom	June
Coral Eclipse Stakes	Sandown	July
Norcross July Cup	Newmarket	July
King George VI and Queen Elizabeth Diamond Stakes	Ascot	July
Swettenham Stud Sussex Stakes	Goodwood	July
Scottish Equitable Richmond Stakes	Goodwood	July
Vodafone Nassau Stakes	Goodwood	July
Walmac International Geoffrey Freer Stakes	Newbury	August
Scottish Equitable Gimcrack Stakes	York	August
William Hill Spring Championship	York	August
Waterford Crystal Mile	Goodwood	August
Vernons Sprint Cup	Haydock	September
Kikuka Shoo Park Hill Stakes	Doncaster	September

Laurent Perrier Champagne Stakes	Doncaster	September
Holsten Pils St. Leger	Doncaster	September
Rokeby Farms Mill Reef Stakes	Newbury	September
Hoover Fillies Mile	Ascot	September
Tattersalls Cheveley Park Stakes	Newmarket	October
Tattersalls Middle Park Stakes	Newmarket	October
Cheveley Park Stud Sun Chariot Stakes	Newmarket	October
Ricard Challenge Stakes	Newmarket	October
Three Chimneys Dewhurst Stakes	Newmarket	October
Dubai Champion Stakes	Newmarket	October
William Hill Futurity Stakes	Doncaster	October

HANDICAPS

William Hill Lincoln Handicap	Doncaster	March
Ladbroke European Free Handicap	Newmarket	April
Insulpak Victoria Cup	Ascot	April
Ladbroke Chester Cup	Chester	May
Newcastle 'Brown Ale' Northumberland Plate Handicap	Newcastle	June
Coral Eclipse Stakes	Sandown	July
William Hill Stewards Cup	Goodwood	July
Exchange Telegraph Extel Stakes	Goodwood	July
Tote Diamond Ebor Handicap	York	August
Tote Portland Handicap	Doncaster	September
Ladbrokes Ayr Gold Cup	Newbury	September
William Hill Cambridgeshire	Newmarket	October
Tote Cesarewitch	Newmarket	October
William Hill November Handicap	Doncaster	November

INTRODUCTION

Braddock's Big Race Guide is a study of the most important races in the British Flat Racing calendar. These include the famous Classics, the Derby, the Oaks, the One Thousand and Two Thousand Guineas and St Leger, plus top races such as the King George VI and Queen Elizabeth Stakes, the Eclipse Stakes and similar prestige prizes together with popular handicaps like the Lincoln, the Cambridgeshire and the Ebor. These top races (excluding the handicaps), form the backbone of the British Pattern Race system. The *Big Race Guide* gives statistics and tables of **all results since 1975.** The information in the tables is presented in the following order: **year, winning horse's name, age, weight (in stones and pounds), trainer, odds, and number of runners.**

THE PATTERN RACE SYSTEM

The Pattern Race system as it stands at present numbers just over one hundred top-class races. These are carefully programmed throughout the racing season to provide the essential competition that identifies the best horses of all ages over all distances.

It was established in the late 1960s in response to proposals set up by a Jockey Club committee. The idea was to ensure the maintenance of high-quality racing which would be attractive to the public. In practice this meant retaining the traditions and structure of the five Classic races whose worth had been proven over almost two centuries of racing, whilst paying due regard to the needs of the modern world.

The speed element fundamental to precocious 2-year-old racing was addressed whilst at the same time consideration was given to horses after their 3-year-old season, and the incentives necessary to keep them in training as older horses.

The British Pattern Race system proved so proficient in practice

1

that it served as a model for a European Pattern Race programme that was founded in 1971. Britain, Ireland and France co-ordinated their top-class race programmes (later Germany and Italy also joined) to provide exciting big-race competition which spanned international borders.

However, this wider approach also demanded that an internationally accepted grading of races be instigated, so their value could be recognised. This led to races within the Pattern Race system being divided into three categories of merit: Group I, Group II, and Group III.

GROUP I RACES – are the top grade. They are the Classic races, of championship standard and therefore of international importance.

GROUP II RACES – are the second grade. Whilst not of championship importance or of Classic standard they still hold an international significance.

GROUP III RACES – are the lowest grade. They are not of Classic or championship standard but often serve as trials for these races. Therefore they are principally of domestic interest only.

Group races are easily comparable tests of ability because horses meet each other at basically level weights. There is provision, however, for age and sex allowance.

The weight for age allowance (WFA) is scale of weight where older horses concede weight to younger horses on a continuously decreasing scale as the season progresses.

Sex allowance is where fillies or mares receive a weight allowance from colts and geldings: 2-year-old fillies receive a 5 lb weight concession whilst 3-year-olds and upwards receive a 3 lb weight allowance.

GROUP I RACES – are strictly level weight contests with only WFA allowance and sex allowance and are always run without horses carrying penalties.

GROUP II RACES – are similarly level weight contests with WFA and sex allowance but usually have a weight penalty for horses successful in previous Pattern races.

GROUP III RACES – are also level weight races with WFA and sex allowance but previous Group race winners are invariably penalised and entry conditions sometimes prohibit a previous Group I winner from taking part.

This grading of Pattern Races gives a ready guide to a horse's achievements, and subsequent value should it be sold, or of its standing if it is to be used for breeding. Therefore in the sales catalogue, or breeding record, horses with Group race successes have these entries printed in big black type to distinguish them easily from winners of more ordinary races such as Handicaps.

HANDICAPS AND LISTED RACES

Outside of the Pattern Race system the most common races in the calendar are Handicaps. They exist for horses of all ages over all distances, and horses are qualified to compete in them after having won one race, or if they have run in three races without winning. Horses' abilities thereafter are assessed by the Jockey Club Official Handicapper who allots them weight, in his opinion, in accord with their ability. The better horses carry the most weight and the slower ones least, so theoretically when they compete against each other all have an equal chance of winning.

Although it was thought that within the Pattern Race system three grades of merit were sufficient to identify the abilities of top-class horses it became apparent there was quite a large gap between Group III class performers and better-quality Handicappers. Therefore an unofficial fourth grade, or intermediate stage, outside the Pattern, was instigated.

These are called **listed races** and exist to demonstrate to breeders and bloodstock markets the merits of horses just outside the upper echelons.

Listed races are subject only to a loose form of regulation and internationally their quality can vary somewhat. Listed races along with Group races are easy tests of comparable abilities as horses compete at basically level weights with consideration only for age and sex allowance, and subject to entry conditions that are likely to penalise previous Group race winners or even bar some from entry.

Listed races serve as a useful step for horses upgraded from Handicap class who are seeking to establish themselves on the first rung of the Pattern Race ladder. They are a means of reference, but like Group III races hold no international importance and so have not been included in this *Big Race Guide*.

LINCOLN HANDICAP STAKES
Handicap   1m   4 y.o. and upwards only

The Lincoln Handicap Stakes is a 1 mile Handicap race for 4-year-olds and older horses, and is run on the straight course at Doncaster late in March. It is the first important Handicap in the Flat Race calendar and always arouses a competitive ante-post betting market. On the ante-post betting front, the Lincoln Handicap makes up the first leg of the famous 'Spring Double' where ante-post bets are coupled with The Grand National (which follows usually a week later).

The Lincoln Handicap, however, is not a race to recommend, especially as an ante-post venture, because more than normal luck is needed just to see your selection start on the day! Ailments, setbacks and changes of plan can cause a horse's withdrawal in the weeks leading up to the race.

An added concern is the large number of entrants, there being a maximum safety limit of 26 runners, and the balloting out of the bottom-weighted horses.

The draw, which is not made until the overnight declaration stage, can also play an important role. The lower numbers have dominated in recent seasons, with eight winners since 1980 drawn in the lower half, seven of them in single figures. It has been suggested that any horse drawn higher than 10 might as well stay at home!

The race is always run at a good pace throughout with the large field dividing into two groups, one each side of the track, soon after the start, with one soon holding a distinct advantage. The ground is invariably softish (Soft, or Good to Soft or Yielding), and the 'Lincoln' is a stiff test of a miler. It demands that a horse be not too far off the pace throughout yet still with plenty in reserve to give in the final two furlongs.

The winner, however, usually turns out to be no more than a smart handicapper. Exceptions are K-BATTERY (1986) and SAHER (1981), who went on to win Group races; CATALDI (1985), who was second later in the season in a Group II event;

4

THE LINCOLN HANDICAP – The first big race of the season and a difficult handicap to predict.

Apprentice ridden SOUTHWARK STAR (Richard Fox, No. 19) runs on well to beat the previous season's Cambridgeshire winner FLYING NELLY (No. 8) and provide a shock 33–1 result in the 1975 Lincoln Handicap.

and MIGHTY FLY (1983) who completed an almost unique double of Royal Ascot's Hunt Cup.

The race has been won almost equally often by 4-year-olds and 5-year-olds (seven times and six times). Ten winners carried between 8 st and 8 st 12 lb and three winners under 8 st. Only CATALDI, at 9 st 10 lb, (which was a post-war record) broke the 9 st barrier. This suggests that this is a race for a horse that is not yet fully exposed in the Handicap.

The market has offered little help to the backer, with only two favourites obliging. One was the classy CATALDI, at a very rewarding 10–1, and the other CAPTAINS WINGS (13–2) who won when the race was staged a couple of weeks later than normal in April 1978 over the round course, with the benefit of a previous winning seasonal debut. Two 2nd favourites and two 3rd favourites have also won but the race has been dominated by the outsider with prices from 14–1 to 33–1, although some were far from friendless in the market.

Most runners will be making their seasonal debut in the race and so much depends on the skill and judgement of their trainers to get them to peak fitness on the day. No trainer has won the Lincoln on more than one occasion and the prize usually falls to the lesser known smaller establishments who are used to handling Handicap-class horses.

Programmed so early in the season, the Lincoln Handicap is normally an extremely difficult race to predict, with no constant factors pinpointing the winner. It is usually the subject of much speculation in the Press, coinciding with the opening of the Flat Race season and has been the subject of numerous gambles, especially by the connections of horses, and which usually fail to materialise. A strong case can often be made for a number of runners but with the numerous uncertainties and large fields it is only the inspired or very lucky backer who will be successful in finding the winner.

88	CUVEE CHARLIE	4	0801	H. Collingridge	33–1		25
87	STAR OF A GUNNER	7	0808	R. Holder	9–1 Jt 2nd Fav.		25
86	K-BATTERY	5	0804	W. Elsey	25–1		25
85	CATALDI	4	0910	G. Harwood	10–1 Fav.		26
84	SAVING MERCY	4	0809	D. K. Weld (Ire.)	14–1		26
83	MIGHTY FLY	4	0804	D. Elsworth	14–1		26
82	KINGS GLORY	4	0803	P. Mitchell	11–1 Co-2nd Fav. of 3	26
81	SAHER	5	0812	R. Sheather	14–1		19
80	KINGS RIDE	4	0812	W. Wightman	10–1		18
79	FAIR SEASON	5	0810	I. A. Balding	8–1		23
78	CAPTAINS WINGS	5	0710	R. Boss	13–2 Fav.		25
77	BLUSTERY	5	0711	M. Smyly	20–1		26
76	THE HERTFORD	5	0806	B. Swift	20–1		26
75	SOUTHWARK STAR	4	0703	G. Peter-Hoblyn	33–1		24

EUROPEAN FREE HANDICAP
Handicap 7f 3 y.o only

The European Free Handicap is a race, for 3 year-olds only, over a distance of 7 furlongs during the three-day Craven meeting at Newmarket in the second week in April. It is the Handicap in which the official handicapper has sought to rate the leading 2-year-olds of the previous season in order of merit, so the top weight ought to be the horse considered by the handicapper to be the best of its generation. On this basis the weights for the European Free Handicap are compiled and the race proposed to be run.

However, the very best horses of the 2-year-old generation seldom take part in the Free Handicap but contest instead Group races considered more appropriate to possible Classic contenders. So this race is usually contested by horses originally much further down the handicap and does not usually hold much influence as a Classic trial.

Only one winner, MRS McARDY (1977), has gone on to capture a Classic race, although NOBLE MINSTREL (1987) finished second in the French Two Thousand Guineas. Also REMAINDER MAN (1978), after winning this race, finished second in the English Two Thousand Guineas, as did CHARMER (1988) who was only second in the Free Handicap.

Perhaps surprisingly, two horses unplaced in the Free Handicap, MATTABOY and BEL BOLIDE (1981), were placed second and third respectively in the Two Thousand Guineas.

However, it should be said that 1981 was one of the better-quality fields of recent times, and included other subsequent Group winners MOTOVATO, THE QUIET BIDDER and TINA'S PET. Besides these horses the best winners of the Free Handicap have undoubtedly been GREEN DESERT (1986) and MOORESTYLE (1980) who developed to become champion sprinters of their respective seasons. Occasionally beaten horses in this race go forward later to achieve Group race success but usually the majority of runners prove to be no better than useful Handicappers at best. A horse will have to improve considerably, probably up to 14 lb, to succeed at Classic level even after winning this race.

*THE EUROPEAN FREE HANDICAP – Promoted as a Classic trial
although it is rarely of any great influence.*

REMAINDER MAID (white face, Michael Wigham) wins the 1978 Free
Handicap from SKYLINER (Brian Rouse, diamonds) and was one of the
race's exceptional winners, subsequently being placed in the English 2,000
Guineas and Derby.

The Free Handicap is always a competitive race, usually with
an exciting and close finish and always attracts a fairly large field
(from 8 to 19 runners). Programmed so early in the season, most
runners will be making their seasonal debut in the race, as has
been the case for ten of the fourteen winners. Form will therefore
be based on the previous season's performances as a juvenile. It
is interesting to note how well the horses with better form (i.e. in
the top half of the Handicap) have fared. Twelve winners carried
above 8 st 7 lb and four winners 9 st or above. Only one winner
has carried below 8 st, suggesting horses will have shown, in
the handicapper's opinion, form worthy of serious consideration
without having been heavily overburdened with weight. Ten of
the fourteen winners had won at least two previous races during

their 2- or 3-year-old careers and eight of these had won at least one race over the distance of 7 furlongs or further.

With the emphasis on preparing a horse to be fully fit for its seasonal racecourse reappearance it is not surprising that the more famous trainers have dominated this race. However, a few less familiar names have also been successful. O. Douieb (who has now returned to his native France) is the only trainer to have won the race more than once.

The market (surprisingly for such a competitive race with large-sized fields) had not been unhelpful in pinpointing the winner with five favourites, one 2nd favourite, four 3rd favourites and four outsiders (13–2, 10–1, 14–1, 20–1) successful. The winning favourites have been 85–40, 9–4, 3–1, 5–1 and 8–1 (of which this was a co-favourite of four). Except for a couple of shock results, the winner is usually far from friendless in the market.

The European Free Handicap is not an easy race for selection. Trust has to be put in a horse's fitness at this early stage of the season and concern for how a horse may have developed in the transition from its 2-year-old career. Results seem to suggest that exposed 2-year-old form holds up well. Class horses with previous Group race experience must always be considered as they are slightly lowered in grade here, and weight may not stop them, even if it is above 9 st. When searching the handicap, the selector must not come down too far. As nine winners have carried 8 st 10 lb and above, this is the area on which to focus.

88	LA PIERRE	3	0901	C. Brittain	10–1	9
87	NOBLE MINSTREL	3	0907	O. Douieb	7–1	11
86	GREEN DESERT	3	0907	M. Stoute	11–2	9
85	OVER THE OCEAN	3	0811	O. Douieb	85–40 Fav.	11
84	CUTTING WIND	3	0808	M. Hinchliffe	20–1	17
83	BOOM TOWN CHARLIE	3	0811	W. O'Gorman	13–2	8
82	MATCH WINNER	3	0904	H. Cecil	9–4 Fav.	13
81	MOTOVATO	3	0813	B. Hills	13–2	13
80	MOORESTYLE	3	0810	R. Armstrong	6–1 2nd Fav.	13
79	LYRIC DANCE	3	0810	J. Tree	3–1 Fav.	14
78	REMAINDER MAN	3	0710	R. Hollinshead	15–2	12
77	MRS McARDY	3	0800	M. W. Easterby	8–1 Co-Fav. of 4	19
76	MAN OF HARLECH	3	0804	J. Dunlop	14–1	19
75	GREEN BELT	3	0809	H. Wragg	5–1 Fav.	15

TRUSTHOUSE FORTE MILE

Group II   1m   4 y.o. and upwards   Colts, geldings and fillies
Level weights, sex allowance with a penalty for a winner of a
Group I or II race after a prescribed date

The Trusthouse Forte Mile is a Group II race for 4-year-olds and older horses over a distance of 1 mile, staged at Sandown Park on the first day of the Whitbread Gold Cup meeting, usually in the final week of April.

First run in 1985, the inaugural race was won by the great filly PEBBLES, already the winner of a Group I prize in the shape of the previous season's One Thousand Guineas. 1988 winner SOVIET STAR similarly held a Group I scalp having won the previous season's French Two Thousand Guineas. Both these champion milers were promoted to favourite and duly obliged on their seasonal debuts.

The other two contests have shown the more problematic nature of the race, with VERTIGE and FIELD HAND successful. Both these wins were gained by two very fit horses who had run only 12 and 9 days previously, and were opposed by favourites who were not champion milers (i.e. TELEPROMPTER and SCOTTISH REEL) and were making their seasonal debuts.

The Trusthouse Forte Mile promises to fill a needed role in the Pattern Race calendar. It is the first Group II race of the season for the older generation of milers, and allows them to show their current worth against their peers before they clash with the new generation of 3-year-olds for the champion miler's crown.

Although only the future is likely to reveal the full essence of this race, early trends suggest the winner will be a horse that has contested the very top Group race prizes of the previous season. Also with two winners having been trained in France, any runners from across the Channel deserve close attention.

88	SOVIET STAR	4	0906	A. Fabre (Fr.)	5–4 Fav.	6
87	VERTIGE	5	0900	P. Biancone (Fr.)	8–1	8
86	FIELD HAND	4	0900	B. Hills	11–2	7
85	PEBBLES	5	0904	C. Brittain	11–8 Fav.	7

VICTORIA CUP
0–115 Handicap   7f   4 y.o. and upwards

The Victoria Cup is a 0–115 handicap for 4-year-olds and upwards run over 7 furlongs on the straight mile Hunt Cup course at Ascot, during the first Flat Race meeting there, at the end of April or beginning of May.

It is usually a very competitive handicap which attracts large fields (13–22 runners, on average 17 runners) who represent the leading mile handicappers from the older generation of horses. The Victoria Cup produces a keen betting market with both a strong ante-post interest and lively exchanges on the day of the race.

It has been won by some useful handicappers including TREMBLANT (1985), MUMMYS PLEASURE (1984) (who both completed the double with Newmarket's Bunbury Cup) and RHODOMANTADE (1975).

Four other winners progressed to gain Group race successes: INDIAN KING (1982), who developed into a major contender for the champion sprinter honours of that season, KAMPALA (1980), PRIVATE LINE (1978) and RECORD TOKEN (1976). Perhaps it is not surprising that the winner of this race is likely to be found among horses well regarded by the handicapper. Eight of the thirteen winners (1983 race abandoned) carried above 8 st 7 lb and six of these 9 st or more. These were thus all proven horses with a recognised ability to accelerate in the closing stages of a race, which is an essential quality to triumph in this competitive contest.

As it is programmed early in the season, the Victoria Cup will be one of the early races in a horse's seasonal campaign. Four winners made their seasonal debut in the race whilst two is the maximum number of prior races of the other winners. Only one winner had won a previous race that season, so it would appear that the winner of the Victoria Cup is likely to be a horse about to come into form rather than one which has peaked already.

The most influential race on the Victoria Cup has been the 1 mile Newbury Spring Cup, usually run 11 days previously, which has seen two winners – THE ADRIANSTAN (1979) and RECORD TOKEN (1976) compete, in both cases unplaced. Negatively, however, eight other horses promoted to favourite after running in the Newbury Spring Cup (two winning and four finishing second) were beaten. It would therefore appear that the form of the Newbury Spring Cup race must be treated with caution. It is, of course, over a furlong further distance, and on a round rather than straight track.

The going for this Spring contest on Ascot's first Flat meeting of the season has varied from Yielding to Firm, and although the race attracts large fields the influence of the draw has varied. Eight winners have been drawn 6 or below, and five have been in the upper third of the draw. It seems best to avoid a middle draw.

The market has only a very partial influence in pinpointing the winner, with one favourite, four 2nd favourites, two 3rd favourites and six outsiders (14–1, 18–1, 20–1, 22–1, 25–1, 25–1) successful.

As befits a competitive handicap, the Victoria Cup has fallen to a wide spectrum of trainers, but C. Brittain and P. Walwyn (two wins each) are the only stables with more than a single success.

The Victoria Cup is always a competitive race only won by a good-class handicapper who may develop to achieve greater heights as the season progresses. Recent records suggest that the area where selection can be most profitably focused is upon the horses well exposed in the Handicap who are likely to be coming into form rather than those who have already peaked.

88	WING PARK	4	0901	A. Bailey	7–1 Jt 2nd Fav.	16
87	FUSILIER	5	0709	C. Brittain	20–1	20
86	READY WIT	5	0713	R. Hannon	7–1 Jt 2nd Fav.	14
85	TREMBLANT	4	0805	R. Smyth	8–1 2nd Fav.	22
84	MUMMYS PLEASURE	5	0809	P. Haslam	14–1	13
83				——— ABANDONED ———		
82	INDIAN KING	4	0903	G. Harwood	4–1 Fav.	13
81	COLUMNIST	4	0913	J. Tree	8–1	14
80	KAMPALA	4	0903	P. Walwyn	8–1	16
79	THE ADRIANSTAN	4	0806	J. Sutcliffe	25–1	18
78	PRIVATE LINE	5	0813	C. Brittain	25–1	16
77	DUKE ELLINGTON	4	0901	H. R. Price	18–1	16
76	RECORD TOKEN	4	0904	P. Walwyn	6–1 2nd Fav.	14
75	RHODOMANTADE	4	0803	P. Makin	22–1	20

ONE THOUSAND GUINEAS
Group I   1m   3 y.o. fillies only
Level weights

The One Thousand Guineas is the first Classic race of the English Flat Race season. It is run over a distance of 1 mile on the straight Rowley Course at Newmarket, on the Thursday of the three-day Guineas meeting in late April or early May. It is confined to 3-year-old fillies. The competition for this race is always fierce, attracting large fields (12–25 runners) and will only be won by a filly who is very smart on the day. It is therefore perhaps surprising to note that five winners of the Thousand Guineas afterwards failed to win another race. This suggests that being the fittest and most forward on the day was the prominent factor responsible for victory.

Only two winners, ENSTONE SPARK (1978) and MIDWAY LADY (1986), have overcome the fitness disadvantage and won the race on their seasonal debut as 3-year-olds. All the others had at least one prior race, with ten successful; and even two making their seasonal debuts had won their final race as 2-year-olds. Good recent winning form is therefore of the uppermost importance and it is not surprising to note that nine winners had previously won at Newmarket on its daunting open and straight course. These included two recent French-trained winners, RAVINELLA (1988) and MA BICHE (1983).

A most significant race in this respect has been Newmarket's Nell Gwynn Stakes (Group III, 7 furlongs, 13–14 days earlier). Five horses, OH SO SHARP (1985), PEBBLES (1984), FAIRY FOOTSTEPS (1981), ONE IN A MILLION (1979) and FLYING WATER (1976), won before completing the double, whilst ON THE HOUSE (1982) was unplaced at Newmarket. Negatively, two fillies promoted to favourite after winning the Nell Gwynn Stakes were beaten in the One Thousand Guineas.

The market trends have been either extremely accurate or very misleading in pinpointing the winner, with seven favourites, one 2nd favourite and six outsiders (whose prices ranged from 20–1 to 35–1) being successful. It appears from these statistics that the

13

obvious form lines which are the main guide to a horse's position in the market are either predictably upheld or else they have been badly misinterpreted, resulting in a surprise win for an outsider, who either improves to reverse proven form, or emerges with form credentials that were underrated or unconsidered. Also, three fillies who were only placed in their first Classic, FAIR SALINIA (1978), TIME CHARTER (1982) and DIMINUENDO (1988), went on to capture the English Oaks.

The One Thousand Guineas is invariably won by a top trainer, with the winners list having an international flavour of English, Irish and French names, but with only H. Cecil (three wins) and Mme C. Head (Fr.) (two wins) having more than a single success. The race itself is usually most exciting with the winner in a challenging position as the field of runners come towards and pass the bushes (a landmark at the side of the course near the two-furlong marker) and then sweep down into the dip before running on strongly in the final uphill finish to the winning post.

The One Thousand Guineas is not an easy race for the purpose of selection with 3-year-old fillies' form always subject to a degree of unpredictability, and unless there appears an outstanding candidate who has the proven form to overshadow her rivals, the backer will be advised to bet with caution.

88	RAVINELLA	3	0900	Mme C. Head (Fr.)	4–5 Fav.	12
87	MIESQUE	3	0900	F. Boutin (Fr.)	15–8 Fav.	14
86	MIDWAY LADY	3	0900	B. Hanbury	10–1	15
85	OH SO SHARP	3	0900	H. Cecil	2–1 Fav.	17
84	PEBBLES	3	0900	C. Brittain	8–1 Jt 2nd	15
83	MA BICHE	3	0900	Mme C. Head (Fr.)	5–2 Fav.	18
82	ON THE HOUSE	3	0900	H. Wragg	33–1	15
81	FAIRY FOOTSTEPS	3	0900	H. Cecil	6–4 Fav.	14
80	QUICK AS LIGHTNING	3	0900	J. Dunlop	12–1	23
79	ONE IN A MILLION	3	0900	H. Cecil	1–1 Fav.	17
78	ENSTONE SPARK	3	0900	B. Hills	33–1	16
77	MRS MCCARDY	3	0900	M. W. Easterby	16–1	18
76	FLYING WATER	3	0900	A. Penna (Fr.)	2–1 Fav.	25
75	NOCTURNAL SPREE	3	0900	H. Murless (Ire.)	14–1	16

THE ENGLISH 1,000 GUINEAS — The first Classic race of the season and confined to fillies. Results alternate between the predictable and the unexpected. Beaten fillies however cannot be lightly disregarded in subsequent races. The winner is often only the filly that was simply the best on the day.

RAVINELLA (Gary Moore, right), brilliantly wins the 1988 English 1,000 Guineas, trouncing her rivals DABAWEYAA (Walter Swinburne, striped cap), yet DIMINUENDO (Steve Cauthen, star on cap) only third, later won the English and Irish Oaks, and MAGIC OF LIFE (white nose) reversed the form with the winner at Royal Ascot.

JOCKEY CLUB STAKES

Group II 1½m 4 y.o. and upwards colts, geldings and fillies
Level weights, sex allowance, with a penalty for a winner
of a Group I or Group II race since a 2 y.o.

The Jockey Club Stakes is a Group II race for 4-year-old and older horses run over a distance of 1½ miles, on part of the Cesarewitch Course at Newmarket during the three-day Guineas meeting. It usually attracts some of the best of the older generation of stayers who have remained in training for another season. It has been won by a couple of real top-class horses, ARDROSS (1982) and MASTER WILLIE (1981), although normally the winners are not quite of this high calibre. Horses competing meet at basically level weights and so with no allowances for horses of inferior stature, a natural dearth of older top-class stayers, fields have been of a compact size with an average of seven runners.

The outcome of the race would therefore seem to be quite predictable but results testify that the selector should be wary of the obvious. Two Derby winners (SLIP ANCHOR (1986), HENBIT (1981)), and an Oaks winner (CIRCUS PLUME (1985)), each promoted to favourite on their reappearance here as 4-year-olds, were all beaten and in effect ended their racing careers.

The market reflects this with only two favourites successful, whilst five 2nd favourites, two 3rd favourites and five outsiders have won. Six winners won on their seasonal debut, three of these providing a shock result – AL MAARAD (13–2), KIRMANN (11–1) and ELECTRIC (12–1).

The daunting 1½ mile course at Newmarket is a severe test of a horse's stamina and fitness and competitors without the help of a preparation race to bring them to peak fitness will need the experience of a skilful trainer. As may be expected, all the contests have been won by the top trainers normally associated with top group races, with P. Walwyn (three wins), G. Harwood, responsible for PHARDANTE's consecutive victories, and the now retired Bruce Hobbs (two wins) the only trainers with more than a single success.

The two most influential races for the eight winners with a

THE JOCKEY CLUB STAKES – The first important stayers race for the older generations of horses.

ARDROSS (Lester Piggott, No. 1) wins the 1982 Jockey Club Stakes on his seasonal debut, beating GLINT OF GOLD (John Mathias, No. 2), the previous season's Derby runner-up. ARDROSS later in the season won his second Ascot Gold Cup and ended his racing career, finishing second in the Prix de l'Arc de Triomphe.

prior race have been the John Porter Stakes (Group III, Newbury, 1½ miles, 13 days earlier), and the Earl of Sefton at Newmarket (Group III, 1 mile 1 furlong, 16 days earlier). But of three winners contesting the John Porter Stakes only one completed the double, GAY LEMUR (1984) and negatively, four other horses promoted to favourite after competing in the Newbury race were beaten in the Jockey Club Stakes. Two horses have won after contesting in the Earl of Sefton, PHARDANTE (1986 and 1987), and ORANGE BAY (1976) but neither did better than third in the earlier race, which seemed to serve mainly as a useful sharp pipe opener to bring a stayer to complete fitness.

Whilst the record suggests a previous outing may be an advantage, only two winners have won their previous race, so the selector will be best served examining a horse's less recent form to see what it may really be capable of.

The Jockey Club Stakes is a fair test of selection skills with the backer needing to balance carefully the proven form of last season with current form, fitness, and likely improvement of horses with the benefit of a previous race in the current season.

88	AL MAARAD	5	0810	J. Dunlop	13–2		4
87	PHARDANTE	5	0812	G. Harwood	7–1		7
86	PHARDANTE	4	0807	G. Harwood	11–2 Jt 2nd Fav.		3
85	KIRMANN	4	0804	R. Houghton	11–1		8
84	GAY LEMUR	4	0807	B. Hobbs	8–1		6
83	ELECTRIC	4	0810	M. Stoute	12–1		11
82	ARDROSS	6	0812	H. Cecil	1–1 Fav.		6
81	MASTER WILLIE	4	0812	H. Candy	2–1 2nd Fav.		6
80	MORE LIGHT	4	0811	W. Hern	4–1 2nd Fav.		8
79	OBRAZTOVY	4	0811	H. R. Price	5–1		9
78	CLASSIC EXAMPLE	4	0905	P. Walwyn	11–4 2nd Fav.		7
77	OATS	4	0901	P. Walwyn	9–4 Fav.		11
76	ORANGE BAY	4	0908	P. Walwyn	3–1 2nd Fav.		8
75	SHEBEEN	4	0810	B. Hobbs	5–1		6

TWO THOUSAND GUINEAS

Group I   1m (straight)   3 y.o.   entire colts and fillies* only
Level weights with sex allowance
*Fillies seldom take part.

The Two Thousand Guineas is the second Classic race of the season. It is run at Newmarket over the straight 1 mile course on the third day, or Saturday, of the Guineas meeting. It takes place in late April or the first week in May and is the first Classic race for 3-year-old colts.

As a Group I race it is the top prize or championship race for 3-year-old horses whose best racing distance will usually be 1 mile. It is second only to the Derby as a prestigious prize for the 3-year-old generation and therefore is always very competitive, attracting fields ranging from 9 to 26 runners, with an average of 17.

The more open the race appears (i.e. there being no outstanding contenders), the larger the field; and the more outstanding or dominating the contenders, the smaller the field. In the six races with 15 or less runners, four have been won by the favourite.

The number of runners has had no affect on the quality of the race. One of the most intriguing and exciting was in 1971 where there was the smallest size field in living memory. BRIGADIER GERRARD won an epic struggle with his two main rivals MILL REEF and MY SWALLOW.

The winner of the Two Thousand Guineas usually turns out to be the best or almost best miler of his generation, as exemplified by winners such as BOLKONSKI (1975), WOLLOW (1976), TO-AGORI-MOU (1981) and SHADEED (1985). Occasionally a very good or champion miler does get beaten – CHIEF SINGER (1984) and KRIS (1979) were both second, POSSE (1980), promoted on the winner's disqualification, and of course the disqualified NUREYEV (1980) himself.

Beaten horses, if they are to prove champions, will do so over longer distances. This was the case with MILL REEF (1971), GRUNDY (1975), VIGTES (1976), THE MINSTREL (1977) and more recently with ADJAL (1987) but as a sprinter.

With the fantastic rewards for winners of the colts' Classics in

19

THE ENGLISH 2,000 GUINEAS – The second Classic race of the season and the first for colts. It is a race where shocks can occur or else conforms very much to the predictable.

Jubilant Freddie Head aboard ZINO is led into the winners' enclosure after his 2,000 Guineas victory in 1982.

terms of Stud Syndication value it is not surprising that horses have been bred only for the specific distance and few have been adaptable or brilliant enough to be champion at different distances (i.e. Guineas, Derby and St Leger) at varying stages of their career. The legendary NIJINSKY who completed the famous Triple Crown in 1970 is the only colt to do so since before the Second World War. Few horses have the necessary stamina to be champion at 1½ miles or further after proving their worth as a miler. DANCING BRAVE (1986) was another very rare exception.

To win the Two Thousand Guineas a horse will most likely have competed prominently in the best Group races for his generation as a 2-year-old or 3-year-old. Without experience at this level of competition a horse will suddenly be faced with being raised considerably in class, a move which is likely to ruthlessly expose its deficiencies. Previous top-class form therefore becomes the essence in the selection of the Guineas winner.

All winners of the Two Thousand Guineas had a previous race that season, with nine horses also having won that race. Surprisingly, therefore, the record of the market leaders is mixed. Six favourites have won and seven outsiders, whose prices ranged from 9–1 to 33–1, plus one 3rd favourite.

Recently (1985–88) the Craven Stakes has had a positive influence on the Two Thousand Guineas, with three horses completing the double. The Craven Stakes (Group III), run over the exact course and distance 16 days earlier, would seem the perfect dress rehearsal but until Shadeed's victory in 1985 the race had been the kiss of death for the winner's chances in the Guineas. Eight winners were beaten, with only two of them even managing to finish third.

Winners have come from widely ranging sources (English, Irish, French) with H. Cecil, G. Harwood, M. O'Brien (Ire.) and M. Stoute (two wins each) the only trainers with more than a single success. Horses from various training centres will have had different preparation races and this perhaps explains why assumed superiority can fail to be confirmed in the actual test of the race. The Two Thousand Guineas frequently bursts the bubble of a high-flown reputation.

As a 2-year-old a prospective Guineas winner is likely to have been lightly raced. Only three winners had more than four races. Also twelve winners won over 7 furlongs or further as a 2-year-old. Since the early 1980s most of the Two Thousand Guineas winners have not made their racecourse debut until the end of August or later in their first season of racing.

To win the Two Thousand Guineas, run over the daunting open straight mile at Newmarket, a horse will need the speed to remain in contention from early in the race (the race is always run at a fast pace throughout), to be able to see out the mile distance, and also be able to quicken inside the final furlong. A horse will not be able merely to gallop opponents into submission at this level of competition; and whether the challenge comes from behind or the horse races from the front, all winners have demonstrated that priceless asset: to accelerate dramatically in the last 2 furlongs.

The Two Thousand Guineas either from the spectator or selector viewpoint is always a race full of interest. It provides a good challenge of selection skills, where the backer is advised to consider the facts provided only in proven top-class form, and not become beguiled with assumptions unsupported by proven racecourse form.

88	DOYOUN	3	0900	M. Stoute	4–5 Fav.	9
87	DON'T FORGET ME	3	0900	R. Hannon	9–1	13
86	DANCING BRAVE	3	0900	G. Harwood	15–8 Fav.	15
85	SHADEED	3	0900	M. Stoute	4–5 Fav.	14
84	EL GRAN SENOR	3	0900	M. V. O'Brien (Ire.)	15–8 Fav.	9
83	LOMOND	3	0900	M. V. O'Brien (Ire.)	9–1	16
82	ZINO	3	0900	F. Boutin (Fr.)	8–1	26
81	TO-AGORI-MOU	3	0900	G. Harwood	5–2 Fav.	19
80	KNOWN FACT	3	0900	J. Tree	14–1	14
79	TAP ON WOOD	3	0900	B. Hills	20–1	20
78	ROLAND GARDENS	3	0900	D. Sasse	28–1	19
77	NEBBILO	3	0900	K. Prendergast (Ire.)	20–1	18
76	WOLLOW	3	0900	H. Cecil	1–1 Fav.	17
75	BOLKONSKI	3	0900	H. Cecil	33–1	24

CHESTER CUP HANDICAP STAKES

0–115 Handicap   2m 2f 97 y   4 y.o. and upwards

The Chester Cup is a handicap for 4-year-olds and older horses over approximately 2¼ miles, which is two complete circuits of Chester's unique tight-turning racetrack. It is staged on the second day of the mid-week meeting in May. With a history dating back to 1824 it is one of the oldest handicap races still in the calendar. It is a popular race with a keen ante-post betting market and usually attracts some of the best long-distance handicappers in training, occasionally with horses of better class. (For example, GILDORAN (1984), the Ascot Gold Cup winner who unsuccessfully competed carrying a mammoth burden of 9 st 13 lb.) Most competitors are not of such calibre and the race attracts fairly large fields (10 to 22 runners with an average of 15) who usually span a full weight range in the handicap.

It is a gruelling test around Chester's tight bends with one or two horses always setting a fast pace throughout. To win requires a tough horse with plenty of stamina, but also a burst of speed in the final home straight, and not burdened too heavily by weight.

The race seems to suit the more mature horses. Ten winners were 5-year-olds or older, and four winners, CONTESTER (1984), DONEGAL PRINCE (1981) and SEA PIGEON (1978 and 1977) were horses that had been National Hunt campaigners during that current season.

All the winners had had a prior flat race that season (three winners having run within the previous seven days) or else had completed a recent National Hunt campaign. The form of winners varied considerably but only two winners, ARAPHOS (1980) and MORGANS CHOICE (1985), won their previous race, and only one winner, DONEGAL PRINCE (1981), defied the extra 3 lb weight burden given to winners after the closing date of the race. Most of the winners have been in the top half of the handicap with only three carrying less than 8 st, suggesting that the winner is likely to be a horse whose abilities are exposed to the handicapper.

The market has been little guide to the selection with only two favourites (one of which was co-favourite of three) successful.

*THE CHESTER CUP – A testing 2¼ mile Handicap around two
circuits of Chester's tight turning track. It is a race that can often suit
a dual purpose Flat and National Hunt horse.*

SEA PIGEON (Mark Birch), the perfect example of the sort of horse at home
in Flat or National Hunt racing, won the Chester Cup for a second time as
an 8 y.o., in 1978, carrying what was then a record weight of 9 st 7 lb.

Other winners have included one 2nd favourite, two 3rd favourites
and eight outsiders with prices ranging from 10–1 to 33–1.

There can be no definite pointers in what is always a competitive
handicap except to suggest that most winners have proven ability
and are known to be able to see out the distance. Tough versatile
dual-purpose horses have fared well but the selector is advised
to be wary of mammoth weights and most particularly of horses
carrying a penalty.

The Chester Cup is not an easy race for successful selection and
has the habit of upsetting some of the better-laid plans, so do not
be surprised if upsets occur.

88	OLD HUBERT	7	0708	A. Bailey	33–1	17
87	JUST DAVID	4	0908	A. Stewart	10–1	13
86	WESTERN DANCER	5	0900	C. Horgan	14–1	22
85	MORGANS CHOICE	8	0711	C. J. Hill	13–2	16
84	CONTESTER	4	0802	P. Cundell	22–1	19
83				ABANDONED		
82	DAWN JOHNNY	5	0808	M. Stoute	14–1	16
81	DONEGAL PRINCE	5	0804	P. Kelleway	12–1	15
80	ARAPHOS	5	0905	B. Hills	7–2 Fav.	10
79	CHARLOTTES CHOICE	4	0804	W. Wightman	10–1	13
78	SEA PIGEON	8	0907	M. H. Easterby	10–1	13
77	SEA PIGEON	7	0808	M. H. Easterby	7–1	15
76	JOHN CHERRY	5	0904	J. Tree	5–1 2nd Fav.	15
75	SUPER NOVA	5	0707	W. Hall	11–2 Fav.	15

DANTE STAKES

Group II   1m 2½f   3 y.o. only   colts, geldings and fillies
Level weights and sex allowance with a penalty for a winner of a
Group I race since a 2 y.o.

The Dante Stakes, held on the second day of York's May meeting, is a race for 3-year-old colts, geldings and fillies only over a distance of 1 mile 2½ furlongs. It was upgraded in 1980 from Group III to Group II status and serves as an important trial for the Derby.

In common with a number of trials for the Derby it is a race that quickly separates the true contenders from the mere pretenders. A number of horses with classic aspirations will have their shortcomings ruthlessly exposed in a trial such as the Dante Stakes where horses race against each other principally at level weights. Beaten horses will usually prove to be below top class although a notable exception was the beaten favourite KALAGLOW (1981) who, after having a disappointing 3-year-old career, attained great heights as a 4-year-old, capturing the Eclipse Stakes and Ascot's King George VI and Queen Elizabeth Stakes.

The influence of the Dante Stakes on the Derby has grown recently, with REFERENCE POINT (1987) and SHAHRASTANI (1986) having victories in the Premier Classic and DAMISTER (1985) finishing third. Previously only SHIRLEY HEIGHTS (1978) had completed the double and the Dante winners consistently disappointed in the Derby with beaten horses often reversing form – perhaps due to a lack of stamina. This trend was repeated in 1988 when Derby favourite and Dante winner RED GLOW finished behind a horse previously beaten in the York race.

Surprisingly perhaps the Dante Stakes has consistently been a race where horses promoted to favourite in the betting market, either on form or by reputation, have been found to be wanting. Only four favourites, two 2nd favourites and one 3rd favourite have won and the prices of six outsiders who won ranged from 5–1 to 50–1. This is all the more surprising as nine of these contests had less than ten runners.

All the winners except two had a previous race that season yet

THE DANTE STAKES – An important trial for the Epsom Derby over a slightly shorter distance, 1 mile 2 furlongs and 110 yards.

HOBNOB (noseband) with Willie Carson riding, beats CORBY (Pat Eddery) and gives the Wragg stable the first of their four wins in the 1975 Dante Stakes. HOBNOB ran in the Derby but was unplaced down the field.

only five horses won their previous race. In fact three winners (interestingly all trained by the Wragg stable) were maidens before gaining this Group prize. The Dante Stakes is certainly a race dominated by the top trainers but Henry Cecil (five wins) and the Wragg stable (four wins) are the only handlers with more than a single success.

Three races have had a particular influence on the outcome of the Dante Stakes. The Newmarket Stakes, a listed race at Newmarket (1¼ miles, 12–13 days earlier), has produced four winners, although only two completed the double. Sandown's Group III Classic Trial (1¼ miles, 18 days earlier), produced two winners, both completing the double; whilst two horses beaten in Newmarket's Two Thousand Guineas (Group I, 11 days earlier) have won the Dante. The most influential 2-year-old race has been Doncaster's Group I Futurity Stakes (1 mile) in which three winners have completed the double.

The Dante Stakes is normally an interesting race but one which can hold a number of pitfalls. It is advisable to examine the form of all the probables closely and pay due regard to form of any horses who have raced in Group I events – as the Dante Stakes for a number of runners will represent a raising in class. The distance of the Dante Stakes should also be closely considered, as the 1 mile 2½ furlongs will often be too long for the milers, and possibly too sharp for the more stoutly bred who would be better suited to 1½ miles.

88	RED GLOW	3	0900	G. Wragg	7–1	7
87	REFERENCE POINT	3	0900	H. Cecil	13–8 Fav.	8
86	SHAHRASTANI	3	0900	M. Stoute	10–11 Fav.	7
85	DAMISTER	3	0900	J. Tree	5–1	5
84	CLAUDE MONET	3	0900	H. Cecil	2–1 Fav.	15
83	HOT TOUCH	3	0900	G. Wragg	11–1	9
82	SIMPLY GREAT	3	0900	H. Cecil	11–10 Fav.	6
81	BELDALE FLUTTER	3	0900	M. Jarvis	11–1	6
80	HELLO GORGEOUS	3	0900	H. Cecil	4–1 2nd Fav.	8
79	LYPHARDS WISH	3	0900	H. Cecil	10–3 2nd Fav.	14
78	SHIRLEY HEIGHTS	3	0900	J. Dunlop	10–1	9
77	LUCKY SOVEREIGN	3	0900	H. Wragg	20–1	15
76	TRASI'S SON	3	0900	M. Tate	50–1	11
75	HOBNOB	3	0900	H. Wragg	15–2	12

YORKSHIRE CUP

Group II   1m 6f   4 y.o. and upwards   colts, geldings and fillies
Level weights and sex allowance with a penalty for a winner of a
Group I or II race since a 2 y.o.

The Yorkshire Cup is a Group II race for 4-year-olds and upwards
over 1 mile 6 furlongs and is staged at York on the third and final
day of the May meeting. It is the first in the quartet of Cup races
but serves in some ways more as a trial for the other big three (the
Ascot, Goodwood and Doncaster Cups) which are contested later
in the season over distances in excess of 2¼ miles.

To win the Yorkshire Cup a horse, whilst not lacking in
stamina, must be more than a resolute stayer and have the
powers of acceleration in the latter stages of the race; a quality
ably demonstrated by that very versatile horse ARDROSS (1982
and 1981) who was the only winner also to capture the premier
staying prize the Ascot Gold Cup in two successive years. Only a
very good horse can win at this level of competition over such a
range of distance.

With the recent dearth of top-class horses who have staying
potential remaining in training as 4-year-olds or older, the
Yorkshire Cup attracts only small fields, 4 to 10 runners with an
average of 7. The records of the market leaders have been quite
positive with seven favourites, three 2nd favourites and one 3rd
favourite successful. However, three outsiders, whose prices were
10–1, 12–1 and 33–1, have triumphed on each occasion when
the race was more numerically competitive and often without a
dominant market leader.

Only three winners of true Group I standard have won the
race MOON MADNESS (1988), ARDROSS (1982 and 1981) and
BRUNI (1976) but other good-class performers have included
BAND (1984) and SMUGGLER (1978). The latter two emphasise
the good record W. Hern has held in the race along with H. Cecil
(three wins).

Winners have been almost equally divided between horses
making their seasonal debut (six winners) and horses having had
a previous race (eight winners). The pointer from winners who had

29

the benefit of a previous race was that five of these had contested Newmarket's Jockey Club Stakes (Group II) 13 days earlier; yet only one, ARDROSS (1982), completed the double and only one other winner who had a prior race won it.

The Yorkshire Cup is an intriguing race from the selection point of view with the backer best served by focusing attention only upon the proven Group I or Group II race performers.

88	MOON MADNESS	5	0900	J. Dunlop	6–5 Fav.	8
87	VERD-ANTIQUE	4	0809	H. Cecil	7–4 Fav.	7
86	EASTERN MYSTIC	4	0809	L. Cumani	9–4 Fav.	7
85	ILLIUM	4	0809	H. Thomson-Jones	5–1 Jt 2nd Fav.	10
84	BAND	4	0810	W. Hern	9–4 Fav.	9
83	LINE SLINGER	4	0804	W. Elsey	33–1	10
82	ARDROSS	6	0901	H. Cecil	2–5 Fav.	6
81	ARDROSS	5	0812	H. Cecil	2–1 2nd Fav.	6
80	NOBLE SAINT	4	0901	R. Armstrong	10–1	8
79	PRAGMATIC	4	0807	R. Houghton	12–1	10
78	SMUGGLER	5	0810	W. Hern	4–1	7
77	BRIGHT FINISH	4	0810	J. Tree	10–30 Jt Fav.	7
76	BRUNI	4	0901	H. R. Price	7–4 Fav.	5
75	RIBOSON	4	0805	W. Hern	11–2 2nd Fav.	4

LOCKINGE STAKES

Group II 1m (straight) 3 y.o. and upwards colts, fillies and geldings
Sex allowance, WFA with a penalty for a winner of a Group I or II race

The Lockinge Stakes is a Group II race demoted to Group III status in 1984 and re-elevated to Group II in 1985. It is for 3-year-olds and upwards and is staged at Newbury over a distance of 1 mile on the straight course in the middle of May. It is the first meeting of the 3-year-old generation of milers with their older-generation counterparts who have remained in training, but it is hardly a real trial of strength as 3-year-olds are always numerically outnumbered by the older horses, and in any case are usually not the best representatives of their generation.

The last thirteen races (1975 race abandoned) have produced fourteen winners, with the 1984 race a dead heat, and has been won by horses of varying quality; the best being dead-heaters CORMORANT WOOD (1984), winner of the previous season's Champion Stakes (Group I, 1¼ miles), and WASSL (1984), winner of the previous season's Irish Two Thousand Guineas (Group I, 1 mile). Also NOALCOHOLIC (1983), subsequent winner of the Sussex Stakes (Group I, 1 mile); champion miler KRIS (1980); and RELKINO (1977), subsequent winner of York's Benson and Hedges Stakes (Group I, 1¼ miles). Only one 3-year-old of note, YOUNG GENERATION (1979), has won the Lockinge and the race regularly falls to the older horses with ten 4-year-olds and two 6-year-olds successful. Usually the race is won by a specialist miler, but occasionally a good-class middle-distance horse (as for instance BROKEN HEARTED (1988), CORMORANT WOOD (1984) and RELKINO (1977)) has the speed necessary to win over the strenuous track.

Only four winners have made their seasonal debut in the Lockinge Stakes and normally a horse will need the benefit of a previous race to succeed here. However, no previous race has had more than a fleeting influence on the outcome. Horses have run over distances of 7 furlongs to 1 mile 2 furlongs in their prior

31

race before success in the Lockinge and perhaps this as much as anything else reveals the uncertainties of winning this race.

Even with the compact size fields of 5–11 runners, the market reflects how divided opinions have been in pinpointing the winner, with four favourites, four 2nd favourites, four 3rd favourites and two outsiders successful. Top trainers invariably win the Lockinge with H. Cecil (three wins) followed by B. Hills (two wins) the most successful trainers on this Berkshire course, where that famous Newmarket trainer's record is second to none.

With the Lockinge Stakes attracting a varying quality of contestant it is not an easy race on which to give positive guidance. It is often a case of finding the horse that is cherry-ripe on the day rather than one who is setting forth on a championship trail. Previous Group I form obviously demands special consideration, as do any runners from Henry Cecil's stable. But with only two winners having won their previous race this is a race to be approached with caution as the expected rarely occurs, and a watching rather than betting brief may be best advised.

88	BROKEN HEARTED	4	0904	P. Cole	8–1	5
87	THEN AGAIN	4	0904	L. Cumani	9–2 2nd Fav.	9
86	SCOTTISH REEL	4	0901	M. Stoute	4–1 2nd Fav.	8
85	PRISMATIC	3	0713	H. Cecil	10–1	11
84 {	CORMORANT WOOD*	4	0905	R. Hills	7–1	
84 {	WASSL*	4	0908	J. Dunlop	9–2	6
83	NOALCOHOLIC	6	0804	G. Pritchard-Gordon	7–2 2nd Fav.	10
82	MOTOVATO	4	0900	B. Hills	7–4 Fav.	7
81	BELMONT BAY	4	0900	H. Cecil	11–10 Fav.	6
80	KRIS	4	0907	H. Cecil	4–9 Fav.	7
79	YOUNG GENERATION	3	0804	G. Harwood	4–1 2nd Fav.	10
78	DON	5	0904	W. Elsey	5–1	10
77	RELKINO	5	0900	W. Hern	4–1 Jt Fav.	9
76	EL RASTO	6	0900	A. Penna (Fr.)	9–2	8
75				———— ABANDONED ————		

*Dead Heat

TEMPLE STAKES

GROUP II   5f   3 y.o. and upwards   colts, fillies and geldings
Level weights, sex allowance, WFA with a penalty for a winner of a
Group I or II race

The Temple Stakes is a Group II race (up to 1986 a Group III
race) for 3-year-olds and upwards over a distance of 5 furlongs
and staged at Sandown Park during the Whitsun holiday meeting
late in May. It is a race that usually fits nicely in the race schedule
for those horses challenging for the honour of being acclaimed
champion sprinter and it has been won by a number of good horses.
HANDSOME SAILOR (1988), DOUBLE SCHWARTZ (1986), NEVER
SO BOLD (1985), FEARLESS LAD (1983), SHARPO (1980), DOUBLE
FORM (1979), LOCHNAGER (1976) and BLUE CASHMERE (1975)
subsequently or previously gained a Group I or Group II prize.

The 5-furlong course at Sandown is the stiffest sprinting track in
the British Isles, having a gradual but steep uphill rise throughout,
with a particularly testing final furlong that mercilessly finds out
any short runners. So it is most suitable for a sprinter adept at a
late final challenge rather than the front-running trail-blazer who
runs out of gas at the end of the race.

Although a glance at the recent winners of the Temple Stakes
reveals an impressive array of successful horses, actually predicting
the winner on the day has been more problematic. It would seem
that it is often in this race that horses reveal their true worth
for the first time. SHARPO (1980) made its English debut, while
DOUBLE FORM (1979) and LOCHNAGER (1976) won their first
Group race before going on to greater honours. The difficulty in
confidently predicting the winner may be explained in that the
thirteen races (1981 was abandoned) produced fifteen winners,
two being dead heats (1984 and 1978). Only three winners won
their previous race, suggesting it is the horse coming into form
rather than the one which has already peaked who will win on
the day.

The Temple Stakes always attracts fair-sized fields (6–15 runners
and on average 11). Although won by 3-, 4- and 5-year-olds it is the

younger age group, with six wins, who just hold sway over the two older groups.

The two Group races programmed earlier in the season, Newmarket's Palace House Stakes (Group III), over 5 furlongs, 23 days earlier), and York's Duke of York Stakes (Group III, 6 furlongs, 18 days earlier), are the races with the greatest influence. Eight winners ran in the Newmarket race with two of them winning it. Negatively, four horses promoted to favourite, two after winning and two finishing in the Newmarket race, were beaten in the Temple Stakes. Two winners ran in the York race but only HANDSOME SAILOR (1988) completed the double, and three horses promoted to favourite, one after winning, and two finishing second at York, were beaten at Sandown.

As with other top sprints, winners of the Temple Stakes are not confined to just the most famous stables but share equally with lesser-known trainers able to demonstrate their abilities if fortunate enough to get a quality horse in their care. W. O'Gorman and M. Stoute, with two wins each, and both responsible for one of the dead heats, are, the only trainers with more than one success.

The market results show wins by five favourites, four 2nd favourites, three 3rd favourites and three outsiders whose prices were 14–1, 16–1 and 33–1.

The Temple Stakes offers quite a stiff challenge to the backer with the race having thrown up a few surprises, although in recent seasons results have been more predictable. However, sprinters are renowned, especially with the smaller margins responsible for victory or defeat over short distances, for reversal of form against rivals, and this is a feature which has not changed. Sandown's unique uphill sprint course also is a striking contrast to the tracks of York and Newmarket where the principals for this race are likely to have last raced. The improving horse who will be challenging for the top sprint race honours as the season progresses is likely to be the one that holds the answer to winning the Temple Stakes.

88	HANDSOME SAILOR	5	0903	B. Hills	7–2 2nd Fav.	10
87	TREASURE KEY	4	0903	P. Makin	16–1	9
86	DOUBLE SCHWARTZ	5	0903	C. Nelson	10–3 Fav.	10
85	NEVER SO BOLD	5	0905	R. Armstrong	9–4 Fav.	6
84	REESH*	3	0806	W. O'Gorman	9–2	9
	PETORIUS*	3	0806	M. Stoute	4–1 Jt 2nd Fav.	9
83	FEARLESS LAD	4	0908	R. D. Peacock	5–4 Fav.	11
82	MUMMYS GAME	3	0802	W. O'Gorman	4–1 Fav.	13
81				ABANDONED		
80	SHARPO	3	0802	J. Tree	33–1	10
79	DOUBLE FORM	4	0811	R. Houghton	5–2 2nd Fav.	12
78	OSCILIGHT*	3	0802	J. Sutcliffe	9–2 Jt Fav.	15
	SMARTEN UP*	3	0902	W. Wightman	14–1	15
77	VILGORA	5	0900	A. Stevens	13–2 Jt 2nd Fav.	6
76	LOCHNAGER	4	0904	M. W. Easterby	5–1	8
75	BLUE CASHMERE	5	0908	M. Stoute	5–1	12

*Dead heat

THE DERBY

Group I   1½m   3 y.o.   entire colts and fillies only
Level weights, sex allowance

The Derby, run at Epsom on the first Wednesday in June, is a Group I race for 3-year-old colts and fillies. The latter, although qualified to run under the entry conditions, seldom do so, and the race was in fact last won by a filly in 1900. It is over the classic stayer's distance of 1½ miles. It is the most glamorous and prestigious race to win in the British calendar with the winner likely to be claimed as the champion stayer of his generation, immediately becoming an extremely highly valued property in his immediately ensuing stud career. Only three Derby winners raced again after their 3-year-old racing season.

The essential qualities necessary to win the Derby, which is always a searching test of speed, stamina and temperament, are:

1.   Good top-class form
2.   Breeding of the highest quality
3.   The stamina to last out the very testing 1½ mile distance
4.   The ability to accelerate devastatingly quickly during the last two furlongs of the race

The Derby is always a competitive race attracting large fields of 14 to 25 runners. With the form of the horses always well exposed it is perhaps not surprising that the obvious form candidates who become the leaders in the betting market have dominated the race. Five favourites, seven 2nd favourites and two outsiders have won the race.

In considering what constitutes top-class form in respect of the Derby, it may immediately be stated that no single race has held a total influence. The winners almost all had a different programme of races prior to the Derby, with the recognised trials all shedding some light on the eventual outcome even if only in a negative way. The only races to have produced the winner on more than one occasion are:

The Dante Stakes, York (Group II, 1 mile 2½ furlongs, 21

days earlier), and responsible for REFERENCE POINT (1987), SHAHRASTANI (1986) and SHIRLEY HEIGHTS (1978).

The Lingfield Derby Trial (Group III, 1½ miles, run 25 days earlier), and responsible for KAHYASI (1988), SLIP ANCHOR (1985) and TEENOSO (1983), with all these completing the double.

The Irish Two Thousand Guineas (Group I, 1 mile, run 18 days earlier), and producing SECRETO (1984), THE MINSTREL (1977) and GRUNDY (1975), but with only GRUNDY completing the double.

The Chester Vase (Group III, 1½ miles, run 29 days earlier), and responsible for SHERGAR (1981) and HENBIT (1980), who both completed the double.

As would be expected, winning form is essential to succeed in the Derby, with eleven winners successful in their prior race. The three other winners were placed in Group I races in their previous contest, all over a shorter distance than the Epsom classic. Of the eleven winners, one won a Group I race, four won a Group II and five a Group III.

Looking at the 2-year-old form of Derby winners, the present trend is definitely to give them an easy first season. Since TROY (1979) who had four races as a juvenile and competed in a Group race in his final outing, no Derby winner has had more than three runs as a 2-year-old. Only SHERGAR and REFERENCE POINT competed in a Group race in their final outing. Similarly, no recent Derby winner since HENBIT (1980) has seen a racecourse until late August, with all except TEENOSO competing over no less than 1 mile as 2-year-olds, showing that all the winners have been trained to exploit their potential stamina to the full rather than any speed they may possess.

The winners have almost without exception been bred in the 'purple' (i.e. by a top-class sire who has won a Group I race or a foreign equivalent, and with a top-class grand sire on the dam's side of the pedigree, that also suggests an adequate premium of stamina). Two sires have dominated the Derby in recent seasons. Firstly, the legendary veteran NORTHERN DANCER, responsible in more recent years for SECRETO (1984) and THE MINSTREL (1977), and in an earlier era for NIJINSKY (1970), who himself has successfully carried on the line, being the sire of GOLDEN FLEECE (1982), SHAHRASTANI (1986) and the paternal grandsire of KAHYASI (1988) whose sire was ILE DE BOURBON. Secondly, the late MILL REEF, sire of REFERENCE POINT (1987) and SHIRLEY HEIGHTS (1978), who also has carried the line forward through SLIP ANCHOR (1985). The only other sire with any influence, hav-

THE DERBY – The most famous race in the world. It is a race that normally runs true to form with every horse's abilities fully exposed to public scrutiny, so the race is usually won by the first or second favourite.

The Maestro, Lester Piggott, in 1983, rides his final Derby winner, on the favourite TEENOSO, beating the white faced CARLINGFORD CASTLE (Michael Kinane).

ing produced two Derby winners, is GREAT NEPHEW, responsible for GRUNDY (1975) and the ill-fated SHERGAR (1981).

Winners of the Derby will need that touch of speed and brilliance of acceleration. This is a quality normally only passed on to them by the highest calibre of sire, who themselves possessed similar powers, which were recognised and fully proven in their racing and/or subsequent stud career.

It can be noted how a number of the most brilliant Derby winners, SLIP ANCHOR (1985), GOLDEN FLEECE (1982),

SHERGAR (1981), TROY (1979) and GRUNDY (1975), displayed a fantastic acceleration within a couple of strides during the last two furlongs of the race to leave their rivals trailing in their wake. Other winners who won in less all-conquering style yet displayed considerable acceleration in the closing stages have been KAHYASI (1988), SHAHRASTANI (1986), SECRETO (1984), HENBIT (1980), SHIRLEY HEIGHTS (1978) and THE MINSTREL (1977), who all showed the traits of a quality not always immediately associated with Derby winners, being that of extreme courage and a determined will to win.

Besides these elements that are essential to a Derby winner it is also necessary for a horse to have the stamina to see out the full distance of the race. Many of the beaten favourites in the Derby were beaten principally because the 1½ mile distance was just beyond their limit. These horses were EL GRAN SENOR (1984) who was beaten only by the smallest margin, but others such as SHADEED (1985) winner of the Two Thousand Guineas, and three horses NIKOLI (1980), BLUSHING GROOM (1977) and WOLLOW (1976) whose brilliant form promoted them to favourite, had only been up to a mile. Other factors are a horse's temperament to withstand pre-race tensions of the preliminaries in the presence of the noise and excitement of a massive crowd.

The best horses usually win the Derby, and although excuses may abound, beaten horses seldom reverse the form with the winner if they ever meet again at level weights over the same distance. A rare exception was the brilliant DANCING BRAVE (1986), definitely the best horse not to win a Derby

The Derby is in many ways a unique race and with its universal appeal is always a most alluring challenge for the backer. The key to finding the winner of the turf's blue riband is a horse with top-class winning form, bred by a top-class sire, proven to see out the distance of 1½ miles. Coupled with these factors is the fact that twelve of the last fourteen winners have been first or second favourite.

88	KAHYASI	3	0900	L. Cumani	11–1		14
87	REFERENCE POINT	3	0900	H. Cecil	6–4 Fav.		19
86	SHAHRASTANI	3	0900	M. Stoute	11–2 2nd Fav.		17
85	SLIP ANCHOR	3	0900	H. Cecil	9–4 Fav.		14
84	SECRETO	3	0900	D. O'Brien (Ire.)	14–1		17
83	TEENOSO	3	0900	G. Wragg	9–2 Fav.		21
82	GOLDEN FLEECE	3	0900	M. V. O'Brien (Ire.)	3–1 Fav.		18
81	SHERGAR	3	0900	M. Stoute	10–11 Fav.		18
80	HENBIT	3	0900	W. Hern	7–1 2nd Fav.		24
79	TROY	3	0900	W. Hern	6–1 2nd Fav.		23
78	SHIRLEY HEIGHTS	3	0900	J. Dunlop	8–1 2nd Fav.		25
77	THE MINSTREL	3	0900	M. V. O'Brien (Ire.)	5–1 2nd Fav.		22
76	EMPERY	3	0900	M. Zilber (Fr.)	10–1 2nd Fav.		23
75	GRUNDY	3	0900	P. Walwyn	5–1 2nd Fav.		18

CORONATION CUP
Group I 1½m 4 y.o. and upwards colts, geldings and fillies
Level weights, sex allowance

The Coronation Cup is a Group I race for 4-year-olds and older horses over a distance of 1½ miles and staged at Epsom on the Derby course usually on the Thursday of the four-day Classic meeting in June. It is an important race for the older generation of horses who have stayed in training for a further season and who will later be aimed at the other prestigious all-age prizes such as the Eclipse Stakes, King George VI and Queen Elizabeth Stakes or Prix de l'Arc de Triomphe.

With there being usually so few quality stayers of Group I standard in training after their 3-year-old race season the Coronation Cup (1975–88) has been contested by only very small select fields of 4–10 runners with an average of 6. It may be expected therefore, that the race is easily predictable and whilst 11 of the 14 races have been won by the 1st or 2nd favourite with eight favourites, three 2nd favourites, and three outsiders successful, a closer review suggests a note of caution. Since 1982 three outsiders have won, at 8–1, 20–1 and 20–1, with the two biggest priced winners when the largest sized fields contested the race. This may be the time to be cautious, for when the race attracts a larger sized field, the race comes up for grabs from the least likely quarter. Two of these shock winners, BE MY NATIVE (1983) and EASTER SUN (1982), were horses not readily associated with Group I prizes.

However, the race has also seen winners obviously of such status, notably TRIPTYCH (1988 and 1987), the third mare to join the select ranks of the immortal PETITE ETOILE and the pre-First World War heroine PRETTY POLLY, who won the race in consecutive seasons. When it is considered that she was also only beaten by a short head in her first challenge for the race in 1986, it can be seen she was only a whisker away from smashing the record books. Other notable winners have been RAINBOW QUEST (1985) subsequently the Prix de l'Arc de Triomphe winner; TIME CHARTER (1984), Oaks Winner in 1982; MASTER WILLIE (1981),

THE CORONATION CUP – The first Group I race of the season for the older generations of horses.

RAINBOW QUEST seen here as a 3 y.o. developed greatly as a 4 y.o. to win the 1985 Coronation Cup and finished the season by winning the Prix de l'Arc de Triomphe.

ILE DE BOURBON (1979), and previous St Leger winners CROW (1978) and BUSTINO (1975). The quality of horse which usually wins this race can be clearly seen.

Only two winners have won this race on their seasonal reappearance and of the twelve who had a previous outing, eight won the prior race. The recent French successes have meant that the Prix Ganay (Group I, 1 mile 2 furlongs at Longchamp, 32 days earlier) is a race to hold great influence, being responsible for four victories. Goodwood's Festival Stakes (formerly Clive Graham Stakes, Listed race, 1¼ miles), which has produced three winners, is the next most influential.

Until TIME CHARTER (1984) and most recently the TRIPTYCH wins, colts had dominated the Coronation Cup, with the fair sex having no success since LUPE (1971) and PARK TOP (1969).

Top trainers of course dominate this race but only P. Biancone (Fr.), J. Tree and H. Candy (two wins each) have had more than a single triumph.

The Coronation Cup with its small fields and normally good betting value is a race to be strongly considered for selection. The backer will normally be able to analyse the race quite quickly and conclude that the outcome rests between only a couple of probables. So paying due regard to top-class form which tends to work out reliably well, will usually be the path to success.

88	TRIPTYCH	6	0811	P. Biancone (Fr.)	11–8 Fav.	4
87	TRIPTYCH	5	0811	P. Biancone (Fr.)	4–5 Fav.	5
86	SAINT ESTEPHE	4	0900	A. Fabre (Fr.)	20–1	10
85	RAINBOW QUEST	4	0900	J. Tree	8–15 Fav.	7
84	TIME CHARTER	5	0811	H. Candy	10–3 Jt 2nd Fav.	6
83	BE MY NATIVE	4	0900	R. Armstrong	8–1	6
82	EASTER SUN	5	0900	M. Jarvis	20–1	8
81	MASTER WILLIE	4	0900	H. Candy	1–2 Fav.	5
80	SEA CHIMES	4	0900	J. Dunlop	5–4 2nd Fav.	4
79	ILE DE BOURBON	4	0900	R. Houghton	4–6 Fav.	4
78	CROW	5	0900	P. Walwyn	9–4 2nd Fav.	5
77	EXCELLER	4	0900	F. Mathet (Fr.)	13–8 Fav.	6
76	QUIET FLING	4	0900	J. Tree	5–2 Fav.	6
75	BUSTINO	4	0900	W. Hern	11–10 Fav.	6

THE OAKS
Group I 1½m 3 y.o. fillies only
Level weights

The Oaks, first run in 1779, is one of the oldest Classic races, being second only to the St Leger. It is the premier Classic for 3-year-old staying fillies; a Group I race run over the full 1½ mile Derby course and usually staged on the Saturday which is the fourth and final day at the June Derby meeting at Epsom.

The Oaks requires many of the qualities identified as being necessary to win the Derby; good top-class form, stamina to last out the distance, yet speed to accelerate in the final quarter-mile of the race. Early June is not the highest point of the season for many 3-year-old fillies and the Oaks may not always (unlike the Derby) be won by the best staying horse of the generation but by the filly who is most forward on the day. Fillies tend to thrive with the warmth of summer sunshine as the natural season reaches its height and therefore some fillies who were beaten in the Oaks often produce better performances later as the summer progresses. The fillies who have dominated their generation at this Classic stayers' distance when entered have gone on to complete the double of the Irish Oaks Classic – DIMINUENDO (1988), UNITE (1987), BLUE WIND (1981), FAIR SALINIA (1978) JULIETTE MARNY (1975) – whilst five fillies who were beaten in the English Oaks then won the Irish Oaks – COLORSPIN (1986), SWIFTFOOT (1982), SHOOT A LINE (1980), GODETIA (1979) and OLWYN (1977). Three winners of the Oaks have completed the double of the final English Classic The St Leger: OH SO SHARP (1985), who is so doing clinched the triple crown, (only the second filly since the War to do so), SUN PRINCESS (1983) and DUNFERMLINE (1977); and two winners have also won Ascot's King George VI and Queen Elizabeth Stakes: PAWNESE (1976) as a 3-year-old and TIME CHARTER (1982) who won it as a 4-year-old.

When adding the achievements of three other horses who were beaten in their respective years as Oaks challengers: ALL ALONG (1982) who as a 4-year-old in 1983 won The Arc de Triomphe and Washington International, MADAM GAY (1981) French Oaks

THE OAKS – The second fillies classic. A race where the unexpected does happen and fillies beaten in the race often improve as the season progresses.

DIMINUENDO and Steve Cauthen are easy winners of the 1988 English Oaks from SUDDEN LOVE (Ray Cochrane). DIMINUENDO later dead-heated in the Irish Oaks, and won the Yorkshire Oaks.

winner (1981), CORMORANT WOOD (1983) Champion Stakes winner (1983) and International Stakes winner (1984), it becomes obvious that beaten competitors in the English Oaks can not always be later safely ignored. Unlike their counterparts in the Derby who competed and had their limitations on the day fully exposed, many 3-year-old Oaks fillies bred on classic staying lines will have been very lightly raced as 2-year-olds and still be open to continued improvement in their 3-year-old season as the summer progresses, and especially in the early Autumn. By September and October they have physically matured on a par with colts and can use their 3 lb sex allowance to great advantage.

The previous race programme of Oak's winners, while quite varied, can be limited to three influential contests: the English One Thousand Guineas (Newmarket, Group I, 1 mile, 37 days earlier), in which five winners ran, four as their immediate prior race, two winning, MIDWAY LADY (1986), OH SO SHARP (1985), and two finishing second; the Sir Charles Clore Stakes (Listed race, 1¼ miles run at Newbury 22 days earlier), in which three fillies ran, two winning, CIRCUS PLUME (1984) and SCINTILATE (1979), and another, SUN PRINCESS (1983), finishing second; the Musidora Stakes (York, Group III, 1 mile 2½ furlongs, 25 days earlier), which DIMINUENDO (1988) and BIREME (1980) both won.

Retrospectively it is easy to recognise the good prior form shown by winners of the Oaks. At the time of the race, however, this appears less obvious, especially as there are a number of lightly raced (and not fully proven) contenders offering challenges for the crown, and with often no major candidates of proven ability who overshadow their rivals. The record of the market leaders is therefore only average with five favourites, three 2nd favourites and six outsiders (6–1, 6–1, 11–1, 12–1, 12–1, 20–1).

The beaten favourites in the Oaks, except for the very narrowly defeated DANCING MAID (1978) who later triumphed in the Group I Prix Vermille, have been an uninspiring bunch and hardly memorable.

The sizes of the fields for the Oaks have not been particularly large, 11 to 16 runners and an average of 13, but are always competitive to provide a wide range of interest.

The winner of the Oaks, like her male Derby counterpart, will need that essential burst of acceleration in the final 2 furlongs of the race, plus the stamina to last out the distance. She will need also to be brave and have no weakness of temperament, as the Oaks is never won by the temperamentally unsound or the faint-hearted.

The Oaks is as severe a test for selection as it is for the horse, and with the unpredictability of improving early season 3-year-old fillies likely to be the issue, it is a race which the backer should approach with caution. As would be expected of a Classic race this is the exclusive domain of the top trainers, with W. Hern (three wins), H. Cecil and J. Tree (two wins each) the leading English trainers.

88	DIMINUENDO	3	0900	H. Cecil	7–4 Fav.	12
87	UNITE	3	0900	M. Stoute	11–1	11
86	MIDWAY LADY	3	0900	B. Hanbury	15–8 Fav.	15
85	OH SO SHARP	3	0900	H. Cecil	6–4 Fav.	12
84	CIRCUS PLUME	3	0900	J. Dunlop	4–1 2nd Fav.	15
83	SUN PRINCESS	3	0900	W. Hern	6–1	15
82	TIME CHARTER	3	0900	H. Candy	12–1	13
81	BLUE WIND	3	0900	D. K. Weld (Ire.)	3–1 Jt Fav.	12
80	BIREME	3	0900	W. Hern	9–2 2nd Fav.	11
79	SCINTILATE	3	0900	J. Tree	20–1	14
78	FAIR SALINIA	3	0900	M. Stoute	8–1 2nd Fav.	15
77	DUNFERMLINE	3	0900	W. Hern	6–1	13
76	PAWNESE	3	0900	A. Penna (Fr.)	6–5 Fav.	14
75	JUILETTE MARNY	3	0900	J. Tree	12–1	12

ROYAL ASCOT

The Royal Ascot meeting is a four-day event commencing on the Tuesday and finishing on the Friday, staged in the middle of June when the English summer should be reaching its first bloom and the conditions for horses and spectators are hopefully ideal. It represents the finest quality of four consecutive days' flat racing to be found throughout the season and is graced by the daily attendance of the Queen and leading members of the Royal Family, earning it the famous regal title.

Besides the racing aspect, Royal Ascot represents an important event in the year's social diary, being the place where the wealthy and class-conscious go to see and be seen. The Royal Enclosure is a specially vetted members-only area, where entry is obtained only by application some time earlier and where the prescribed dress is military uniform or morning dress for men and glamorous but conservative costume the desired attire for ladies. The Queen or the other female members of the Royal Family set the tone in fashion for the ladies with their daily change of wardrobe throughout the week, which is marked by their arrival on the course each day in their resplendent open carriage procession up the centre of the racetrack before the start of racing.

Royal Ascot may be considered the flat-race equivalent of Cheltenham National Hunt Festival where there are championship-type races for different age groups of horses over varying distances. Whereas the Cheltenham meeting comes at the culmination of the season and the winner of each type of race may be crowned as worthy champion, the Royal Ascot meeting is programmed just as flat racing settles into top gear, and although winners gain immense prestige the crowning of champions has to wait until other later races.

A win at Royal Ascot represents a step on the path to championship acclaim rather than a confirmation of title, but good form shown at this meeting can never be lightly dismissed. There are only three Group I races: the Gold Cup (2½ miles), St James

48

ROYAL ASCOT – A feast of top races over four days at the height of mid-summer in June. The best horses, the best trainers and jockeys compete for the most prestigious prizes.

A typical Royal Ascot finish, horses and jockeys battle for supremacy against a backdrop of fashion and social status.

Palace Stakes (1 mile) and Coronation Stakes (1 mile); six Group II races: Queen Anne Stakes (1 mile), Prince of Wales Stakes (1½ miles), King's Stand Stakes (5 furlongs), Ribblesdale Stakes (1½ miles), King Edward VII Stakes (1½ miles) and the Hardwicke Stakes (1½ miles); plus five Group III races, four Listed races and a number of popular handicaps which all go to make up a feast of racing that is full of interest to suit the appetite of almost every racing fan.

QUEEN ANNE STAKES

Group II   1m (straight course)   3 y.o. and upwards (but limited
to 3 y.o.s which had not previously won a Group I race)   colts,
geldings and fillies
Level weights, sex allowance, WFA with a penalty for a winner of a
Group I or II race

The Queen Anne Stakes is a Group II race for 3-year-olds and
older horses over the straight mile course and traditionally serves
as the opening race of the Royal Ascot meeting in mid-June. Raised
in 1984 to Group II status, it has attracted a slightly better standard
of horse and consequently better-quality winners among the older
generation of milers who have dominated this race. With the entry
conditions restricting the very best 3-year-olds from taking part,
the race has been won only four times by the younger generation
as opposed to ten occasions by the older horses.

The race is invariably run at a fast pace on the lush,
well prepared Ascot turf and is a searching test for any horse over
this unrelenting straight mile. Any horse short of fitness will soon
be found out and consequently only two winners, ROUSILLON
(1985), who later was acclaimed top miler of that season, and the
enigmatic RADETZSKY (1978), who returned to the racetrack
after serving as a stallion at stud, overcame the disadvantage of
making their seasonal reappearance here.

Since its elevation in status the Queen Anne Stakes has also
been won more by the specialist milers in slightly smaller fields,
and consequently has become a much more predictable event
with favourites or 2nd favourites winning on each occasion where
hitherto results were much more problematic when only three
favourites but also three 3rd favourites and three outsiders at 11–2,
8–1 and 25–1 were successful. Since 1984 three of the four winners
who had at least one previous race (ROUSILLON (1985) made
a seasonal debut) won it, whereas before only four winners out
of eight (RADETZSKY (1978) made a seasonal debut) won their
prior race. Two races (1975–88) have been of most influence. One
is the Diomed Stakes (Group III, Epsom, 1 mile 110 yards, some
13 days before), in which three winners ran, WAAJIB (1988) and

THE QUEEN ANNE STAKES – Traditionally the opening race of the Royal Ascot meeting, is a Group II event for 3 y.o. and older horses over the straight mile course, and often presents a tricky choice for the backer.

WAAJIB (Michael Roberts) just holds on to win from the well backed French challenger SOVIET STAR (Cash Asmussen, No. 1) and gets favourite backers off to a bad start at the 1988 Royal Ascot.

PENNINE WALK (1986) completing the double, whilst VALIYAR (1983) was placed at Epsom. Negatively, two horses promoted to favourite after contesting the Diomed Stakes were beaten here. The second influential race is the Lockinge Stakes (Group II, Newbury, 1 mile, 31–32 days earlier), in which three winners ran – THEN AGAIN (1987) and BELMONT BAY (1981) completed the double, whilst TROJAN FEN (1984) was unplaced after unseating its jockey. The Lockinge Stakes was also in the prior race programme of four other winners who failed to win there. Negatively, three horses promoted to favourite after competing in the Lockinge Stakes in their previous race were beaten in the Queen Anne Stakes.

The Queen Anne Stakes is normally won by the very top trainers but H. Cecil, with four consecutive wins (1981–84) and J. Tree, two wins, are the only stables with more than a single winner. Any runner from Henry Cecil's yard deserves the closest inspection as he has a great record at Royal Ascot and likes nothing better than to start the meeting on a successful note.

The Queen Anne Stakes, although recently having displayed a more predictable nature, is a race that has often got the backer off to a bad start at the Royal meeting, and unless you are very confident (don't forget the demise of the beaten favourite SOVIET STAR in 1988) it is advisable that you wait for later races to test your betting skills.

88	WAAJIB	5	0905	A. Stewart	5–2 2nd Fav.	5
87	THEN AGAIN	4	0905	L. Cumani	4–5 Fav.	6
86	PENNINE WALK	4	0902	J. Tree	5–2 2nd Fav.	9
85	ROUSILLON	4	0905	G. Harwood	11–4 Jt Fav.	8
84	TROJAN FEN	3	0805	H. Cecil	9–4 2nd Fav.	6
83	VALIYAR	4	0905	H. Cecil	10–1	10
82	MR FLUOROCARBON	3	0806	H. Cecil	3–1 Jt Fav.	10
81	BELMONT BAY	4	0911	H. Cecil	4–1	10
80	BLUE REFRAIN	4	0908	C. Benstead	8–1	11
79	BAPTISM	3	0805	J. Tree	6–1	9
78	RADETZSKY	5	0905	C. Brittain	25–1	10
77	JELLABY	4	0908	H. R. Price	9–4 Jt Fav.	8
76	ARDOON	6	0811	G. Pritchard-Gordon	11–2	9
75	IMPERIAL MARCH	3	0710	M. V. O'Brien (Ire.)	2–1 Fav.	11

PRINCE OF WALES STAKES

Group II 1¼m 3 y.o. and upwards colts, geldings and fillies
Level weights, sex allowance, WFA with a penalty for a winner of
a Group I or II race since a 2 y.o.

The Prince of Wales Stakes, run on the first day of Royal Ascot,
is a Group II race over 1¼ miles for 3-year-olds and upwards.
It is one of the first encounters of the season for the current
3-year-old generation with their older counterparts. The record
suggests that the older horses are still superior at this time in the
season over this distance, 4-year-olds or 5-year-olds winning all the
races in the period under review.

It normally attracts some useful middle-distance performers
and has been won by a number of top-class horses, dual
winner MTOTO (1988 and 1987), who was also a subsequent dual
Eclipse Stakes winner, STANERRA (1983) (who completed a
notable double by capturing the Hardwicke Stakes later during
the meeting), ELA-MANA-MOU (1980) who won both the Eclipse
Stakes and King George VI and Queen Elizabeth Stakes of that
season, and GUNNER B (1978) who also completed the double of
the Eclipse Stakes. In fact the Prince of Wales Stakes is the most
informative guide to the Eclipse Stakes staged a few weeks later.
Besides three horses completing the double, four other winners,
MORCON (1984), CRIMSON BEAU (1979), LUCKY WEDNESDAY
(1977) and ANNE'S PRETENDER (1976), were all placed in the
Sandown race.

The Prince of Wales Stakes therefore is won only by a very
good horse, and sometimes by one of the very highest standard.
This means that winners have usually come to this race with very
solid form credentials. Eleven have won their previous race and
only one winner was unplaced in the prior race.

The most influential race has been the Brigadier Gerard
Stakes (Group III, Sandown, 1¼ miles, usually 21 days earlier),
in which four winners ran and completed the double. However, a
cautionary note is that four horses promoted to favourite also ran
the Sandown race, two of them winning, but were beaten here.
An earlier Sandown race, the Gordon Richards Stakes (Group III,

*THE PRINCE OF WALES STAKES – A Group II 1¼ mile race
which often proves a useful guide to the Eclipse Stakes.*

The white faced MTOTO in 1988 gives jockey Michael Roberts and
trainer Alec Stewart their second successive win in the Prince of Wales
Stakes beating BROKEN HEARTED and Richard Quinn against the rails.
MTOTO subsequently won a second successive Eclipse Stakes to become
the first horse since the war to do so.

formerly Westbury Stakes, 1¼ miles, 52 days earlier) has been
another race to have an influence, with two winners contesting
this as the prior race to this Royal fixture. This earlier Sandown
race has also been the springboard for five other winners in their
programme leading up to the Prince of Wales, with two of them
winning it. Epsom's Diomed Stakes (Group III, 1 mile 110 yards,
11–13 days earlier) and Goodwood's Festival Stakes (Listed race,
1¼ miles, 27–28 days earlier) have been the only other races
with more than a fleeting influence. The Goodwood race has
produced three winners: MTOTO (1988), MORCON (1984) and
LUCKY WEDNESDAY (1977), who completed the double (although
the 1988 race for technical reasons was declared void), and negatively, a horse promoted to favourite after winning was beaten in
the Prince of Wales Stakes.

The Prince of Wales Stakes attracts nicely compact sized fields, of 4 to 11 runners, and with its number of positive pointers offers a fair challenge for selection. The market trends, with six favourites, two 2nd favourites, two 3rd favourites and four outsiders – especially with a couple of recent shock winners (14–1 and 33–1) gives the backer the hint of the unexpected to warn against overconfidence, but points to results being well within the realms of predictability.

A. Stewart, H. Cecil and W. Hern (two wins each) are the only trainers with more than single success in a race that holds encouragement for less well known trainers aspiring to top honours.

88	MTOTO	5	0908	A. Stewart	8–15 Fav.	4
87	MTOTO	4	0904	A. Stewart	7–2 Jt Fav.	10
86	ENGLISH SPRING	4	0812	I. Balding	14–1	9
85	BOB BLACK	4	0907	M. Jarvis	33–1	4
84	MORCON	4	0901	W. Hern	11–8 Fav.	5
83	STANNERA	5	0812	F. Dunne (Ire.)	7–1	11
82	KIND OF HUSH	4	0901	B. Hills	4–1	7
81	HARD FOUGHT	4	0904	M. Stoute	3–1 2nd Fav.	9
80	ELA-MANA-MOU	4	0904	W. Hern	10–3 Fav.	10
79	CRIMSON BEAU	4	0901	P. Cole	11–2	7
78	GUNNER B	5	0901	H. Cecil	4–5 Fav.	7
77	LUCKY WEDNESDAY	4	0901	H. Cecil	5–6 Fav.	5
76	ANNE'S PRETENDER	4	0901	H. R. Price	10–3 2nd Fav.	8
75	RECORD RUN	4	0902	G. Pritchard-Gordon	12–1	6

ST JAMES PALACE STAKES

Group I   1m (round course)   3 y.o.   colts and fillies only
Level weights, sex allowance

The St James Palace Stakes is a Group I race (elevated to this status in 1988) for 3-year-olds only over the old mile or round mile course at Ascot. It is run on the first day of the Royal meeting and in 1988 had the highest prize money for any race during the four-day programme. It normally attracts the best milers of the current 3-year-old generation and is therefore one of the highest-calibre races of the meeting.

Past winners have included SURE BLADE (1986), CHIEF SINGER (1984), DARA MONARCH (1982), TO-AGORI-MOU (1981), POSSE (1980), KRIS (1979), JAAZEIRO (1978) and BOLKONSKI (1975); the best, or almost the best, milers of their generation. These winners, all of whom had been running in the highest grade, continued to achieve success throughout their later careers at this level of competition

The St James Palace Stakes is the race where competitors from the English and Irish Two Thousand Guineas often renew rivalry and where the challenge is renewed to see if top-class form is upheld. Results suggest that normally it is, with winners of the English Two Thousand Guineas TO-AGORI-MOU (1981), BOLKONSKI (1975) and winners of the Irish Two Thousand Guineas DARA MONARCH (1982), JAAZEIRO (1978) confirming their superiority, and beaten horses such as BAIRN (1985), CHIEF SINGER (1984), POSSE (1980) and KRIS (1979) avenging previous memories of defeat without meeting their previous conquerors again.

Therefore the prior races of consequence have been the English Two Thousand Guineas (Group I, Newmarket, 45 days earlier) and Irish Two Thousand Guineas (Group I, Curragh, 31 days earlier). Four winners contested the English Classic with only BOLKONSKI (1975) winning before coming to claim the St James Palace. However, five other winners competed at Newmarket before taking in other races on their route to the Royal meeting with TO-AGORI-MOU (1981) the only other horse to complete the double.

THE ST. JAMES PALACE STAKES – Raised to Group I status in 1988, this is a race on the round mile course for the current classic 3 y.o. generation.

PERSIAN HEIGHTS (Pat Eddery, No. 8) comfortably draws clear of RAYKOUR (Ray Cochrane, No. 10) to win 1988 St James Palace Stakes. Later, PERSIAN HEIGHTS was the first past the post in York's Group I International Stakes, only to be disqualified.

Four of these next ran in the Irish Two Thousand Guineas, with two winning and completing the double. However, the Irish Two Thousand Guineas has also had a negative influence on the St James Palace, with four other horses (three winners of the Irish Classic) promoted to favourite and then beaten here.

Because a number of winners have avenged defeats in their previous race, only six horses actually won their last race. Three of course were the Classic winners, and whilst the three others, HALF A YEAR (1987), KRIS (1979) and PERSIAN HEIGHTS (1988), ran in non-pattern races, the latter two had both been second in Group I company previously.

As would be expected, the St James Palace is principally the preserve of the very top stables although only H. Cecil and L. Cumani, with two wins each, have had more than one victory. However, the recent successes in the 1980s for a few less famous trainers demonstrates that reputation alone is no guarantee for success and a quality winner can emerge from humbler quarters.

The St James Palace Stakes usually attracts small fields of 5 to 9 runners, but as befits a race of this stature, quality rather than quantity is the order of the day. Surprisingly, although the market leaders have figured prominently in finding the winner, the actual favourite has won only three times, whilst six 2nd favourites, two 3rd favourites and three outsiders have been successful. This suggests, especially with small fields, that have averaged 7 runners, the backer should be wary of the clammering that sometimes promotes horses to favouritism and that a more impartial assessment of the race is demanded.

It is worth remembering that Ascot is quite a different track from the straight course of Newmarket's Two Thousand Guineas, or the sweeping mile of the Irish Guineas at the Curragh, and some horses may be more or less suited to Ascot than the other two tracks. Horses may also now be improving as summer reaches its full bloom, and those horses who were in close proximity to the winner of the mile Classics may now be ready to issue a sterner challenge.

88	PERSIAN HEIGHTS	3	0900	G. Hufter	9–2 2nd Fav.	7
87	HALF A YEAR	3	0900	L. Cumani	11–2	5
86	SURE BLADE	3	0900	B. Hills	9–2 Jt 2nd Fav.	7
85	BAIRN	3	0900	L. Cumani	6–4 Fav.	8
84	CHIEF SINGER	3	0900	R. Sheather	85–40 Fav.	8
83	HORAGE	3	0900	M. McCormack	18–1	7
82	DARA MONARCH	3	0900	L. Browne (Ire.)	7–2 2nd Fav.	9
81	TO-AGORI-MOU	3	0900	G. Harwood	2–1 2nd Fav.	8
80	POSSE	3	0900	J. Dunlop	11–2	8
79	KRIS	3	0900	H. Cecil	11–10 2nd Fav	5
78	JAAZEIRO	3	0900	M. V. O'Brien (Ire.)	5–2 2nd Fav.	8
77	DON	3	0900	W. Elsey	11–2	7
76	RADETZKY	3	0900	C. Brittain	16–1	8
75	BOLKONSKI	3	0900	H. Cecil	4–5 Fav.	8

KING EDWARD VII STAKES

Group II 1½m 3 y.o. colts and geldings only
Level weights with a penalty for a winner of a Group I or II race
over 1¼m or further

The King Edward VII Stakes is a Group II race for 3-year-old colts and geldings over a distance of 1½ miles and is now run on the first day of Royal Ascot. It is often called Ascot's Derby and is programmed just a couple of weeks after the real thing. The King Edward Stakes can offer compensation to horses beaten in the Epsom Classic who will appreciate the ease in grade that this race offers. In recent seasons this is the path which three winners have taken: SHERIFF'S STAR (1988), LOVE THE GROOM (1987) and LANFRANCO (1985). All were unplaced in the blue riband event but triumphed at this Royal meeting.

Similarly, ELA-MANA-MOU (1979) who later went on to much greater successes, after finishing fourth in the Derby, captured the King Edward Stakes. However, unless this recent trend becomes the rule, these are exceptions. Most winners have been horses experiencing a raising in class rather than lowering. For some this race therefore served as a platform to launch them to greater success: SHAREEF DANCER (1983) went on to win the Irish Derby, LIGHT CAVALRY (1980) later in the season won the English St Leger, while ILE DE BOURBON (1978) won the King George VI and Queen Elizabeth Stakes. HEAD FOR HEIGHTS (1984), one of the rare winners to have previously run in better class, later captured Newmarket's Group II Princess of Wales Stakes.

Although the majority of winners, except the Derby contenders, had quite different previous race engagements, the common factor among all winners is that they have been lightly raced as 3-year-olds. Only two had three prior races, and the others two or less, with only BUSTOMI (1981) making his season's reappearance in the race. The King Edward Stakes can be ideally programmed for the improving horse who seizes this opportunity before progressing to even better things, and although won by a few relatively inexperienced horses, it has fallen to only one

THE KING EDWARD VII STAKES – often called Ascot's 'Derby' is a Group II race for 3 y.o.'s over 1½ miles.

The improving SHAREEF DANCER is driven out by Walter Swinburn to win the 1983 King Edward VII Stakes from RUSSIAN ROUBLES (Willie Carson, No. 10) and the grey HAWA BALDI (Steve Cauthen). In his next race SHAREEF DANCER won the Irish Derby.

maiden, ILE DE BOURBON (1978), although three others began their 3-year-old careers as such.

In the past, with the race often won by the improving horse, rather than one with proven abilities, the King Edward VII Stakes has not been an easy race to predict even though the fields, of 5 to 13 runners, have been of a desirable size. This has been reflected by the market where only three favourites and two 2nd favourites have won, whilst four 3rd favourites and five outsiders have been successful.

The King Edward Stakes is an interesting race to consider for selection but perhaps that is where the backer should leave it, because invariably the choice will be between the improving horse raised in class and the more exposed horse seeking to redeem higher expectations. This is often a most difficult decision with no consistent positive pointers, except that the King Edward Stakes is invariably won by the very top trainers who are expert in the development of stayers, such as W. Hern (four wins) and H. Cecil (three wins), who have dominated the race.

The advice to backers unless they have very strong views is to maintain a watching brief paying due regard to the winner of the

61

King Edward VII Stakes in its future races where, with its ability now proven, it may be supported with confidence.

88	SHERIFF'S STAR	3	0808	Lady Herries	9–2	8
87	LOVE THE GROOM	3	0808	J. Dunlop	7–1	8
86	BONHOMIE	3	0808	H. Cecil	9–4 Fav.	13
85	LANFRANCO	3	0806	H. Cecil	13–8 Fav.	10
84	HEAD FOR HEIGHTS	3	0806	W. Hern	5–1 2nd Fav.	10
83	SHAREEF DANCER	3	0806	M. Stoute	10–1	7
82	OPEN DAY	3	0806	W. Hern	9–1	11
81	BUSTOMI	3	0806	W. Hern	13–2	11
80	LIGHT CAVALRY	3	0806	H. Cecil	9–2	10
79	ELA-MANA-MOU	3	0806	G. Harwood	11–10 Fav.	9
78	ILE DE BOURBON	3	0806	R. Houghton	11–1	10
77	CLASSIC EXAMPLE	3	0806	P. Walwyn	14–1	10
76	MARQUIS DE SADE	3	0810	H. R. Price	6–1	5
75	SEA ANCHOR	3	0810	W. Hern	4–1 2nd Fav.	8

CORONATION STAKES

Group I   1m (round course)   3 y.o. fillies only

The Coronation Stakes is a Group I race (elevated from Group II status in 1988) for 3-year-old fillies only, run over the round mile course on the second day of Royal Ascot. It is second only in importance to the English and Irish One Thousand Guineas for 3-year-old fillies racing over a mile, and often serves as a re-match for those who have already met in the Classics, whilst occasionally being a prize for a previously underrated filly who missed those races.

The key to the Coronation Stakes is therefore invariably found in the form of these mile Classics, with the Irish One Thousand Guineas (Group I, Curragh, 25 days earlier) as the immediate one holding greater influence. Eight winners of the Coronation Stakes ran in the Irish race with four fillies, SONIC LADY (1986), AL BAHATHRI (1985), KATIES (1984) and CAIRN ROUGE (1980) completing the double. On the negative side, two other winners of the Irish Classic were promoted to favourite in the Coronation Stakes but were beaten.

The English Guineas, programmed three weeks before the Irish, has only twice served as a previous race for this Ascot contest, with ONE IN A MILLION (1979) completing the double and MAGIC OF LIFE (1988) dramatically reversing Newmarket form with the brilliant and previously unbeaten French filly RAVINELLA. PEEBLES (1984) was the other English Guineas winner promoted to favourite and beaten here. However, five fillies only placed in the English Classic won the Coronation Stakes, three of them competing in the Irish Classic on the way. With form of this magnitude it is not surprising that only two fillies who had not previously competed at this high level, CHALON (1982) and ROUSALKA (1975), were able to bridge the gap successfully and gain victory here.

The Coronation Stakes therefore attracts very select fields, of 6 to 14 runners, as only the very best fillies have any chance of winning what is always a competitive race. The market has been reasonably accurate in pinpointing the winner, with six favourites (four of which were odds-on) and one 2nd favourite successful,

63

THE CORONATION STAKES – only elevated to Group I status in 1988, it is always won by a top class filly.

CAIRN ROUGE with Tony Murray on their way to the start before winning the 1980 Coronation Stakes. In her previous race she won the Irish 1,000 Guineas, and ended her 3 y.o. campaign winning Newmarket's Champion Stakes (Group I).

whilst four 3rd favourites and three outsiders have triumphed. The strength of the record of the third choice in the market gives rise to the backer guarding against any overconfidence in the obvious. Due regard must be paid to the filly who has shown semblance of very useful form without previously quite fulfilling that promise.

The top trainers win the Coronation Stakes, with H. Cecil (three wins) and M. Stoute (two wins) the only handlers with more than a single success, although four winners have been trained in Ireland. These were all by different trainers but give warning of the influence the Emerald Isle has on this race.

The Coronation Stakes is a race of quality where the best fillies meet and only a very good one wins. It is a race to be strongly considered for selection, with a focus to be directed towards the filly who is at or about to reach the top of her form, and with this aspect firmly in mind the backer is likely to strike the winning chord.

88	MAGIC OF LIFE	3	0900	J. Tree	16–1	8
87	MILLIGRAM	3	0900	M. Stoute	4–5 Fav.	6
86	SONIC LADY	3	0904	M. Stoute	8–15 Fav.	7
85	AL BAHATHRI	3	0904	H. Thomson-Jones	4–6 Fav.	7
84	KATIES	3	0904	M. Ryan	11–2	10
83	FLAME OF TARA	3	0900	J. Bolger (Ire.)	11–2	6
82	CHALON	3	0900	H. Cecil	9–4 Fav.	8
81	TOLMI	3	0900	B. Hobbs	4–1	10
80	CAIRN ROUGE	3	0904	M. Cunningham (Ire.)	6–5 Fav.	8
79	ONE IN A MILLION	3	0904	H. Cecil	10–11 Fav.	13
78	SUTTON PLACE	3	0900	D. K. Weld (Ire.)	14–1	14
77	ORCHESTRATION	3	0900	A. Maxwell (Ire.)	12–1	10
76	KESAR QUEEN	3	0900	A. Breasley	7–2 2nd Fav.	10
75	ROUSALKA	3	0900	H. Cecil	9–1	11

ROYAL HUNT CUP
0–115 Handicap   1m straight course   3 y.o. and upwards

The Royal Hunt Cup is a handicap for 3-year-olds and older horses over the straight mile course. It is staged on a Wednesday, the second day of the Royal Ascot meeting, and traditionally is one of the most competitive betting races of the season with a healthy ante-post market that is set to capture public interest in the intervening weeks since the Derby. The Hunt Cup always attracts a large field, as owners of mile handicappers (often of widely varying abilities but ever hopeful of success) run their horses to try to win a famous Ascot prize that would normally be out of reach.

A number of good horses have won this race: VAGUE SHOT (1987), MIGHTY FLY (1983), TENDER HEART (1980), JUMPING HILL (1976) and GOVERNORSHIP (1988), all of whom carried 9 st or more. When you add the slightly unpredictable BUZZARDS BAY (1982) who was later to win the Queen Elizabeth Stakes (then Group II) over the course and distance, it shows that only a smart handicapper wins this race.

The large fields of 15 to 31 runners which regularly contest this race mean that the runners split into two, sometimes even three, groups across the track, but the draw has no consistent influence; horses can win from a high, low or middle draw. The only consistent factor in the draw is that the winner seldom races alone, but is in a group that figures prominently throughout the race. In fact nine winners were drawn within six positions of the second, giving them a horse to race against in the closing stages, rather than facing challengers out of view across the track.

Although contested by 3-year-olds and upwards the Hunt Cup is usually won by a 4-year-old. Eleven have won the last fourteen races. The pointers to finding the Hunt Cup winner are broad rather than specific and occasionally contradictory. All the winners except one have carried above 8 st with nine carrying 8 st 7 lb or higher, so it would be unusual to find the winner too far down the handicap. A horse needs that vital burst of acceleration in the final quarter to win a race like the Hunt Cup, and this is a quality which

THE ROYAL HUNT CUP – One of the most competitive handicap races of the Royal Ascot meeting with a very strong betting market.

Apprentice ridden HAWKLEY (Tyrone Williams) defies a 7 lb penalty to win the 1984 Royal Hunt Cup in typical stirring finish from TELEPROMPTER (Willie Carson, white cap) with favourite BASIL BOY (Lester Piggott, No. 2) third.

is hardly likely to have been unnoticed by the official handicapper. So look to the proven performers.

Winning form, however, is not necessarily a prerequisite to win. Only six horses were successful in their previous race, four defying a penalty, yet five others promoted to favourite were beaten by their penalty. Eight horses had failed to win any prior races during the season. This means the market has been a very limited guide, with a win for only one favourite (who was co-favourite of three), three 2nd favourites (one however being TENDER HEART (1980) who landed a tremendous gamble for its connections), four 3rd favourites and six outsiders whose prices ranged from 10–1 to 33–1.

The Royal Hunt, whilst being obviously a most competitive handicap, is not a race to be dismissed completely out of hand and careful consideration of the horses with recent good, improving or winning form may set the backer on the correct path. It is a race in which a few successful gambles have been landed by the connections of winners and which often gives the less famous trainers a chance to have a big race winner. Only J. Sutcliffe's Epsom yard has had more than a single victory and any runner from this stable in the race deserves close inspection.

88	GOVERNORSHIP	4	0906	O. Nelson	33–1	27
87	VAGUE SHOT	4	0905	R. Casey	10–1 Jt 2nd Fav.	25
86	PATRIARCH	4	0712	J. Dunlop	20–1	32
85	COME ON THE BLUES	6	0802	C. Brittain	14–1	27
84	HAWKLEY	4	0806	P. Haslam	10–1	18
83	MIGHTY FLY	4	0903	D. Elsworth	12–1	31
82	BUZZARDS BAY	4	0812	H. Collingridge	14–1	20
81	TEAMWORK	4	0806	G. Harwood	8–1	20
80	TENDER HEART	4	0900	J. Sutcliffe	13–2 2nd Fav.	22
79	PIPEDREAMER	4	0805	H. Candy	14–1	24
78	FEAR NAUGHT	4	0800	J. Etherington	12–1	19
77	MY HUSSAR	5	0810	J. Sutcliffe	10–1	15
76	JUMPING HILL	4	0907	M. Murless	6–1 Co-Fav. of 3	16
75	ARDOON	5	0803	G. Pritchard-Gordon	9–1 2nd Fav.	18

GOLD CUP

Group 1   2½m   4 y.o. and upwards   colts, geldings and fillies
Level weights, sex allowance, WFA

The Ascot Gold Cup is a Group I race for 4-year-olds and upwards over the marathon distance of 2½ miles, and serves as the feature race on the Thursday or 'Ladies Day' at the Royal Ascot meeting. It is a severe test of stamina; the winner will need to see out every yard of the race and yet be more than a one-paced stayer.

The start of the Gold Cup is a couple of furlongs from the beginning of the long mile straight, and the finish is only after the horses have swept past the winning post for a second time, having completed a circuit of the round course. Although there is a premium on stamina, a unique feature of a really good Gold Cup winner is to be able to quicken appreciably in the final 2 furlongs of the race. This was ably demonstrated by the luckless disqualified ROYAL GAIT (1988), dual winners ARDROSS (1982 and 1981) and LE MOSS (1980 and 1979), and the great SAGARO (1977, 1976 and 1975), the only horse to have won three Gold Cups. All of them had a blistering turn of pace to leave their rivals stranded in the latter stages of the race.

Formerly the Gold Cup, as a Group I race, had entry limited to entire horses and fillies and a dearth of long-distance stayers capable of challenging for the very top honour meant there were small fields. Since 1986 the race has been opened to geldings and as a consequence a slight rise in the numbers taking part with on average 10 or 11 runners as opposed to 7 or 8 previously. This puts a more competitive edge to a race which has too often been dominated by an outstanding horse.

Preparing a horse to tackle this extreme distance, with the possibility of the other Cup races to follow, has ensured that all the winners have had fairly light preparation. Only five winners had the maximum of three prior races, and LE MOSS (1980) was expertly prepared by Henry Cecil to make his seasonal reappearance in the race and claim his second Gold Cup.

One of the two prior races of greatest influence has been the Henry II Stakes (Group III, Sandown, 2 miles, usually about

THE ASCOT GOLD CUP – The marathon 2½ mile race that crowns the champion stayer.

ROYAL GAIT (Cash Asmussen) easily beats SADEEM (Greville Starkey) in 1988, in record time. However after a stewards' enquiry the winner was disqualified for interference to EL CONQUISTADOR and SADEEM announced the winner. A lucky result in a lucky race for favourite backers.

17–24 days earlier), in which five winners ran but only LONGBOAT (1986) and ARDROSS (1982) completed the double. Negatively, two winners of the Sandown race promoted to favourite in the Gold Cup were beaten. The other prior race is the Prix du Cadran (Group I, Longchamp, 2½ miles, 25 days earlier), in which triple winner SAGARO ran on each occasion, but won only once, to complete the double on the second of his Ascot victories. Since the domination of the Gold Cup by dual winners ARDROSS and LE MOSS and triple winner SAGARO, when previous race winning form was almost essential, only one winner since 1982 has won its previous race. However, all winners have shown themselves to be proven stayers, having won previously over 2 miles or further.

As staying ability at the very highest level is an easily recognisable attribute, the market has been an extremely reliable guide to pinpointing the winner; with eight favourites, three 2nd favourites and three 3rd favourites successful. After the disqualification of easy winner ROYAL GAIT (1988) it can be said that the Gold Cup has become a 'lucky' race for favourite-backers, and this is a tag which cannot be hung on many races.

As the premier long-distance stayers' race in the calendar, it is always won by older-generation horses who alone have the strength for this stamina-sapping contest. They are always trained by the very top trainers, with the master at the art of handling stayers being H. Cecil (five wins), leading F. Boutin (three wins – gained by Sagaro) and W. Hern and B. Hills (two wins each).

88	SADEEM	5	0900	G. Harwood	7–2 Fav.	13
87	PAEAN	4	0900	H. Cecil	6–1	8
86	LONGBOAT	5	0900	W. Hern	1–1 Fav.	11
85	GILDORAN	5	0900	B. Hills	5–2 Fav.	12
84	GILDORAN	4	0900	B. Hills	10–1	9
83	LITTLE WOLF	5	0900	W. Hern	4–1 2nd Fav.	12
82	ARDROSS	6	0900	H. Cecil	1–5 Fav.	5
81	ARDROSS	5	0900	H. Cecil	30 100 Fav.	4
80	LE MOSS	5	0900	H. Cecil	3–1 Fav.	6
79	LE MOSS	4	0900	H. Cecil	7–4 2nd Fav.	6
78	SHANGAMUZO	5	0900	M. Stoute	13–2	10
77	SAGARO	6	0900	F. Boutin (Fr.)	9–4 2nd Fav.	6
76	SAGARO	5	0900	F. Boutin (Fr.)	8–15 Fav.	7
75	SAGARO	4	0900	F. Boutin (Fr.)	7–4 Fav.	8

RIBBLESDALE STAKES

Group II 1½m 3 y.o. fillies only
Level weights with a penalty for a winner of a Group I or II race
over 1¼m or further

The Ribblesdale Stakes is a Group II race for 3-year-old fillies only, over 1½ miles and now staged on a Thursday, the third day of the Royal Ascot meeting. It has been called the 'Ascot Oaks' but is a race certainly below the class of the Epsom race and is usually an alternative event for fillies below top class, or for later-maturing horses. With the very top-class fillies of proven ability over the longer distances penalised by the conditions of the race, the Ribblesdale Stakes is seldom contested by them. SHOOT A LINE (1980) is the only one to have successfully defied a penalty. In fact for most winners the Ribblesdale will be the pinnacle of their career. The exceptions have been SALLY BROWN (1985), who later won the Yorkshire Oaks (Group I); HIGH HAWK (1983), Doncaster's Park Hill Stakes (Group II); and SHOOT A LINE (1980), Irish Oaks (Group I).

The form of the winners has varied considerably, with two winners, MISS BONIFACE (1988) and SHOOT A LINE (1980), finishing unplaced in the English Oaks, in their previous race. HIGH HAWK (1983) finished second in the Italian Oaks and NANTICIOUS (1977) finished fourth in the Irish One Thousand Guineas, whilst all the other winners experienced varying degrees of elevation in class to win this Group II event. All those except QUEEN MIDAS (1987), previously beaten in the Lingfield Oaks 1½ miles Trial, were tackling a longer distance for the first time and were very much in uncharted territory. So with most winners tackling a longer distance and better horses for the first time, it is no wonder the Ribblesdale has been a selector's nightmare.

The market has been quite uninformative with only one favourite (who was joint favourite), one 2nd favourite, four 3rd favourites and eight outsiders (with prices ranging from 11–2 to 16–1) successful. This suggests that this race is one to leave alone. Five beaten favourites had previously run in the English Oaks, three of these finishing in the first four, whilst another beaten

THE RIBBLESDALE STAKES – A race for 3 y.o. staying fillies and a notoriously difficult race to predict.

DISH-DASH (left-breast girth), with Bruce Raymond, just gets the better of SING SOFTLY (Lester Piggott) to win the 1983 Ribblesdale Stakes.

favourite had finished fourth in the English One Thousand Guineas. This shows that a drop in class holds no certain key to victory in the Ribblesdale.

The fillies competing in the Ribblesdale are invariably extremely well bred, and late-maturing types, with stamina their forte, who are trained by the very top trainers, who are looking for prestigious success to make their charges valued property at stud. Therefore masters with the staying type of animal have dominated the race. H. Cecil (three wins), J. Dunlop and W. Hern (two wins each), are the only trainers with more than one victory. Three other winners were all trained by different handlers in Ireland whose form was equally difficult to assess.

The keynote to winning the Ribblesdale Stakes is to be found in the improving filly, a most unpredictable venture to contemplate, as fillies often progress most individually and at varying rates. The backer is therefore strongly advised to maintain a watching brief, as selection can only be made with much trepidation.

88	MISS BONIFACE	3	0808	P. Kellaway	12–1	11
87	QUEEN MIDAS	3	0808	H. Cecil	9–1	6
86	GULL NOOK	3	0808	J. Dunlop	8–1	12
85	SALLY BROWN	3	0807	M. Stoute	7–1	10
84	BALLINDERRY	3	0807	J. Tree	9–2 2nd Fav.	9
83	HIGH HAWK	3	0807	J. Dunlop	7–1	14
82	DISH DASH	3	0807	R. Armstrong	6–1	10
81	STRIGIDA	3	0807	H. Cecil	5–1	9
80	SHOOT A LINE	3	0811	W. Hern	5–2 Jt Fav.	9
79	EXPANSIVE	3	0807	W. Hern	11–2	7
78	RELFO	3	0810	P. Prendergast (Ire.)	12–1	12
77	NANTICIOUS	3	0810	D. K. Weld (Ire.)	15–2	9
76	CATALPA	3	0810	H. Cecil	16–1	7
75	GALLINA	3	0810	M. V. O'Brien (Ire.)	7–1	6

HARDWICKE STAKES

Group II   1½m   4 y.o. and upwards   horses, geldings and fillies
Level weights, sex allowance with a penalty for a winner of a Group I or II race since a 2 y.o.

The Hardwicke Stakes is a Group II race for 4-year-olds and older horses over a distance of 1½ miles and staged on a Friday, the final day of the Royal Ascot. It is a race for the older generations of proven performers, whose form is well exposed to the public's gaze and whose abilities are well recognised.

The Hardwicke Stakes attracts only a select band of top-class international stayers. The size of the fields has ranged from 4 to 11 runners and this cosmopolitan assembly has been reflected in the results, ten winners being trained in England, two in France and two in Ireland. As would be expected for a race of this standard, the most famous trainers have dominated the race but only two trainers H. Cecil and P. Walwyn, with two wins each, have gained more than a single victory.

The entry conditions of the Hardwicke Stakes require only winners of a Group I or Group II race (since their 2-year-old season) to carry a penalty. This allows the horses which previously had not gained success at this higher group race level the chance to succeed. This may have led to the general standard of winners being somewhat disappointing. Only three winners, ALMAARAD (1988), JUPITER ISLAND (1985) and STANERRA (1983), went forward to win a major prize; JUPITER ISLAND and STANERRA, who broke the course record, both captured the international Japan Cup (Gd. I) on the other side of the globe, and ALMAARAD winning a Group I prize in Germany. There are few other races of similar standard in the calendar at this distance and most horses will be retired to take up stud duties, and this may also explain their subsequent lack of racing success.

As would be expected by this time in the season, every winner of the Hardwicke Stakes has had at least one prior race. Ten winners have won at least one previous race, with seven of these winning

THE HARDWICKE STAKES – A race for top class older horses over 1½ miles.

A pulsating finish between CHARLIE BUBBLES (Pat Eddery (right)) who just got the better of ARTHURIAN (Lester Piggott) to win the 1975 Hardwicke Stakes.

their immediately previous race. Winning form is therefore likely to be of some consequence.

However, by contrast, four other winners failed to win a prior race that season, although three of these, KHAIRPOUR (1984), CRITIQUE (1982) and MONTCONTOUR (1978), had contested a Group I or Group II prize in their previous race, and now challenged for this race with the weight concessions turned to their advantage.

Only two races have had more than a fleeting influence on the Hardwicke Stakes, the Jockey Club Stakes (Group I, Newmarket, 1½ miles, 49–52 days earlier), in which three winners ran; and the Grand Prix d'Evry (Group II, Evry, 1½ miles, 13 days earlier), which the two French winners contested. A notable feature has been that seven winners had not run for at least 35 days previously, and therefore arrived for this race quite fresh.

The market has only been moderately helpful in pinpointing the winner. Three favourites, five 2nd favourites, two 3rd favourites and four outsiders whose prices have been 6–1, 13–2, 12–1 and 25–1, have been successful. This suggests that the backer should beware the obvious and focus upon the horses prominent but not necessarily leaders in the market. Five horses have been promoted to favourite after their performance in Epsom's Group I Coronation Cup and then been beaten, so this would seem to be a race to view cautiously as an influence on the Hardwicke Stakes.

However, the Hardwicke Stakes is a race which can, with a little thought, offer the chance of a reasonably priced winner. It is always won by a horse that thoroughly stays Ascot's stern 1½ mile distance with its tough final furlong finish, yet with a burst of acceleration at the 2 furlong market to leave rivals trailing.

88	ALMAARAD	5	0812	J. Dunlop	6–1	0
87	ORBAN	4	0809	H. Cecil	11–4 2nd Fav.	4
86	DIHISTAN	4	0809	M. Stoute	11–2	10
85	JUPITER ISLAND	6	0809	C. Brittain	85–40 2nd Fav.	4
84	KHAIRPOUR	5	0812	R. Hougton	13–2	7
83	STANERRA	5	0809	F. Dunne (Ire.)	4–1 Jt 2nd Fav.	10
82	CRITIQUE	4	0809	H. Cecil	7–2 2nd Fav.	8
81	PELERIN	4	0812	H. Wragg	7–1	9
80	SCORPIO	4	0900	F. Boutin (Fr.)	2–1 Fav.	7
79	OBRAZTSOVY	4	0809	H. R. Price	9–4 Jt Fav.	6
78	MONTCONTOUR	4	0812	M. Zilber (Fr.)	25–1	6
77	MENEVAL	4	0900	M. V. O'Brien (Ire.)	2–1 Fav.	7
76	ORANGE BAY	4	0900	P. Walwyn	9–2 2nd Fav.	5
75	CHARLIE BUBBLES	4	0810	P. Walwyn	12–1	11

WOKINGHAM STAKES
0–115 Handicap   6f   3 y.o. and upwards

The Wokingham Stakes is a handicap for 3-year-olds and upwards over a distance of 6 furlongs and is staged on the final day of Royal Ascot. It always attracts a very large field of 12 to 30 runners, with an average of 25, usually spread right across the racetrack in what becomes a veritable cavalry charge, and often culminates in an exciting close finish.

It is hardly a race to feel confident of the outcome, yet traditionally attracts great betting interest and a strong ante-post market. Horses in the past have been known to be specially 'laid out' (or prepared) for this race, but the luck of the draw casts a strong influence on the result. Seven winners have come from the lower third of the draw, and four winners from the top third. The middle numbers seem to have had their chances nullified.

The previous race records of the Wokingham winners are contradictory and confusing. Five winners had failed to win a prior race during the season (four of whom failed to make the frame), whilst four other winners won their previous race, and the remaining winners had won at some time earlier in the season. The weight that winners had carried similarly covers almost the full range of the scale, from 7 st 5 lb for MELINDRA (1983) to 10 st for BOONS CABIN (1975).

The trainers involved with the winners have also run from the very top, e.g. M. V. O'Brien, to the lesser lights more usually associated with only handicap successes. P. Cole (three wins) is the only trainer with more than a single success.

There have been some notable winners of the Wokingham Stakes: PETONG (1984), GREAT EASTERN (1981), IMPORT (1976) and BOONS CABIN (1975), all of whom were better class than the average handicapper who competes, and they carried burdens of 9 st 6 lb, 9 st 8 lb, 9 st 4 lb and 10 st respectively.

The market has been, as might be expected, little comfort as a reliable guide to finding the winner. Eight outsiders have been successful although four favourites, one 2nd favourite and one 3rd favourite have also obliged.

THE WOKINGHAM STAKES – A very competitive 6 furlong handicap which generates a lively betting market and invariably ends with a very close finish.

The Vincent O'Brien trained, Robert Sangster owned ROONE'S CABIN, with Lester Piggott, shows how class will out, winning the 1975 Wokingham Stakes by a comfortable ¾ length under a mammoth 10 st from TOLSPRING (Pat Eddery, No. 9) and BLUE STAR (Joe Mercer).

The Wokingham Stakes is not a race in which the backer is advised to speculate, but rather one to watch as a spectator, although the weight-carrying performance of the four noted winners suggests that better class will out and that horses of similar ability cannot be disregarded.

88	POWDER BLUE	6	0805	P. Makin	28–1	30
87	BEL BE YOU	3	0803	P. Cole	11–2 Fav.	29
86	TOUCH OF GREY	3	0808	D. Thom	20–1	28
85	TIME MACHINE	4	0712	P. Hughes (Ire.)	10–1	30
84	PETONG	4	0906	M. Jarvis	11–1 Jt Fav.	28
83	MELINDRA	4	0705	D. Elsworth	7–1 Fav.	27
82	BATTLE HYMN	3	0707	G. Harwood	14–1	24
81	GREAT EASTERN	4	0908	J. Dunlop	16–1	29
80	QUEENS PRICE	4	0713	P. Cole	28–1	29
79	LORD ROCHFORD	4	0808	B. Swift	16–1	28
78	EQUAL OPPORTUNITY	4	0711	R. Arthur	20–1	24
77	CALIBINA	5	0805	P. Cole	14–1	13
76	IMPORT	5	0904	W. Wightman	4–1 Fav.	12
75	BOONE'S CABIN	5	1000	M. V. O'Brien (Ire.)	6–1 2nd Fav.	20

KING'S STAND STAKES

Group II   5f   3 y.o. and upwards   colts, geldings and fillies
Level weights, sex allowance, WFA

The King's Stand Stakes is a Group II race, demoted from Group I status in 1988 after holding the position of perhaps the premier 5 furlong race in the racing calendar. It is for 3 year-olds and upwards and is now open to geldings, whereas before it was restricted to entire colts and fillies. It is run on the final day of the Royal meeting over Ascot's stiff 5 furlong course.

Traditionally the King's Stand Stakes has been one of the races, along with July Cup (Group I, Newmarket, 6 furlongs) and William Hill Sprint Championship (Group I, York, 5 furlongs), which decide who will be acclaimed champion sprinter. It is therefore only won by a very good sprinter. In fact three winners, NEVER SO BOLD (1985), SOLINUS (1978) and LOCHNAGER (1976) completed the treble to become undisputed champions in their respective seasons.

Looking down the list of winners of the King's Stand Stakes the quality of the successful horses immediately becomes apparent. However, the backer, trying to pick the winner on the day, is not equipped with such hindsight and the task is not quite that simple. The market reflects the dilemma posed in selection, with results balanced between the predictable and unexpected. Five favourites and two 2nd favourites have been successful, as opposed to two 3rd favourites and five outsiders (at 10–1 to 33–1).

Examining this more closely it appears that when an outstanding candidate emerges and is consequently promoted to strong favourite (e.g. GODSWALK 4–6 Fav., SOLINUS 4–6 Fav., HABIBTI 4–5 Fav., MARWELL 5–4 Fav. and LOCHNAGER 6–4 Fav.), form is upheld. However, when no such obvious market leader emerges to dominate the proceedings the King's Stand Stakes can become a race up for grabs, with frequent shocks. All the beaten favourites have been 13–8 or longer with the exception of GALLIC LEAGUE (4–6 in the 1988 reconstituted race).

The King's Stand Stakes always attracts a good-sized field, of 8 to 16 runners, with an average of 12. Blinding speed is an essential

THE KING'S STAND STAKES – A race for the best 5 furlong sprinters in training yet where results are evenly balanced between surprises and the predictable.

AFRICAN SONG (Pat Eddery), storms clear for a surprise victory in the 1980 King's Stand Stakes.

quality, plus an ability to quicken inside the stiff final furlong. It is only won by a very good horse on the day. This ability to thoroughly see out every yard of Ascot's 5 furlongs accounts for why nine winners had previously won over 6 furlongs or further. No short runner will succeed here.

Prior winning form also has been a prerequisite to success. Eleven winners also won their previous race. The surprise winners have been exceptions to this rule with CHILIBANG (1988) and SAYF EL ARAB (1983). Winners have had a variety of previous races, with three Irish trained and two French trained, so no set prior race programme has emerged. Only two races have more than a fleeting influence. One is the Temple Stakes (now Group II, 5 furlongs, Sandown, 18–25 days earlier), in which four winners ran, NEVER SO BOLD (1985), DOUBLE FORM (1979) and LOCHNAGER (1976) completing the double, whilst three other horses promoted to favourite, two after winning, were unsuccessful. The other race is the Ballyogan Stakes (Group III, 5 furlongs,

Leopardstown, 13–20 days earlier), with three winners, BLUEBIRD (1987), SOLINUS (1978) and GODSWALK (1977), completing the double, but where two other winners promoted to favourite were beaten in the King's Stand Stakes.

The King's Stand Stakes, with some surprise victories, has enabled a few lesser-known trainers to enter the winners circle, but the Irish maestro Vincent O'Brien (three wins) is leader, ahead of J. Dunlop (two wins) as the only handlers with more than a single victory.

Prior winning form has been the key to success in this Ascot sprint, but unless a very dominant candidate emerges, with impeccable credentials, the backer may need to be wary – especially if there are any doubts about lasting out this punishing 5 furlongs. In the past the King's Stand has been a reliable medium for the astute backer, with speed an easy quality to identify. Provided an air of caution is maintained in accepting only good class Group race form as an essential criterion, the King's Stand Stakes should remain a good betting medium.

88	CHILIBANG	4	0903	J. Dunlop	16–1		8
87	BLUEBIRD	3	0809	M. V. O'Brien (Ire.)	7–2		12
86	LAST TYCOON	3	0809	R. Collett (Fr.)	9–2		14
85	NEVER SO BOLD	5	0903	R. Armstrong	4–1	2nd Fav.	15
84	HABIBTI	4	0900	J. Dunlop	4–5	Fav.	11
83	SAYF EL ARAB	3	0809	W. O'Gorman	33–1		16
82	FEARLESS LAD	3	0809	R. D. Peacock	10–1		14
81	MARWELL	3	0806	M. Stoute	5–4	Fav.	12
80	AFRICAN SONG	3	0809	P. Kellaway	10–1		14
79	DOUBLE FORM	4	0903	R. Houghton	12–1		13
78	SOLINUS	3	0809	M. V. O'Brien (Ire.)	4–6	Fav.	8
77	GODSWALK	3	0809	M. V. O'Brien (Ire.)	4–6	Fav.	11
76	LOCHNAGER	4	0903	M. W. Easterby	6–4	Fav.	13
75	FLIRTING AROUND	4	0904	R. Carver (Fr.)	9–2	2nd Fav.	12

NORTHUMBERLAND PLATE
Handicap 2m 3 y.o. and upwards

The Northumberland Plate Handicap Stakes is a handicap for 3-year-olds and upwards over a distance of 2 miles, staged at Newcastle on the last Saturday in June.

The Northumberland Plate, or 'Pitman's Derby' as it is often called, is one of the oldest handicaps in the racing calendar, having been first run in 1833. It regularly attracts the best staying handicappers in the country who do battle on the testing Newcastle racetrack and has been won by a couple of good horses who were of Group race standard rather than mere handicappers – KARADAR (1984) who carried record weight 9 st 10 lb, and TUG OF WAR (1978 and 1977) who won it for two consecutive seasons.

Most winners have been lightly raced during the season (only one winner had more than four races) and consequently have often been reasonably handicapped (six carried between 8 st and 8 st 9 lb) with only three winners, STAVORDALE (1988), KARADAR (1984) and TUG OF WAR (1978) carrying above 9 st.

The previous race programme of winners has varied, with no one race holding particular influence, although it is interesting to note that eight of the thirteen winners (1982 meeting abandoned) had run in a race at the Royal Ascot meeting 9–11 days before. The races concerned have been the Ascot Gold Cup (Group I, 2½ miles), in which KARADAR and TUG OF WAR ran in without making the frame; the Ascot Stakes (2½ mile handicap) in which four winners ran, although only DAWN JOHNNY was placed; and the Bessborough Handicap (1½ miles), in which STAVORDALE was third and WEAVERS PIN was fourth. However, two other horses promoted to favourite after finishing second in the Bessborough were beaten in the Northumberland Plate. This short span of 9 to 11 days for these winners suggests they were at or close to peak race fitness at the Royal Ascot meeting which may have given them a vital edge over their rivals for this race.

Winning form has not been a major criterion for success in the Northumberland Plate. Only three winners were successful in

NORTHUMBERLAND PLATE – A competitive 2 mile handicap for tough stayers.

The well-backed favourite STAVORDALE (left) tenderly handled by Michael Roberts just gets the better of ZERO WATT (Greville Starkey) in the 1988 Northumberland Plate handicap.

their previous race and there have been only two others with prior wins during the season. Whilst three winners have defied penalties of 4, 6 and 7 lbs to gain victory here, five favourites carrying 6 to 8 lbs have been defeated.

The Northumberland Plate is always a competitive race, attracting 10 to 20 runners, with an average of 14, who will often range the full length of the handicap, and it is a tough race to win. Top stayers of their eras, NICHOLAS BILL (1979), SEA PIGEON (1978 and 1977) and JOHN CHERRY (1975) were all promoted to favourite and beaten, so it says something of KARADAR's feat in 1984 to win with a record weight of 9 st 10 lb, when the previous year he was beaten with 9 st 4 lb. The bare form figures may not have accounted for much, as a couple of winners were dropped from Group I class, and all the beaten favourites were first or second in their prior race. This is definitely a race for the older horses. No 3-year-old has been successful and nine races have fallen to

5-year-olds and upwards, probably through their greater strength and stamina.

The market gives some indication as to where the winner might be found, but with a betting and an ante-post market quite competitive there has been no positive or consistent guide, with three favourites, two 2nd favourites, two 3rd favourites and six outsiders (whose prices were 17–2, 16–1, 20–1, 20–1, 20–1 and 40–1) being successful.

The Northumberland Plate is a race shared equally between the very top stables and the lesser known ones who are usually only associated with handicap prizes. M. Stoute, M. Jarvis and the retired D. Whelan (two wins each) are the only trainers with more than one success.

The Northumberland Plate is a most interesting race to consider and usually provides an exciting spectacle to watch. It has been shown in recent seasons that really top-class stayers can succeed despite the burden of weight. It is, however, not an easy handicap on this testing Newcastle course and unless the backer is convinced of a horse's quality and staying powers, it would be advisable to maintain a watching brief. The form of the race often works out very well subsequently, with a number of horses winning their next contest, especially if lowered in class, so the backer may be advised to take careful note from this point of view.

88	STAVORDALE	5	0902	H. Thomson-Jones	9–4 Fav.	10
87	TREASURE HUNTER	8	0707	J. Fitzgerald	20–1	20
86	SNEAK PREVIEW	6	0812	H. Candy	4–1 Fav.	15
85	TRADE LINE	4	0713	R. Sheather	17–2	13
84	KARADAR	6	0910	M. Stoute	10–1	19
83	WEAVERS PIN	6	0808	M. Francis	20–1	14
82				———— ABANDONED ————		
81	DAWN JOHNNY	4	0806	M. Stoute	5–1 Fav.	18
80	MONS BEAU	5	0707	E. Beeson	40–1	15
79	TOTOWAH	5	0802	M. Jarvis	5–1 2nd Fav.	11
78	TUG OF WAR	5	0902	D. Whelan	11–2	10
77	TUG OF WAR	4	0807	D. Whelan	11–2	15
76	PHILOMINSKY	5	0800	W. Marshall	20–1	11
75	GREY GOD	4	0809	M. Jarvis	8–1 Jt 2nd Fav.	12

OLD NEWTON CUP
0–115 Handicap   1m 4f   3 y.o. and upwards

The Old Newton Cup is a 0–115 handicap race over 1½ miles for 3-year-olds and upwards. It is staged on the Saturday of the two-day meeting at Haydock at the beginning of July.

It attracts comfortable sized fields of 4 to 12 runners, with an average of about 8, who are likely to be experienced performers, from both the older and the current 3-year-old generation. It has been won by the older generations in ten of the fourteen contests, with 5-year-olds winning on seven occasions. This suggests that the race is well suited to the seasoned campaigner. All the winners except ROUSHAYD (1988) and RAKAPOSHI KING (1986) had won at least one prior race in the season, with CLANRALLIER (1985) undefeated in four previous contests. Nine other winners had won at least two previous races before gaining success here. This suggests that a horse's abilities are likely to be well exposed in the handicap and are there for all to assess, but with the winner able to defy the handicapper's hold. In fact the weight carried by winners has fallen into two distinct categories. Eight winners carried 9 st or above and the remaining six winners 8 st 6 lb or less. This suggests that the top-weighted winners have successfully withstood their handicap rating whilst the lower-weighted winners may have been slightly ahead of the assessment. The mid-weight range of horses have been unable to succeed because their abilities would seem to have been correctly assessed.

A number of winners have been obviously improving horses (a handicapper's nightmare), with six winners defying penalties for a previous race success. These included the gallant winner VALENTINIAN (1982) who carried a mammoth burden of 10 st 3 lb including a 3 lb penalty. On the weight issue it is also interesting to note that six winners were apprentice ridden, showing that the skilful use of good apprentice's allowance can be a telling factor on Haydock's galloping track.

The key to finding the winner of the Old Newton Cup at the height of the summer season would seem to lie in the careful assessment of a horse's immediate previous race form. Nine winners won their prior race and so this is the area on which to focus. The most significant races have been the Coopers and Lybrand Summer Cup (formerly the Newbury Summer Cup), staged 23 days earlier, in which three winners competed: VALENTIANIN (1982) who won the Newbury race, RAKAPOSHI KING (1986) and SHADY NOOK (1980), who were third; and the Bessborough Stakes at Royal Ascot, 17 days earlier. The latter race is certainly the more significant. Four winners of the Old Newton Cup have competed in it with three completing the double, CLANRALLIER (1985), ST BRIAVELS (1979) and FOOL'S MATE (1975). However, five other horses were promoted to favourite after their performance in this Royal Ascot race only to be defeated here (three of these five were joint favourites), and only one of these actually won the Bessborough Stakes.

The market in this competitive handicap has been a reasonably helpful guide with three favourites, five 2nd favourites, two 3rd favourites and four outsiders (7–1, 15–2 and 14–1) successful. No major shocks have occurred and selection needs to be focused towards the two leaders in the market. Only H. Cecil (two wins) has had more than one victory. Successes have been gained by both Northern and the more well-known Southern training establishments.

Although not an easy race for the backer, the abilities of most of the competitors are well exposed. Previous race-winning form would appear to be the keynote, as previous winners have consistently overcome the handicapper's clutches to gain a further success.

88	ROUSHAYD	4	0910	R. Houghton	6–1		9
87	PIPSTED	3	0800	G. Wragg	7–1		9
86	RAKAPOSHI KING	4	0907	H. Cecil	9–2 2nd Fav.		10
85	CLANRALLIER	5	0803	J. W. Watts	7–2 Jt Fav.		10
84	BISHOPS RING	3	0806	M. Stoute	7–2 2nd Fav.		4
83	REGAL STEEL	5	0802	R. Hollinshead	14–1		9
82	VALENTINIAN	4	1003	W. Hern	4–1 2nd Fav.		10
81	DOGBERRY	3	0705	H. Wragg	10–3 2nd Fav.		8
80	SHADY NOOK	5	0905	H. Blagrave	8–1		10
79	ST BRIAVELS	5	0903	G. Pritchard-Gordon	7–1		7
78	MOVE OFF	5	0904	J. Calvert	15–2		12
77	MINT	3	0707	W. Elsey	11–4 Fav.		11
76	PEACEFUL	5	0900	J. Tree	9–2 2nd Fav.		8
75	FOOL'S MATE	4	0902	H. Cecil	7–4 Fav.		9

ECLIPSE STAKES

Group I   1½m   3 y.o. and upwards   colts, geldings and fillies
Level weights, sex allowance, WFA

The Eclipse Stakes is a Group I race for 3-year-olds and older horses over a distance of 1½ miles. It is run at Sandown Park in early July and is the first Group I meeting of the season for the present 3-year-old generation at this middle distance. Thus it serves to suggest which may be the superior generation in later encounters during the season.

The record in this sphere in regard to the Eclipse Stakes is almost divided, with six victories to the current 3-year-old generation and eight victories to the 4-year-old and 5-year-old age group. Sometimes a victory here (often by what is usually considered to be the second team of the leading 3-year-olds) will signal further victories in the other national and international 1½ mile races later in the season.

The Eclipse Stakes attracts a select field of internationally trained horses of 4 to 16 runners, with an average number of 9. The largest size field during this time, of 16 runners (1975), resulted in the biggest upset, with victory going to STAR APPEAL (20–1). However, the race is only won by a very good horse, as a glance at the list of recent winners quickly reveals; and often by a horse who is adept at both 1¼ miles and 1½ miles, with the speed and stamina to succeed at either distance. This observation is confirmed by the success of MTOTO (1988), DANCING BRAVE (1986), KALAGLOW (1982) and ELA-MANA-MOU (1980), who completed the double of this race and the King George VI and Queen Elizabeth Stakes. Also MASTER WILLIE (1981) won the Eclipse after winning the Coronation Cup of the same year, and STAR APPEAL (1975) completed the rare double (MILL REEF (1971) did so earlier) of capturing the Eclipse and Prix de l'Arc de Triomphe in the same season, as of course did DANCING BRAVE.

Sandown Park's turning racetrack with its stiff 3½ furlong run-in demands that a horse be able to accelerate during the last 2 furlongs. However fast the race is run, either by a specially engaged front-running pace-setter or more naturally, as the race unfolds horses invariably close up together in the final 1½ furlongs. Here that vital burst of acceleration can be the key factor that defeats horses more suited to the 1½ mile distance.

The form of the winners of the Eclipse is invariably very good. Nine winners have won their previous race whilst of five other horses who were second in their prior race, four had been achieved in Group I company. The race programme that horses will have had before the Eclipse depends upon their age, and no particular race has influenced the result of the Eclipse, especially with the competition being international. Eight English-trained, four Irish-trained and one French and one German-trained horses have won. The selector must inspect the form closely of all runners in the top international Group I races. The only races with more than a fleeting influence have been: (i) the Prince of Wales Stakes (Group II, 1¼ miles, Royal Ascot, 18 days earlier), in which five winners ran, with three, MTOTO (1988 and 1987), ELA-MANA-MOU (1980) and GUNNER B (1978) completing the double; (ii) the French Derby (Group I, 1½ miles, Chantilly, 3 to 4 weeks earlier), in which three horses all trained by Vincent O'Brien ran, but with only SOLFORD (1983) completing the double.

The market has generally been a reliable guide in pinpointing the winner with six favourites, five 2nd favourites, two 3rd favourites and one outsider being successful. The prices of five of the favourites has been odds against, (6–4, 11–10, 6–4, 85–40, 7–4) generally representing fair value.

Until PEBBLES's brilliant victory in 1985, when she trounced the opposition (which included subsequent Arc de Triomphe winner RAINBOW QUEST), the race had never been won by a filly since it was founded in 1886. Whilst not always having been contested by fillies of the highest quality, it is noticeable that fillies as eminent as PARK TOP (1969), DAHLIA (1974) and TIME CHARTER (1983, 1984) and TRIPTYCH (1988, 1987, 1986) were all beaten in the race. It is understandable at this stage in the season that 3-year-old fillies are not yet on par with colts of their own generation, and certainly not with older horses; but it is surprising that the older fillies also have not been more successful and suggests the maxim of waiting until later in the summer to see fillies beating colts.

As would be expected the Eclipse is only won by very top trainers, with M. V. O'Brien (three wins), H. Cecil, G. Harwood and A. Stewart (two wins) the only trainers with more than a single victory.

The Eclipse Stakes is a fair race for selection. Top-class form usually works out extremely well and the backer who pays careful attention to current form and trends is likely to be rewarded.

88	MTOTO	5	0907	A. Stewart	6–4 Fav.	9
87	MTOTO	4	0907	A. Stewart	6–1	8
86	DANCING BRAVE	3	0808	G. Harwood	4–9 Fav.	8
85	PEBBLES	4	0904	C. Brittain	7–2 Jt 2nd Fav.	4
84	SADLERS WELLS	3	0808	M. V. O'Brien (Ire.)	11–4 2nd Fav.	9
83	SOLFORD	3	0808	M. V. O'Brien (Ire.)	3–1 Jt 2nd Fav.	9
82	KALAGLOW	4	0907	G. Harwood	11–10 Fav.	9
81	MASTER WILLIE	4	0907	H. Candy	6–4 Fav.	8
80	ELA-MANA-MOU	4	0907	W. Hern	85–40 Fav.	6
79	DICKENS HILL	3	0808	M. O'Toole (Ire.)	7–4 2nd Fav.	7
78	GUNNER B	5	0907	H. Cecil	7–4 Fav.	9
77	ARTAIUS	3	0808	M. V. O'Brien (Ire.)	9–2	10
76	WOLLOW*	3	0808	H. Cecil	9–4 Fav.	10
75	STAR APPEAL	5	0907	T. Greiper (Ger.)	20–1	16
*76	TREPAN	4	0907	F. Boutin (Fr.)	3–1 2nd Fav.	

(TREPAN for betting purposes declared winner – disqualified for technical reasons some time later)

BUNBURY CUP
0–115 Handicap   7f   3.y.o. and upwards

The Bunbury Cup is a 7 furlong handicap for 3-year-olds
and upwards, rated 0–115 by the handicapper over the straight
Bunbury course at Newmarket. It is staged on Tuesday the first
day of the three-day Summer meeting in July.

It is a prestigious race for horses basically of Handicap class
and therefore always attracts competitive sized fields of 7 to 19
runners with an average of 15, from the leading 6 furlong to 1
mile handicappers. The Bunbury Cup has been won by some very
useful performers: PATRIARCH (1986), TREMBLANT (1985),
dual winner MUMMY'S PLEASURE (1984 and 1983), PATERNO
(1982), CAPTAIN NICK (1981) and PIPEDREAMER (1979). It
has tended to be a highlight in a horse's career, rather than
a stepping-stone to greater prizes. It is held at a time when
conditions are usually perfect for the horses and correspondingly
favourable for selection. Form at this part of the season is usually
at its most settled. Therefore it is not surprising that all but three
winners had run within the previous 21 days (with six of these at the
Royal Ascot meeting) and five other winners within the previous
10 days.

Recent form and fitness is therefore of paramount importance,
with the winner needing that extra spurt of acceleration to
outspeed its rivals in the stiff final furlong. Toughness and battling
qualities will also be required in abundance against tenacious
rivals. This perhaps explains why the more experienced older
horses have dominated over their 3-year-old rivals. 4-year-olds
have won eight races, 5-year-olds four and a 6-year-old one. It
is also not surprising, with the winner likely to be an experienced
horse whose abilities are well recognised by the handicapper, that
higher weighted horses have fared very well in this race. Eight
winners carried 8 st 10 lb or above.

The draw has had some influence, with seven winners coming
from the upper half of the draw, although two others had the
lowest possible draw!

The previous form of the winners has borne little similarity. Five winners won their immediate prior race, but five others were without a previous victory in the season. However, all the winners except MUMMY'S PLEASURE (1984) (who had not raced for 69 days) and the sole 3-year-old winner PENNY POST (1975) (who had not raced for 39 days) had run quite recently, with the races at Royal Ascot having greatest influence. Five winners had run in the Hunt Cup but only PATRIARCH (1986) and PIPEDREAMER (1979) achieved a double, and PATERNO (1982) was the only victor of the Bunbury Cup to be placed in the Ascot race.

The market has had a mixed influence with five favourites, (one of these was a joint and another co-favourite) three 2nd favourites, one 3rd favourite and five outsiders (11–2, 15–2, 8–1, 11–1, 16–1) successful, suggesting that although no positive guide can be given, no major shocks occurred either.

The leading trainers have tended to dominate this race, although it can be noted that two skilful handlers of handicappers, J. W. Watts and P. Haslam (responsible for dual winner MUMMY'S PLEASURE) along with the more famous M. Stoute, are the only trainers with more than a single victory.

The Bunbury Cup, like most handicaps, is not an easy race to consider for selection; however, there are some helpful factors. The distance of 7 furlongs can be quite specialist and demands that a horse be either very adaptable or especially suited to this distance, which is just between a sprint and a mile. Two recent winners, TREMBLANT (1985) and MUMMY'S PLEASURE (1984), have shown this to be the case, completing the double with Ascot's competitive Victoria Cup (7 furlongs) earlier in the season. A proven ability to quicken in the closing stages of this always competitive race also holds a key to finding the winner of the Bunbury Cup.

88	PINCTADA	6	0803	R. Simpson	6–1 Jt Fav.	16
87	INDIVIDUALIST	4	0805	M. Jarvis	16–1	15
86	PATRIARCH	4	0901	J. Dunlop	6–1 Fav.	16
85	TREMBLANT	4	0812	R. Smyth	4–1 Fav.	18
84	MUMMY'S PLEASURE	5	0903	P. Haslam	11–2 2nd Fav.	17
83	MUMMY'S PLEASURE	4	0903	P. Haslam	9–1 Co-Fav. of 3	19
82	PATERNO	4	0901	R. Armstrong	6–1 2nd Fav.	14
81	CAPTAIN NICK	5	0913	J. Hindley	11–1	11
80	STEEPLE BELL	4	0709	M. Stoute	8–1	14
79	PIPEDREAMER	4	0903	H. Candy	15–2	14
78	GREENHILL GOD	4	0805	M. Stoute	9–2 2nd Fav.	11
77	KINTORE	5	0800	J. W. Watts	5–2 Fav.	8
76	LOTTO GIFT	5	0810	D. Hanley	11–2	7
75	PENNY POST	3	0802	J. W. Watts	7–1	14

PRINCESS OF WALES STAKES

Group II   1½m   3 y.o. and upwards
Level weights, sex allowance, WFA with a penalty for a winner
of a Group I or II race since a 2 y.o.

The Princess of Wales Stakes is a Group II race for 3-year-olds
and upwards over a distance of 1½ miles. It is run on the July
course at Newmarket on the first day of the Summer meeting, and
is the first Group race of the season over the Classic 1½ miles
stayers' distance. Here the present generation of 3-year-olds meet
their counterparts for the first time, which can act as a comparative
guide to the merits of each generation.

With only a small number of horses with the ability to
compete at this level of competition, the Princess of Wales
Stakes has attracted only select sized fields, of 4 to 11 runners,
with an average number of 7. It was raised from Group III
to Group II in 1978 but the standard of winners has not
appreciably altered. Only PETOSKI (1985), who subsequently
won King George VI and Queen Elizabeth Stakes, and LIGHT
CAVALRY (1981), the winner of the previous season's St Leger,
were winners with top-class pretensions. The Princess of Wales
Stakes normally attracts contestants who are below the very highest
grade; 3-year-olds whose once Classic race aspirations have now
been tempered to gaining a Group race honour and 4-year-olds
and upwards who are either consistent lower-grade Group race
performers, or handicappers still attempting to bridge the gap.

The entry conditions of the race can provide a wide range
in the weight horses carry, and possibly favour the improving
3-year-old (with or without penalty). Eight races were won by
3-year-olds, five by 4-year-olds and one by a 5-year-old.

Winners are always trained by the top trainers and special
attention should be paid to the runners of W. Hern, who has
captured the race on six occasions.

The Princess of Wales Stakes is a race whose outcome is not
always as predictable as records may suggest, with six favourites,
four 2nd favourites, one 3rd favourite and two outsiders being
successful, for there have also been a couple of major surprises,

in the defeat of ARDROSS (1982) (1–5 Fav.), and HOT GROVE (1978) (1–3 Fav.). In both these instances there were only very small fields of four runners, producing a muddling sort of race on the wide-open Newmarket course which may produce a false result. The previous form of winners has also been fairly difficult to assess, with only two winners, HEAD FOR HEIGHTS (1984) and HEIGHT OF FASHION (1982) successful in their prior race. The form generally has varied as much as the winners, ranging from horses unsuccessful in Group I races lowered in class, to a horse having unsuccessfully competed in a handicap at Brighton.

The Princess of Wales Stakes is a race which offers a challenge for selection with the backer advised to focus on horses proven at the distance who have previously competed at this level or in a higher class.

88	UNFUWAIN	3	0000	W. Hern	6–4 Fav	5
87	CELESTIAL STORM	4	0900	L. Cumani	13–8 Fav.	9
86	SHARDARI	4	0900	M. Stoute	5–2 2nd Fav.	6
85	PETOSKI	3	0800	W. Hern	8–1	5
84	HEAD FOR HEIGHTS	3	0806	W. Hern	10–3 Fav.	9
83	QUILTED	3	0800	M. O'Toole (Ire.)	7–2 Fav.	11
82	HEIGHT OF FASHION	3	0711	W. Hern	4–1 2nd Fav.	4
81	LIGHT CAVALRY	4	0909	H. Cecil	11–4 Fav.	8
80	NICHOLAS BILL	5	0902	H. Candy	12–1	9
79	MILFORD	3	0802	W. Hern	11–8 Fav.	6
78	POLLERTON	4	0902	H. Thomson Jones	7–1	4
77	LORD HELPUS	4	0902	B. Hills	5–1 2nd Fav.	8
76	SMUGGLER	3	0711	W. Hern	11–4 Jt 2nd Fav.	6
75	LIBRAS RIB	3	0711	R. Houghton	8–1	10

CHILD STAKES

Group II 1m 3 y.o. and upwards fillies and mares only
Level weights, WFA with a penalty for a winner of a Group
I or II race since a 2 y.o.

The Child Stakes is a Group II race (elevated from Group III in 1987) for 3-year-olds and older fillies only, over the 1 mile July course, and run on the second day of the Summer meeting at Newmarket. It is one of the few top-class 1 mile races confined to fillies and gives the opportunity for two generations of fillies to meet. As one would expect, the 3-year-old generation usually provides the winner as most top-class fillies do not race after their 3-year-old season. Three-year-olds have won on eleven occasions. SONIC LADY (1987) winning as a 4-year-old for the second time was a rare exception.

The Child Stakes (up to 1974 it was called the Falmouth Stakes) attracts only a select number of runners who are fillies considered to be the leading milers of their generation. The race therefore often attracts an international entry, with fillies from England, Ireland and France, although English-trained fillies have dominated, winning twelve of the races, with only a single success each to a French- and Irish-trained runner. The top trainers associated with Group class horses have reigned supreme here, although M. Stoute (three wins) is the only one to have gained more than a single victory.

Most of the runners will have been competing at the highest level, the 3-year-olds taking on the best milers of their generation with the English and Irish One Thousand Guineas and Royal Ascot's Coronation Stakes looming large in their racing engagements. Royal Ascot's Coronation Stakes 21 days earlier is the previous race with most influence – five winners competing, and three fillies, SONIC LADY (1986), AL BAHATHRI (1985) and CHALON (1982) capturing both. The immediate prior race form of the winners of the Child Stakes may not look impressive, with only three Coronation Stakes winners having winning form, but herein is probably the key to the race. The eleven other winners were unpenalised because they had no previous group race victories and

96

were therefore able to turn this few pounds weight concession to their advantage. When it is considered that INCHMURRIN (1988), MEIS EL-REEM (1984), ROYAL HEROINE (1983), STAR PASTURES (1981) and CISTUS (1978) had been second in Group I events, it is no wonder they were able with their weight advantage to gain their first Group race victory here.

July is also the time in the season when fillies may begin to blossom and the successful early season filly may be superseded by an improving rival, especially if previous differences between them were only slight.

The Child Stakes is a most interesting race to consider, and, as the market reflects with seven favourites, two 2nd favourites, four 3rd favourites and one outsider (16–1) successful, quite a predictable one.

The backer is advised to view the race carefully and not become beguiled into a rash conclusion without due consideration of all the factors, especially not to place overwhelming faith in clockwork consistency in 3-year-old fillies. A due regard in this respect and general appraisal of top-class form should, however, result in a successful and rewarding selection.

88	INCHMURRIN	3	0806	G. Wragg	4–1	7
87	SONIC LADY	4	0910	M. Stoute	11–10 Fav.	4
86	SONIC LADY	3	0811	M. Stoute	4–9 Fav.	8
85	AL BAHATHRI	3	0811	H. Thornton-Jons	6–5 Fav.	9
84	MEIS EL-REEM	3	0805	C. Brittain	6–1	5
83	ROYAL HEROINE	3	0805	M. Stoute	2–1 Fav.	8
82	CHALON	3	0811	H. Cecil	8–15 Fav.	8
81	STAR PASTURES	3	0803	J. Hindley	11–2 2nd Fav.	10
80	STUMPED	3	0712	B. Hobbs	5–1	9
79	ROSE ABOVE	4	0810	M. Cunningham (Ire.)	10–3 Jt 2nd Fav.	7
78	CISTUS	3	0802	W. Hern	7–4 Fav.	10
77	RIVER DANE	3	0805	A. Paus (Fr.)	11–8 Fav.	6
76	DUBOFF	4	0906	B. Hills	16–1	5
75	SAUCEBOAT	3	0801	N. Murless	6–1	6

JULY CUP
Group I   6f   3 y.o. and upwards   colts, geldings and fillies
Level weights, sex allowance, WFA

The July Cup is a Group I race for 3-year-olds and older horses over a distance of 6 furlongs on the July course at Newmarket on the third and final day of the Summer meeting in early July. It was raised to Group I status in 1978 and until 1988 was the only Group I race for 3-year-olds and older horses over 6 furlongs.

The July Cup is therefore a most important race in deciding who will be considered champion sprinter of the year. It has been won by such brilliantly fast horses as NEVER SO BOLD (1985), HABIBTI (1983), SHARPO (1982), MARWELL (1981), MOORESTYLE (1980), THATCHING (1979), SOLINUS (1978) and LOCHNAGER (1976), who could all be said to have gained that crown. The consistent feature of all these winners was blinding acceleration in the final furlong which left rivals stranded.

The July Stakes is a race where the best meet the best. Competition is likely to be international and different generations of horses meet, often to confirm which is the superior generation. In this respect each age group has had it moments of glory with six 3-year-old winners, five 4-year-old winners and two 5-year-old winners. Not surprisingly, no older horse has won in this time as horses with major stallion or stud ambitions hardly ever race past their season as a 5-year-old. The older horse winners with the exception of SOVIET STAR (1988) have all been confirmed sprinters, but six of the 3-year-old winners, AJDAL (1987), GREEN DESERT (1986), CHIEF SINGER (1984), HABIBTI (1983), MARWELL (1981) and MOORESTYLE (1980), have been horses running over distances of 7 furlongs or 1 mile, who reverted for this race to display their forte as sprinters. The form of the winners of the July Stakes has often been vividly exposed to reveal the right credentials in the case of the seven winners who had won their previous race (four of these at Group I level). However, three other winners had failed to win previously during the season.

With nearly all the 3-year-olds reverting to the 'speed game' after varying success over longer distances, the prior race programme

*THE JULY CUP – The highlight of Newmarket's mid-week meeting
in early July attracting an international array of top sprinters and has
considerable influence on who will be considered champion.*

French trained SOVIET STAR (Cash Asmussen) beat Irish trained BIG
SHUFFLE (Michael Kinane) in 1988 and demonstrates how a horse
with speed, yet a non-specialist sprinter, can sometimes succeed in the
July Cup.

of winners has often been quite different. However, for all horses
the King's Stand Stakes (Group I, 5 furlongs, Royal Ascot, 20 days
earlier) has been the race of greatest influence. Five winners ran
in the Ascot race and four – NEVER SO BOLD (1985), MARWELL
(1981), SOLINUS (1978) and LOCHNAGER (1976) – completed
the double. The only exception was GENTILHOMBRE (1977)
who was unplaced at Ascot and only gained the July Cup on
the disqualification of the actual winner. On the negative side,
two other King's Stand Stakes winners – BLUEBIRD (1987) and
HABIBTI (1984) (seeking a second July Cup victory) – were both
beaten.

Competition is always fierce for the July Cup with many
connections believing their sprinters hold some sort of chance,
so fields have ranged from 5 to 16 runners, with an average
of 11 runners. Victory has been shared by English-, Irish- and
two French-trained winners, with M. Stoute (three wins) and R.
Armstrong and M. V. O'Brien (two wins each) as the only handlers
with more than a single success.

Speed is the definable factor responsible for winning the July Cup and at this top level of competition it is an element more discernible and reflected by the market influence with eight favourites, one 2nd favourite, two 3rd favourites and three outsiders (8–1, 10–1 and 10–1) being successful.

The July Cup is most certainly a good race for the backer to consider for selection, with the quality of horses of proven ability likely to reward logical reasoning with success.

88	SOVIET STAR	4	0906	A. Fabre (Fr.)	15–8 Fav.	9
87	AJDAL	3	0811	M. Stoute	9–2	11
86	GREEN DESERT	3	0811	M. Stoute	7–4 Fav.	5
85	NEVER SO BOLD	5	0906	R. Armstrong	5–4 Fav.	9
84	CHIEF SINGER	3	0811	R. Sheather	15–8 2nd Fav.	9
83	HABIBTI	3	0808	J. Dunlop	8–1	15
82	SHARPO	5	0906	J. Tree	13–2	16
81	MARWELL	3	0808	M. Stoute	13–8 Fav.	14
80	MOORESTYLE	3	0811	R. Armstrong	3–1 Fav.	14
79	THATCHING	4	0906	M. V. O'Brien (Ire.)	2–1 Fav.	11
78	SOLINUS	3	0811	M. V. O'Brien (Ire.)	4–7 Fav.	14
77	GENTILHOMME	4	0906	N. Adam	10–1	8
76	LOCHNAGER	4	0906	M. W. Easterby	3–1 Fav.	10
75	LIANGA	4	0904	A. Penna (Fr.)	10–1	13

KING GEORGE VI AND QUEEN ELIZABETH STAKES

Group I 1½m 3 y.o. and upwards colts, geldings and fillies
Level weights, sex allowance, WFA

The King George VI and Queen Elizabeth Stakes is a Group I race for 3-year-olds and older horses over a distance of 1½ miles and is run at Ascot at the end of July. It is the most prestigious race in the British calendar (besides the Derby) and gives the opportunity for the current generation of 3-year-olds to meet and test their prowess against the best older horses over the classic stayer's distance. It normally attracts a very select field of internationally trained runners; fields have ranged in size from 7 to 14, with an average of 10 runners. It attracts larger fields when the race appears more open and smaller fields when the race seems to be dominated by one or two horses.

The King George VI and Queen Elizabeth Stakes is only won by a very good horse and recent winners include great horses such as MTOTO (1988), DANCING BRAVE (1986), SHERGAR (1981), TROY (1979), THE MINSTREL (1977), PAWNESE (1976) and GRUNDY (1975).

The winner will have shown form of the highest calibre. Twelve out of the fourteen winners competed in a Group I race immediately previous to this race, and ten of these twelve winners won it.

The generations are divided in winning this race with 3-year-olds winning on nine occasions, 4-year-olds on four, and a 5-year-old once.

The successful 3-year-old colts (with the exception of ILE DE BOURBON (1978) had all competed in the Epsom Derby, and all but DANCING BRAVE (1986) (the best horse not to have won a Derby) and the late-maturing PETOSKI (1985) were Classic winners. SHERGAR, TROY, THE MINSTREL and GRUNDY were winners of both the English and Irish premier Classics whilst PAWNESE (1976), the only successful 3-year-old filly, had won both the English and French Oaks. These races serve as the itinerary of almost every prospective 3-year-old King George VI

THE KING GEORGE VI QUEEN ELIZABETH STAKES – A most prestigious race where the classic generation of 3 y.o. stayers meet their older counterparts to decide the merits of each.

DANCING BRAVE (Pat Eddery, against rails) beats subsequent International Stakes winner SHADARI (Steve Cauthen, hoops) and TRIPTYCH (Yves St. Martin) proving his ability to see out 1½ miles and avenging his Epsom Derby defeat by SHAHARSTANI (white blaze, centre), to win the 1986 King George VI Queen Elizabeth Stakes.

and Queen Elizabeth Stakes winner, with the Irish Derby serving as the previous race in the programme of four winners. On the negative side, two other winners and a second in the Irish Derby, subsequently promoted to favourites in the King George VI and Queen Elizabeth Stakes, were then beaten in the Ascot race.

The immediate prior race which holds greatest influence for all generations is the Eclipse Stakes over 1 mile 2 furlongs at Sandown 21 days earlier. Six contested it and MTOTO (1988), DANCING BRAVE (1986), KALAGLOW (1982) and ELA-MANA-MOU (1980) completed the double. In contrast, only one horse promoted to favourite after good performance in the Eclipse has failed to collect, and that was TIME CHARTER attempting as a 5-year-old to win the race in successive seasons, and emulate the great DAHLIA, the only horse to achieve this feat since the race was founded in 1951.

The race is invariably run at a very fast pace throughout, with some leading contenders also having a pacemaker to ensure the race is a true test of speed and stamina. The then record-breaking time set by GRUNDY (1975) in an epic struggle with the gallant BUSTINO is the most graphic example of this, but with a fast pace throughout and a testing short straight it is only a horse with the finest powers of acceleration in the last 2 furlongs who comes out victorious here.

The King George VI and Queen Elizabeth Stakes, being a race of such quality and with extremely exposed public form, has been a good race for the backer following the market trends, with five favourites, five 2nd favourites, two 3rd favourites and two outsiders (whose prices were 12–1 and 13–2) successful. The note of caution, however, is that three of the winning favourites have been at the uneconomic odds of 2–5, 2–5 and 4–5. Three of the seven beaten favourites were French-trained, suggesting their form was either overrated or that they failed to adapt to English racing conditions. As would be expected, the winner is always trained by a top trainer. However, only W. Hern (four wins) and G. Harwood (two wins) trained the winner on more than a single occasion.

The King George VI and Queen Elizabeth Stakes is a most searching test of horse and rider where the very best of respective generations meet the very best. As only top-class form will suffice here, and this is well exposed to the public gaze, the market leaders will accurately reflect the horses' chances.

88	MTOTO	5	0907	A. Stewart	4–1 2nd Fav.	10
87	REFERENCE POINT	3	0808	H. Cecil	11–10 Fav.	9
86	DANCING BRAVE	3	0808	G. Harwood	6–4 2nd Fav.	9
85	PETOSKI	3	0808	W. Hern	12–1	12
84	TEENOSO	4	0907	W. Wragg	13–2	13
83	TIME CHARTER	4	0904	H. Candy	5–1 2nd Fav.	9
82	KALAGLOW	4	0807	G. Harwood	13–2	9
81	SHERGAR	3	0808	M. Stoute	2–5 Fav.	7
80	ELA-MANA-MOU	4	0907	W. Hern	11–4 2nd Fav.	10
79	TROY	3	0808	W. Hern	2–5 Fav.	7
78	ILE DE BOURBON	3	0808	W. Hern	12–1	7
77	THE MINSTREL	3	0808	M. V. O'Brien (Ire.)	7–4 Fav.	11
76	PAWNESE	3	0805	A. Penna (Fr.)	9–4 2nd Fav.	10
75	GRUNDY	3	0807	P. Walwyn	4–5 Fav.	10

THE GOODWOOD FESTIVAL

The Goodwood Festival Meeting is five days of quality racing staged at the most picturesque English racecourse at the height of the national holiday season, in the last week of July or the first week in August. The five days of 'Glorious Goodwood', as it is known, commence on the Tuesday and end on the Saturday after what is usually a most enjoyable week of racing. While Royal Ascot's social convention demands top hat and tails, Goodwood reflects the holiday mood of panama hats and blazers or light summer suits, and attracts, besides the racing officiandos, a large number of summer holiday makers.

The more relaxed atmosphere, however, does nothing to lessen the competition of a programme of racing that includes a Group I race, a number of Group II and Group III prizes and a few popular and competitive handicaps (Steward's Cup and Extel Handicap, etc.). This is the middle of the Flat Race season and a time which also heralds the commencement of the jumping season. Already training plans are being provisionally arranged for the late summer and early autumn campaigns of contestants who figure prominently in the important races here. Early-season form can be superseded as horses improve and 'come to themselves' with benefit of time and the summer warmth, and also as the going now rides very fast.

The 'Glorious Goodwood' meeting, with its thirty races spread over the five days, covers a range of races from the marathon 2 mile 5 furlongs of the Goodwood Cup (Group III) which means the contestants must cover the complete circuit of the twisting undulating course, to the furious 5 furlong dash for 2-year-olds (Molecombe Stakes, Group III).

THE GOODWOOD FESTIVAL MEETING – is five days of high quality racing at the height of summer in late July on the most picturesque of English racecourses, Goodwood. While Royal Ascot's dress is formal high fashion, 'Glorious' Goodwood's response is a relaxed holiday atmosphere of shirt sleeves and ice cream and for those seeking a formal uniform, panama hats.

A typical view at the Goodwood meeting shows the field streaming past the winning post with the famous Trundle Hill and the rolling Sussex Downs in the background.

105

STEWARD'S CUP
0–115 Handicap   6f   3 y.o. and upwards

The Steward's Cup is a Handicap for 3-year-olds and upwards, rated 0–115, over 6 furlongs, and is staged at Goodwood on the Tuesday and is the first day of the festival meeting. It is a popular and competitive handicap, that attracts lively ante-post betting, and a number of horses are betted on at long odds some time before the race in the hope of landing a hefty gamble.

The race always attracts large fields (16 to 30 runners) who cover the whole range of the weights, and the race often resembles a cavalry charge as horses in a line abreast cover the whole width of the course. With such large fields the race can end up with the runners splitting into two groups soon after the start, one group tracking over to the stand-side rails while others keep to the far side. There is no conclusive evidence to say which is the favoured position.

The race has been won recently by some good sprinters; probably the best was PETONG (1984), who later was to win Vernons Spring Cup (Group II, 6 furlongs), especially when it is considered he broke the 20th century weight record, carrying 9 st 10 lb. GREEN RUBY (1986), SOBA (1982), CREWS HILL (1981) and AHONOORA (1978) were other winners who were much better than the average sprint handicapper normally associated with winning a Steward's Cup.

Although this sprint handicap is a race of pure speed from beginning to end, the winner will still need that burst of acceleration inside the final furlong to withstand challenging rivals or to draw it from the pack of more one-paced horses. While weight in handicaps can be a great leveller, it is usually only horses at the top end of the weight scale who possess this vital finishing speed, and a class horse over Goodwood's easy 6 furlongs should be able to withstand the burden relatively easily. However, only two winners, PETONG (9 st 10 lb) and CREWS HILL (9 st 9 lb), have broken the 9 st barrier, and looking strictly at the weight carried by recent winners, the well-handicapped horse would seem

THE STEWARDS CUP – A competitive 6 furlong handicap with a healthy Ante Post market and hefty wagers on the day.

The apprentice ridden grey STANDAAN (Paul Bradwell) forges clear from toiling rivals in the 1979 Steward's Cup to strike a blow for favourite backers and get them off to a good start on the first day of Goodwood week.

to hold sway. Ten winners carried 8 st 5 lb or less, and four below 7 st 11 lb.

The form of winners has varied. Only four winners won their previous race, yet all but three winners had won at least one race previously that season, and SOBA had won six prior races, AL TRUI five prior races, and AUTUMN SUNSET three races, showing that their form was well exposed to public gaze.

No immediate prior race has held more than a slight influence over the outcome of the Steward's Cup, not surprisingly when the winners have come from very varied backgrounds. No trainer has had more than one success and these range the breadth of the profession. The age of winners has been divided amongst all generations – 3-year-olds six wins, 4-year-olds three wins, 5-year-olds four wins and a 6-year-old one win. The most significant previous race has been the Wokingham Stakes, a 6 furlong handicap at Royal Ascot 39 days earlier, with two winners, PETONG (1984) and CALIBINA (1977), completing the double, and AL TRUI (1985) finished third and IMPORT (1975) fourth at Ascot. AL TRUI was the only one of the quartet to have raced again before the Steward's Cup. The only other prior race to hold any influence is the 6 furlong handicap at Kempton (Prix Hippodrome D'Evry) twelve days earlier, in which GREEN RUBY and AL TRUI both finished third.

For such an obviously competitive handicap the market has been quite a useful guide to pinpointing the winners, with five winning favourites (one joint), but at the rewarding odds of 5–1, 6–1, 8–1, 8–1 (Jt Fav.), and 9–1; one 2nd favourite, and of course eight outsiders whose prices ranged from 14–1 to 50–1.

The Steward's Cup is not an obvious race for the prudent backer to consider. The list of probables often gains in number, the more the intricacies of weight are pondered. The race, however, is seldom won by a complete no-hoper, and a horse which has a touch of class about it, whether an improving 3-year-old (which often holds the solution) or a proven older horse, the reward for successful selection will be an attractively priced winner.

88	ROTHERFIELD GREYS	6	0808	C. Wall	14–1	28
87	MADRACO	4	0702	P. Calver	50–1	30
86	GREEN RUBY	5	0812	G. Balding	20–1	24
85	AL TRUI	5	0801	S. Mellor	9–1 Fav.	28
84	PETONG	4	0910	M. Jarvis	8–1 Jt Fav.	26
83	AUTUMN SUNSET	3	0802	M. Stoute	6–1 Fav.	23
82	SOBA	3	0804	D. Chapman	18–1	30
81	CREWS HILL	5	0909	F. Durr	11–1 2nd Fav.	30
80	REPETITIOUS	3	0702	G. Harwood	15–1	28
79	STANDAAN	3	0710	C. Brittain	5–1 Fav.	16
78	AHONOORA	3	0800	B. Swift	50–1	23
77	CALIBINA	5	0805	P. Cole	8–1 Fav.	24
76	JIMMY THE SINGER	3	0708	B. Lunness	15–1	17
75	IMPORT	4	0800	W. Wightman	14–1	21

SUSSEX STAKES
Group I   1m   3 y.o. and upwards   colts, geldings and fillies
Level weights, sex allowance, WFA

The Sussex Stakes is a Group I race for 3-year-olds and upwards over a distance of a mile and is staged at Goodwood on the second day of the festival meeting. It marks the meeting of the current generation of 3-year-old milers with their older counterparts and the likelihood of the winner being claimed as the season's champion miler. A look at recent winners: WARNING (1988), SONIC LADY (1986), ROUSILLON (1985), CHIEF SINGER (1984), KINGS LAKE (1981), POSSE (1980), KRIS (1979), JAAZEIRO (1978), WOLLOW (1976), BOLKONSKI (1975), may confirm this view.

The Sussex Stakes attracts a select field of 5 to 13 runners, usually the best milers in training, with entrants from England, Ireland and France. The record of the successful trainers in this race demonstrates an international flavour, with M. V. O'Brien (Ire.) (three wins), H. Cecil (three wins), G. Harwood (two wins) and A. Fabre (Fr.) (one win). Other trainers, with only a single success, have all been English based.

As it is rare for the cream of the previous season's milers to remain in training as 4-year-olds, the Sussex Stakes has been dominated by the current season Classic contenders, with 3-year-olds winning all but two races which fell to 4-year-old ROUSILLON (1985) and 6-year-old NOALCOHOLIC (1983). By this time in the season 3-year-olds will be getting on a par with their older contenders, who will have to be very smart to withstand the challenge at the weight-for-age scale.

To win the Sussex Stakes form will normally need to be first class. Nine horses won their previous race, although only two of them were successful at Group I standard over different distances. CHIEF SINGER won the Newmarket 6 furlong July Stakes, and WOLLOW (albeit at the technical disqualification of the winner) won Sandown's 1 mile 2 furlong Eclipse Stakes. With 3-year-olds dominating Royal Ascot's St James Palace Stakes (now Group I but formally Group II), this has been the race of almost total influence. Six winners ran in it as their immediate prior

110

THE SUSSEX STAKES – The premier race of the meeting where the 3 y.o. Classic generation meet their older rivals to see who will be acclaimed Champion miler.

SONIC LADY (Walter Swinburn) quickens to comfortably win the 1986 Sussex Stakes and maintain the excellent record that favourites hold in the race, beating the other Michael Stoute trained runner SCOTTISH REEL (Greville Starkey, No. 3). EFISIO (Willie Carson, stripes) was last of the five runners.

race and seven horses in all, five completing the double and two finishing second. The fillies' equivalent race at the Royal meeting, the Coronation Stakes, was similarly contested by the two winning fillies but with only SONIC LADY (1986) winning both; yet the beaten ON THE HOUSE (1982) had previously won the English One Thousand Guineas. When it is considered that KINGS LAKE (1981) and JAAZEIRO (1978) were Irish Two Thousand Guineas winners, and WOLLOW (1976) and BOLKONSKI (1975) English Two Thousand Guineas victors, the quality needed to succeed here becomes obvious.

To win this race a horse will need speed to remain in contention throughout the race, yet with a rare brilliance in acceleration to outpace rivals who will be no slouches themselves. It is a case of selecting the best of the best, and with form at this very highest

111

level of competition likely to be extremely reliable, this can be a race in which the backer can do well.

The market has reflected this view, with favourites successful on ten occasions (although unfortunately seven were odds-on – as was one beaten favourite), two 2nd favourites and two outsiders (the only winners not first or second in their previous race).

The Sussex Stakes, with top-class form reliably upheld on the fast ground prevalent at the height of summer, offers the backer a fine opportunity to capitalise fully, apart from the problem of getting value for money in the odds offered by the bookies.

88	WARNING	3	0810	G. Harwood	11–10 Fav.	9
87	SOVIET STAR	3	0810	A. Fabre (Fr.)	3–1 2nd Fav.	7
86	SONIC LADY	3	0807	M. Stoute	5–6 Fav.	5
85	ROUSILLON	4	0907	G. Harwood	2–1 Jt Fav.	10
84	CHIEF SINGER	3	0810	R. Sheather	4–7 Fav.	5
83	NOALCOHOLIC	6	0907	G. Pritchard-Gordon	18–1	11
82	ON THE HOUSE	3	0907	H. Wragg	14–1	13
81	KINGS LAKE	3	0810	M. V. O'Brien (Ire.)	5–2 2nd Fav.	9
80	POSSE	3	0810	J. Dunlop	8–13 Fav.	9
79	KRIS	3	0810	H. Cecil	4–5 Fav.	7
78	JAAZEIRO	3	0810	M. V. O'Brien (Ire.)	8–13 Fav.	6
77	ARTAIUS	3	0810	M. V. O'Brien (Ire.)	6–4 Fav.	11
76	WOLLOW	3	0810	H. Cecil	10–11 Fav.	9
75	BOLKONSKI	3	0810	H. Cecil	1–2 Fav.	9

RICHMOND STAKES

Group II   6f   2 y.o. only   colts, geldings and fillies
Level weights, sex allowance with a penalty for a winner of
a Group I or II race

The Richmond Stakes is a Group II race for 2-year-olds only, over 6 furlongs and is normally staged on the second day of Goodwood's Summer Festival meeting. It is usually only won by a very speedy 2-year-old and a list of some of the winners confirms this: WARNING (1987), PRIMO DOMINE (1984), TENDER KING (1981), YOUNG GENERATION (1978), PERSIAN BOLD (1977) and J O TOBIN (1976). However, perhaps surprisingly, with the exception of J O TOBIN who raced with great success in America as a 3-year-old, only WARNING, PRIMO DOMINE, YOUNG GENERATION and ANOTHER REALM among the winners enhanced their reputation as 3-year-olds with another Group race success.

The Richmond Stakes attracts only a small select field of 4 to 10 runners, with an average of 6, because only the fastest 2 year olds will have any chance of winning this prestigious prize over Goodwood's easy 6 furlong course.

It also comes at a time in the season when the established earlier form of the more precocious two year old can be challenged by potentially classier peers, with less racecourse experience but subject to greater possible improvement. This may explain why there have been a number of form upsets in the race. This may be indicated in the fact that only four winners of this Group II standard race had previously competed in Group race company. For the ten other winners this race represented a raising in class for them and therefore a likely improvement on previous form.

The form of the winners has been variable. Only three horses, WARNING (1987), PRIMO DOMINE (1984) (four previous races) and J O TOBIN (1976), were unbeaten (although J O TOBIN had only one previous race). Ten winners, including the above mentioned, won their prior race and no winner was previously a maiden. Seven winners also had four or more previous races, suggesting that unless a horse is improving or classy enough to outshine its rivals, racing experience will be a very useful asset.

113

Unlike some prestigious 2-year-old races, the Richmond Stakes has been won by stables right across the training spectrum, with G. Harwood (two wins) the only handler with more than a single victory.

The market mirrors the alternatively predictable and unpredictable nature of the Richmond Stakes, with six favourites successful (five of which were odds-on, as were two beaten favourites), one 2nd favourite, one 3rd favourite and six outsiders (8–1, 11–1, 12–1, 12–1, 16–1 and 20–1).

No prior race has proved to be a consistent influence although three of the four winners had previously run in Royal Ascot's Group III 6 furlong Coventry Stakes. Only PRIMO DOMINE managed to complete the double. In fact two winners of the Coventry Stakes – CUTTING BLADE (1986) and VARINGO (1979), promoted to favourite in the Richmond Stakes – were beaten; as was another winner of a Group prize, GREEN DESERT (1985), previously winner of Newmarket's July Stakes Group III 6 furlongs.

The Richmond Stakes can therefore cause problems in selection. The backer is advised to be confident only when there is an outstanding candidate who has stood the test of a number of races at Group standard. One should be wary of any horse that may have gained an inflated reputation without such a solid background. Selection will need to be based on what a horse has actually achieved, and with special consideration for any challenger that has demonstrated a brilliant burst of speed in the final furlong.

With form variable and earlier season form often being overturned, this is not a race to fill the backer with confidence, because even when you get it right the rewards can be scanty. So unless convictions are extremely strong it is a race to leave alone.

88	HEART OF ARABIA	2	0900	C. Brittain	11–1	6
87	WARNING	2	0811	G. Harwood	4–11 Fav.	7
86	RICH CHARLIE	2	0811	C. Nelson	11–4 Jt Fav.	8
85	NOMINATION	2	0811	P. Cole	8–1	10
84	PRIMO DOMINE	2	0811	B. Swift	10–11 Fav.	6
83	GODSTONE	2	0811	P. Haslam	14–1	9
82	GALLANT SPECIAL	2	0811	R. Armstrong	4–6 Fav.	4
81	TENDER KING	2	0811	J. Sutcliffe	11–4 2nd Fav.	7
80	ANOTHER REALM	2	0811	F. Durr	16–1	10
79	CASTLE GREEN	2	0811	M. Stoute	20–1	5
78	YOUNG GENERATION	2	0811	G. Harwood	12–1	5
77	PERSIAN BOLD	2	0811	A. Ingham	4–6 Fav.	5
76	J O TOBIN	2	0811	N. Murless	8–11 Fav.	5
75	STAND TO REASON	2	0811	B. Hills	12–1	9

EXTEL STAKES HANDICAP

0–115 Handicap 1¼m 3 y.o. only

The Extel Stakes Handicap is a race for 3-year-olds only, rated
0–115 in the official Handicap, and run over a distance of 1¼
miles on the Friday, the fourth day of the Goodwood Festival. It is
thought to be one of the most competitive handicaps of the season
for 3-year-old middle-distance performers. It usually attracts a
number of improving horses with recent winning performances
who are likely to be better than the handicapper has rated them.
It has, however, been won by horses carrying weights that range
the full length of the handicap, from 9 st 3 lb carried by BROKEN
HEARTED (1987) down to 7 st 7 lb by KARAMITA (1980). The
weights are divided, with five winners carrying 8 st 11 lb or above,
and nine 8 st 6 lb or below. Also, two winners (both trained by
Barry Hills), defied penalties: INDIAN TRAIL (1981) with 5 lb
extra and DUBOFF (1975) with 6 lb extra, carrying 8 st 3 lb and
8 st respectively.
   Although the Extel Stakes is considered a tough handicap
to crack, a notable feature is that all but three winners had
recent winning form (of these exceptions AD LIB RA (1977) had
competed throughout his season's campaign exclusively in Group
race company, whilst CRIMSON BEAU (1978) had started his season's campaign as a Classic trialist in a Group race, only to have
his sights lowered to handicap grade) and KAZAVIYNA (1988),
a daughter of KARAMITA (1980), who was still a maiden. The
six other winners began their 3-year-old campaign as maidens,
gradually improving to capture this prize. It is these opposing
approaches which make the Extel Handicap a difficult race to predict. This is highlighted by FREE GUEST (1984) (subsequently one
of the best winners), who had only one prior race before winning;
whilst DUBOFF, another filly, had seven prior races winning the
first six consecutively. Similarly, FISH 'N CHIPS (1985) won
four consecutive previous races, MILLFONTAINE (1983) three,
and BROKEN HEARTED (1987) two; and with CHINOISERIE (1986)
and LINDORO (1979) also winning a couple of consecutive races

THE EXTEL HANDICAP – A very competitive handicap for middle distance 3 y.o.'s.

The well-handicapped KARAMITA, (Phillip Robinson), wearing the colours of the Aga Khan, comfortably wins the 1980 Extel Handicap by six lengths. Keeping it in the family her daughter KAZAVIYNA emulated this victory in 1988 with her own success.

it can be seen how most winners have been well exposed to the handicapper.

This shows just how skilled many of the training performances must have been, to keep improving the horse enough to withstand the handicapper's grip. Consequently only the top trainers have succeeded in the Extel Stakes: L. Cumani (three wins) leads from P. Cole, W. Hern, B. Hills and M. Stoute (two wins each). The honours list in fact reads more like one associated with a Group rather than a Handicap race prize.

As most winners had their schedule programmed to their individual needs by their respective trainers, the previous race programmes of most winners has been completely different, with no race holding much influence on the outcome. Only the Duke of Cambridge Handicap (1 mile 2 furlongs at Newmarket, 16–23 days earlier) has had any significance on the Extel Handicap, with three winners competing – INDIAN TRAIL completing the double and defying a penalty, whilst two other horses who finished second won this Goodwood race.

The Extel Stakes regularly attracts competitive sized fields, of 7 to 15 runners, and is usually won by a tough colt or gelding in a hard-fought finish. However, two of the four occasions when it has been won by fillies, FREE GUEST (1984) and KARAMITA (1980), were the easiest and widest-margin victories in memory.

For a race renowned for its competitive character the Extel Stakes has been a medium for some surprisingly hefty and success-ful gambles by connections of winners, notably INDIAN TRAIL's victory. The market therefore has been a not uninformative guide to finding the winner, with five favourites, two 2nd favourites, three 3rd favourites and four outsiders (7–1, 12–1, 14–1, 16–1) successful, showing that most winners have been far from friend-less. The winning favourites, at 6–4, 9–4, 3–1, 4–1 and 4–1, have also been good value.

Although the Extel Stakes is not an easy race for selection the key invariably lies in picking out the improving 3-year-old likely to be still just ahead of the handicapper. This will usually resolve on two or three candidates, but with no collateral form lines between them to judge who is really the best, the backer may need to turn to the market for guidance. Any strong support for one of these, especially if trained by a leading stable with a good record in the race, is likely to put the backer on the right track.

88	KAZAVIYNA	3	0710	M. Stoute	16–1	14
87	BROKEN HEARTED	3	0903	P. Cole	7–2 2nd Fav.	14
86	CHINOISERIE	3	0811	L. Cumani	14–1	13
85	FISH 'N CHIPS	3	0803	L. Cumani	9–4 Fav.	14
84	FREE GUEST	3	0806	L. Cumani	4–1 Fav.	15
83	MILLFONTAINE	3	0813	G. Harwood	6–1	12
82	BUSASCO	3	0901	W. Hern	7–1	10
81	INDIAN TRAIL	3	0803	B. Hills	3–1 Jt Fav.	9
80	KARAMITA	3	0707	M. Stoute	5–1 2nd Fav.	10
79	LINDORO	3	0900	W. Hern	6–4 Fav.	8
78	CRIMSON BEAU	3	0802	P. Cole	4–1	7
77	AD LIB RA	3	0900	R. Houghton	4–1 Fav.	14
76	IL PADRONE	3	0801	J. Sutcliffe	12–1	13
75	DUBOFF	3	0800	B. Hills	7–1	12

NASSAU STAKES

Group II   1m 2f   3 y.o. and upwards   fillies and mares only
Level weights, WFA with a penalty for a Group I or II race
winner in a prescribed year

The Nassau Stakes is a Group II race for 3-year-olds and older
fillies over a distance of 1¼ miles and is staged at Goodwood
on a Saturday, the fifth and final day of the Festival meeting. It
is the last important race of the Goodwood meeting and usually
serves as a fitting finale to the excellent racing which had been
seen earlier in the meeting.

The Nassau Stakes attracts some of the best middle-distance
fillies in training and has been won by some very good fillies, FREE
GUEST (1985), OPTIMISTIC LASS (1984), ACCLIMATISE (1983),
VIELLE (1980), CISTUS (1978), TRIPLE FIRST (1977) and dual
winner ROUSSALKA (1976 and 1975). It is a race dominated by
3-year-olds (all but two winners have been 3-year-olds since it was
opened to older horses in 1975) and ideally it is suited to horses not
quite good enough to win a classic. Five of the 3-year-old winners
had previously run unsuccessfully in the Epsom Oaks but only one
had finished out of the first four.

As a number of fillies may have been previously taking
on opposition that was too good for them or may still be
experimenting to find their best distance, it is not surprising
that only three winners had won their previous race. Two races
of greatest significance have been the Child Stakes (now Group
II, 1 mile, Newmarket 24 days earlier), in which seven winners
raced, although only CISTUS (1978) completed the double. This
was also the race in which the two 4-year-old winners FREE GUEST
(1985) and ROUSSALKA (1976) ran, however. Two winners of the
Child Stakes, AL BAHATHRI (1985) and SAUCEBOAT (1975),
were promoted to favourite but both being milers found the extra
distance of the Nassau Stakes beyond them

In contrast, the Lancashire Oaks (Group III, 1½ miles,
Haydock, 28 days earlier) has seen two winners, PARK EXPRESS
(1986) and VIELLE (1980) complete the double, and second-
placed ACCLIMATISE (1983), go on to capture the Nassau Stakes.

Winners of the Nassau Stakes therefore have been balanced between those fillies going up in distance from a mile, to those who have been tackling the long trip of 1½ miles now trying this middle distance. Horses whose stamina is unproven are always problematic and often places selection in the realms of guesswork. The market, however, has been fairly accurate in gauging the winner, with four favourites and six 2nd favourites successful, and only one 3rd favourite and three outsiders to break their dominance. However, two winning and four beaten favourites have been odds-on; and three of the winning 2nd favourites have been joint, just in case the backer believes this race is all beer and skittles.

The Nassau Stakes regularly attracts only select fields (5 to 11 runners) of the choicest-bred fillies seeking Group race success to enhance their stud value. Therefore the winners only come from the very top drawer of trainers, and especially those adept at handling quality fillies. Henry Cecil (four wins) heads the list from M. Stoute, the Wragg Stable and now retired B. Hobbs, with two wins each.

The Nassau Stakes is an interesting race for selection and although dominated by the market leaders is not without pitfalls. With the summer season now at its height all the fillies should have had some sun on their backs and be reaching full bloom. This will often present the backer with an uncomfortable choice between those who have already blossomed and those just about to. The choice between supporting proven ability that may have reached its peak, or the unproven promising to fulfill its potential, is not one to get right without some luck or even inspiration.

88	ELA ROMANA	3	0806	G. Wragg	10–1	7
87	NOM DE PLUME	3	0806	H. Cecil	11–4 2nd Fav.	5
86	PARK EXPRESS	3	0808	J. Bolger (Ire.)	7–1	7
85	FREE GUEST	4	0908	L. Cumani	11–2 Jt 2nd Fav.	11
84	OPTIMISTIC LASS	3	0808	M. Stoute	5–2 Fav.	5
83	ACCLIMATISE	3	0805	B. Hobbs	4–1 Jt 2nd Fav.	6
82	DANCING ROCKS	3	0805	H. Wragg	12–1	11
81	GO LEASING	3	0808	G. Harwood	15–2	11
80	VIELLE	3	0805	B. Hobbs	8–15 Fav.	7
79	CONNAUGHT BRIDGE	3	0805	H. Cecil	5–1 2nd Fav.	10
78	CISTUS	3	0805	W. Hern	4–7 Fav.	7
77	TRIPLE FIRST	3	0805	M. Stoute	13–2 Jt 2nd Fav.	8
76	ROUSSALKA	4	0906	H. Cecil	15–8 Fav.	10
75	ROUSSALKA	3	0808	H. Cecil	9–4 2nd Fav.	6

GEOFFREY FREER STAKES

Group II   1m 5f 60y   3 y.o. and upwards   colts, geldings and fillies
Level weights, sex allowance, WFA with a penalty for a winner of a Group I or II race since a 2 y.o.

The Geoffrey Freer Stakes is a Group II race for 3-year-olds and older horses over a distance of 1 mile 5 furlongs 60 yards. It is staged on a Saturday, the second day of the two-day meeting at Newbury in mid-August. It is a race that attracts small fields of top-class stayers, 4 to 10 runners with an average of 5, and has been a race that often gives the older stayer a chance of a good class Group prize or heralds the rise of a 3-year-old.

In the former case we can cite MOON MADNESS (1987), SHERNAZAR (1985), KHAIPOUR (1983), ARDROSS (1982 and 1981), NICHOLAS BILL (1980) and SWELL FELLOW (1976), with perhaps surprisingly four of these winners being a 5-year-old or older when successful. For the 3-year-old generation, who have won seven of the races in recent years, the race, while of importance in itself, is often used as a preparation for the final Classic the St Leger. In this respect it has been a disappointment in not producing any double winners, although BAYNOUN (1984) came closest, beaten by only a neck at Doncaster. NINISKI (1979) also was placed but ILE DE BOURBON (1978), an odds-on favourite for the St Leger, and CONSOL (1975) were both well beaten. However, CUT ABOVE (1981), who could only finish third of four to ARDROSS in this race, did win the St Leger, reversing previous form with the red-hot favourite SHERGAR.

The previous race programmes of winners have varied considerably depending to which generation they belong. The Princess of Wales Stakes (Group II, over 1½ miles, Newmarket, 39 days earlier) has the most influence, with NICHOLAS BILL (1980) completing the double of the two races, and ARDROSS (1982) and KHAIRPOUR (1983) were placed in the Newmarket contest.

The only other race of significance has been King George VI and Queen Elizabeth Stakes (Group I, Ascot, 21 days earlier),

120

THE GEOFFREY FREER STAKES – A race for top class stayers over an extended 1½ mile distance.

The magnificent 3 y.o. ILE DE BOURBON (John Reid) on the way to post before winning the Geoffrey Freer Stakes in 1978. Winner of the King George VI Queen Elizabeth Stakes in his previous race he was subsequently promoted to favourite in the St. Leger but beaten.

with ILE DE BOURBON (1978) completing a rare double and MOON MADNESS (1987) fourth in the Ascot race. With eight winners running in similar Group II or higher Group I races, only six winners won their previous race. However, all the winners had been racing over 1½ miles or further and could be expected to stay this 1 mile 5 furlong 60 yard distance. The winners have been divided into those who ran within the last 15–21 days (six winners), or those who had not ran for at least 35 days earlier (eight winners), with stayers often benefiting from this longer break.

The Geoffrey Freer Stakes, over the extended classic stayer's distance, attracts small fields and produces few shocks, and so the market has been a very reliable guide to picking the winner, with seven favourites (although four were odds-on), four 2nd favourites and just three outsiders. The quality of horse needed to win at this

121

level ensures that it is only won by the very top stables. R. Houghton (three wins) is ahead of H. Cecil (two wins) as the only trainers with more than a single victory.

The Geoffrey Freer Stakes is a fair test of selection with an analysis of the small field usually resolving to a couple of easily identified probables and a little careful thought should provide a successful result for the backer.

88	TOP CLASS	3	0803	C. Brittain	20–1	6
87	MOON MADNESS	4	0908	J. Dunlop	11–8 2nd Fav.	4
86	BAKHAROFF	3	0803	G. Harwood	6–4 Fav.	6
85	SHERNAZAR	4	0900	M. Stoute	8–13 Fav.	5
84	BAYNOUN	3	0804	R. Houghton	2–1 2nd Fav.	5
83	KHAIPOUR	4	0900	R. Houghton	9–1 Fav.	7
82	ARDROSS	6	0908	H. Cecil	1–3 Fav.	4
81	ARDROSS	5	0908	H. Cecil	10–11 Fav.	4
80	NICHOLAS BILL	5	0905	H. Candy	15–8 2nd Fav.	5
79	NINISKI	3	0801	W. Hern	7–4 2nd Fav.	7
78	ILE DE BOURBON	3	0809	R. Houghton	11–8 Fav.	7
77	VALINSKY	3	0804	M. V. O'Brien (Ire.)	8–13 Fav.	5
76	SWELL FELLOW	5	0900	J. Hindley	16–1	5
75	CONSOL	3	0806	P. Walwyn	9–1	10

THE YORK FESTIVAL MEETING

The York Festival is a three-day meeting staged on the beautiful Knavesmire racecourse at York in the latter part of August. It commences on a Tuesday and runs through until Thursday, providing a good general spectacle of racing plus three important Group I races: the International Stakes (formerly the Benson and Hedges Gold Cup), the Yorkshire Oaks and the William Hill Sprint Championship, which confirm or begin to establish the leading candidates for the champion honours in the respective types of contest (i.e. middle distance, staying fillies or sprinters).

While not having the same impact in the social diary as the Royal Ascot meeting in June, it is often referred to as 'The North's Ascot', and has a special charm and warmth of its own.

The racing itself, whilst not being quite of the high general overall standard associated with the Royal Ascot, has the three above-mentioned Group I races that are equal rivals to any race at Ascot, plus having The Tote Ebor Handicap which in 1988 had almost the richest prize money for a British Handicap. It also has the unique feature of staging two Group I races on the same day, a characteristic unmatched at any other British racing fixture throughout the season.

The races scheduled at the meeting range from the prestigious Group I prizes down to juvenile selling stakes and present a full array of races in the racing calendar. The top races attract challenges from Ireland and the Continent plus of course from all leading English-trained candidates. The smaller prizes regularly attract a strong challenge from the southern-based stables, which the northern stables (who do not usually get the cream of flat-race bloodstock) often find difficult to repel.

Programmed at the height of summer, the York Festival has a fine mixture of grand races and more domestic events to provide interest for the racing connoisseur and average fan alike.

THE YORK FESTIVAL – A three day mid week meeting staged on the beautiful Knavesmire course at York in late August. It brings quality racing in abundance to the North of England.

The French trained DAHLIA (Lester Piggott) wins in 1975 in the rain, beating another French challenger CARD KING, to gain her second successive victory in the International Stakes.

INTERNATIONAL STAKES
(Formerly BENSON AND HEDGES GOLD CUP)

Group I   1m 2f 110y   3 y.o. and upwards   colts, geldings
and fillies
Level weights, sex allowance, WFA

The International Stakes (until 1985 the Benson and Hedges Gold Cup) is a Group I race for 3-year-olds and upwards over a distance of 1 mile 2 furlongs 110 yards, and staged on a Tuesday, the first day of the Festival Meeting at York. It is a race which has assumed a position of some importance in the British racing calendar since its inception in 1972. Its inaugural running witnessed the dramatic victory of the gallant ROBERTO over the previously unbeaten BRIGADIER GERARD in a course record time for the distance which remained intact until 1988 when the subsequently disqualified PERSIAN HEIGHTS bettered it.

Since that initial race in 1972, racing fans have been treated to numerous other exciting spectacles in the race, and many other notable winners, TRIPTYCH (1987), COMMANCHE RUN (1985), CORMORANT WOOD (1984), CAERLEON (1983), ASSERT (1982), BELDALE FLUTTER (1981), MASTER WILLIE (1980) plus the brilliant dual winner DAHLIA (1975 and 1974), all of whom previously or subsequently were winners of other Group I races. This quality, winning form at the very highest level, is the essential element necessary to win, and all the winners, with the exceptions of SHADY HEIGHTS (1988), SHARDARI (1986), MASTER WILLIE (1980), HAWAIIAN SOUND (1978) and RELKINO (1977), had already gained a Group I race honour. However, the latter three were all second in the English Derby of their respective year, whilst SHADY HEIGHTS was beaten only by the smallest margin by MTOTO in Sandown's Group I Eclipse Stakes and SHARDARI had in its previous race finished second to DANCING BRAVE in Ascot's Group I King George VI and Queen Elizabeth Stakes. The three Derby runners-up also were perhaps better suited to this 1 mile 2½ furlong trip than the classic stayers' distance of 1½ miles.

125

THE INTERNATIONAL STAKES (Formerly Benson and Hedges Gold Cup) – A top class race over the middle distance of 1 mile 2 furlongs and 110 yards attracting an international field and a race which only a very good horse wins.

The intelligent DAHLIA after her 1975 International Stakes race victory.

The race has regularly attracted the best middle-distance performers from England, Ireland and the Continent, with select-sized fields ranging from 6 to 12 runners and on average 8 to 9. It is the meeting of different generations of horses over this distance, with normally not all the best representatives of the older generations contesting the race, and the WFA scale by this time in the season beginning to favour quickly improving members of the younger generation. Three-year-olds have won seven of the fourteen contests.

Top-class form is the criterion to win the International Stakes;

consequently eleven winners ran in a Group I race in their previous race, with Ascot's King George VI and Queen Elizabeth Stakes (Group I, 1½ miles, 24 days earlier) holding the greatest influence. Seven winners ran in Ascot's Diamond Festival race, five of whom were placed, another was inexplicably tailed off, and only TROY (1979) won, matching DAHLIA's dual triumph five years earlier. Conversely, five other horses promoted to favourite in the International Stakes after their Ascot performance were beaten. Four of these were second, with GRUNDY (1975) the only winner who had gained a heart-stopping narrow victory. However, each had been subjected to a very hard race and all possibly needed a slightly longer recovery period between these races than the time allowed. A jaded horse won't win the International Stakes so perhaps it is not surprising that four winners won the York prize after an absence of 45 days or longer from racing. The seven successful graduates from Ascot's premier race (with the exception of ASSERT (1982) who had a rare tussle) were not subject to battle-weary struggles in defeat, nor as in TROY's case a facile victory. So they benefited from their encounters rather than becoming jaded by them.

Another race with some influence on the outcome of the International Stakes has been Goodwood's Sussex Stakes (Group I, 1 mile, 20 days earlier). WOLLOW (1976) completed the double to display his versatility at mile and middle distances, whilst RELKINO (1977), only third, appreciated the further 2½ furlongs of the Knavesmire. In contrast, ARTAIUS (1977), who won the Sussex Stakes when promoted to favourite at York, was unsuccessful.

Whilst top-class form is essential to win the International Stakes, winning the previous race is not. Only four winners were successful in their prior contest. However, all had been contesting Group I or II prizes and only DAHLIA (1975) (winning the race for the second successive season) had not won at least one previous race during the season. Therefore, perhaps, due consideration should be paid to horses about to peak, rather than those who already have. Any contestant expecting to coast to victory on past reputation is in for a shock, as the International Stakes is always hard fought.

It takes a tough horse to win this race, and explains why colts have dominated, and only two brilliant and game mares, the 5-year-olds TRIPTYCH (1987) and DAHLIA (1975) and the 4-year-old filly CORMORANT WOOD (1984) have broken the male hold. The younger 3-year-old fillies at this time in the season have been shown to be not quite up to it, with even the brilliant OH SO SHARP (1985) beaten, as was another good filly MRS PENNY (1980), both when promoted to favourite.

Attracting an international array of runners, the International Stakes has been won by a corresponding array of trainers. W. Hern and B. Hills, with two wins each, are the only handlers with more than one success.

A glance at the record of the market leaders shows six favourites, three 2nd favourites, two 3rd favourite and only three outsiders (9–1, 15–1 and 33–1) successful. However, whilst the market may steer the backer in the right direction, caution remains the watchword. Two successful favourites were odds-on, as have been four beaten ones – notably the 'racing certs' OH SO SHARP (1985), 2–5 favourite, and GRUNDY (1975), 4–9 favourite. The race can therefore hold pitfalls for the unwary.

The distance of 1 mile 2½ furlongs is almost unique and may present a problem to the genuine 1½ mile stayer on this flat galloping track. It may also be the limit of distance for the purely 10 furlong horse, especially if the ground should ride soft in a rain-soaked English summer. Some doubts may therefore be cast on a candidate who might otherwise seem to hold impeccable credentials.

Top class holds the key to picking the winner, but the backer should think carefully should the obvious candidate show any weakness over the distance, or be felt to be weakened by a previous hard-fought race.

88	SHADY HEIGHTS	4	0906	R. Armstrong	7–2	6
87	TRIPTYCH	5	0903	B. Biancone (Fr.)	13–8 Fav.	11
86	SHARDARI	4	0906	M. Stoute	13-8 Fav.	12
85	COMMANCHE RUN	4	0906	L. Cumani	5–1 2nd Fav.	6
84	CORMORANT WOOD	4	0903	B. Hills	15–1	9
83	CAERLEON	3	0810	M. V. O'Brien (Ire.)	10–3 Fav.	9
82	ASSERT	3	0810	D. V. O'Brien (Ire.)	4–5 Fav.	7
81	BELDALE FLUTTER	3	0810	M. Jarvis	9–1	9
80	MASTER WILLIE	3	0810	H. Candy	13–2	12
79	TROY	3	0810	W. Hern	1–2 Fav.	10
78	HAWAIIAN SOUND	3	0810	B. Hills	2–1 Fav.	10
77	RELKINO	4	0906	W. Hern	33–1	8
76	WOLLOW	3	0810	H. Cecil	9–4 2nd Fav.	7
75	DAHLIA	5	0904	M. Zilber (Fr.)	7–2 2nd Fav.	6

YORKSHIRE OAKS STAKES
Group I   1m 4f   3 y.o. fillies only
Level weights

The Yorkshire Oaks is a Group I race for 3-year-old fillies over a distance of 1 mile 4 furlongs and is staged at York on the first day of the Festival Meeting. It is a race for the highest quality 3-year-old staying fillies and attracts fields of 5 to 13 runners, on average 9. The Yorkshire Oaks has been won by four fillies DIMINUENDO (1988), CIRCUS PLUME (1984), SUN PRINCESS (1983) and FAIR SALINIA (1978), who had all previously won the Epsom Oaks to complete a notable double; and by three fillies who previously won the Irish Oaks, DIMINUENDO (1988), SHOOT A LINE (1980) and FAIR SALINIA (1978). However, the Irish Oaks (Group I, 1½ miles at the Curragh 31–38 days earlier) has had quite a negative effect on the Yorkshire Oaks. Five winners promoted to favourite after success at the Curragh were subsequently beaten on the Knavesmire. On the positive side, however, twelve winners had run in the English or Irish Oaks (five running in both) and so had been competing in the very highest class. However, do not expect 3-year-old fillies to reproduce their form like clockwork. As this race demonstrates, four winners – BINT PASHA (1987), UNTOLD (1986), SALLY BROWN (1985) and MAY HILL (1975) reversed their Epsom or Irish Oaks form against their previous conquerors.

With such reversals of form, winning their previous race has not been an essential factor in gaining success in the Yorkshire Oaks. Whilst seven winners had achieved this, three of these were in Group II or III races (and there it will be essential if a filly is to successfully bridge the class difference to win a Group I prize). Nine other horses were promoted to favourite after winning their previous race (six won a Group I race) but were beaten in the Yorkshire Oaks. In these instances winning has appeared almost as a liability and the essential factor has seemed to be a filly that has simply performed creditably at the highest level. Eight winners finished in the first four in a Group I race in their prior engagement before gaining victory on the Knavesmire. It appears

THE YORKSHIRE OAKS – The third race in the 3 y.o. fillies Oaks trilogy, and only ever won by the very highest class staying fillies.

SHOOT A LINE and a very pleased Willie Carson are met by a happy Dick Hern after winning the 1980 Irish Oaks at the Curragh. She became one of the few fillies to complete the double with the Yorkshire Oaks.

that by late August, it is the filly about to blossom rather than one which has already bloomed who will capture the prize. This is a view supported by the fact that winners have tended to be fresh. Eleven winners had not run for 31 days or more (seven of these for 38 days or longer) and were fillies that had progressed in the height of the summer season.

As would be expected it is only the top trainers who usually have these high-class fillies in their charge and the Yorkshire Oaks has therefore been won exclusively by these establishments. M. Stoute (three wins) heads the list from H. Cecil, J. Dunlop, W. Hern and P. Walwyn (two wins each), with two winners also trained in Ireland by different handlers.

The market indicates that the backer should be wary of the favourite, with only three winning (two at odds-on), and three other odds-on shots beaten. It is best to focus on the next two in the market. Six 2nd favourites and three 3rd favourites have been successful, as have two outsiders.

The Yorkshire Oaks, which forms a trilogy with the English and Irish Classics, is an interesting race to consider for selection; yet it is one where reversals of form can and do occur. Fillies that have previously performed with distinction in the Epsom and Curragh Classics may now improve upon their performances in defeat, whilst those previously victorious may not be able to reproduce their triumphs on the flat galloping Knavesmire track, that is quite opposite in type to the other two courses.

Forewarned as to the possibility of reversals of top class form, the backer should look for the less obvious filly just behind the leader in the market. If she is a progressive improving type it is likely she will be the one to capture the spoils in the Yorkshire Oaks.

88	DIMINUENDO	3	0900	H. Cecil	30–100 Fav.	6
87	BINT PASHA	3	0900	B. Cole	5–1	9
86	UNTOLD	3	0900	M. Stoute	5–1	11
85	SALLY BROWN	3	0900	M. Stoute	6–1	7
84	CIRCUS PLUME	3	0900	J. Dunlop	5 6 Fav.	5
83	SUN PRINCESS	3	0900	W. Hern	6–5 Fav.	6
82	AWAASIF	3	0900	J. Dunlop	4–1 2nd Fav.	7
81	CONDESSA	3	0900	J. Bolger (Ire.)	5–1 Jt 2nd Fav.	11
80	SHOOT A LINE	3	0900	W. Hern	13–8 2nd Fav.	7
79	CONNAUGHT BRIDGE	3	0900	H. Cecil	9–2	5
78	FAIR SALINIA	3	0900	M. Stoute	5–1	10
77	BUSACA	3	0900	P. Walwyn	5–1 2nd Fav.	8
76	SARAH SIDDONS	3	0900	P. Prendergast (Ire.)	10–3 2nd Fav.	13
75	MAY HILL	3	0900	P. Walwyn	4–1 2nd Fav.	5

GREAT VOLTIGEUR STAKES

Group II   1m 4f   3 y.o.   colts and geldings only
Level weights with a penalty for a winner of a Group I or
II race since a 2 y.o.

The Great Voltigeur Stakes is a Group II race for 3-year-old colts and geldings over a distance of 1 mile 4 furlongs, and is staged usually on the Wednesday, the second day of the York Festival Meeting. It is a most prestigious race that is considered as an informative trial for the final classic The St Leger, which follows a few weeks later at Doncaster. However, the influence of the actual winners of the Great Voltigeur Stakes on the St Leger has been somewhat limited, no winners since BUSTINO in 1974 completing the double. The main reason for this is that the majority of the winners of the Great Voltigeur have not contested the Doncaster race, and the five who did: SHERIFFS STAR (1988), NISNAS (1986), ELECTRIC (1982), GLINT OF GOLD (1981) and ALLEGED (1977), were all beaten.

In contrast to these winners who have been defeated in the St Leger, three horses beaten in the Great Voltigeur: MOON MADNESS (1986), TOUCHING WOOD (1982) and LIGHT CAVALRY (1980), have redressed the balance by gaining victory in the St Leger, thereby showing that this race is not to be lightly dismissed as a Classic trial.

The Great Voltigeur has been won by a number of good horses, REFERENCE POINT (1987), RAINBOW QUEST (1984), GLINT OF GOLD (1981) and ALLEGED (1977), who was probably the best winner in recent times and captured The Arc de Triomphe in two consecutive seasons. With this quality of horse heading the list of recent winners it is not surprising that the race only attracts small fields, 3 to 8 runners with an average of 6.

Only the best stayers of the current 3-year-old generation have any chance of winning a race where contestants basically carry level weights. The race is invariably run at a good pace, and is quite a demanding test of a horse's stamina as the field swings for home up York's 5 furlong sweeping straight. This develops into the battle of who will show sufficient brilliance of acceleration in the final 2 furlongs. For a horse to pass this test and win the race it will need to be of a high quality, and therefore, it is not surprising that six winners had contested a Group I prize in their previous race, five of these either winning or being placed. Of the eight other winners, who had not competed in a Group I contest in their previous race, all except shock winner outsider NOBLE SAINT (1979) had won their prior race ably. Therefore with eight winners successful in their previous race, winning form has been an important feature.

The most significant immediate prior race has been the Grand Prix de Paris Group I (then 1 mile 7 furlongs) at Longchamp some seven weeks earlier, in which three winners ran, GLINT OF GOLD (1981) alone completing the double. The Irish Derby (Group I, 1½ miles, at the Curragh, 53 days before) has two winners, DAMISTER (1985) and RAINBOW QUEST (1984), both placed capturing the Great Voltigeur Stakes. Negatively, two other horses promoted to favourite after being placed in the Irish Classic were beaten here. Two races at the Goodwood Festival some three weeks earlier, the Gordon Stakes (Group III, 1½ miles, 22 days earlier) and the Alcydion Stakes (listed race, 1½ miles, 19 days earlier), have seen four winners, two in each race, ELECTRIC (1982) and PRINCE BEE (1980), and NISNAS (1986) and SEYMOUR HICKS (1983) respectively. Negatively, two winners and a second of the Gordon Stakes were promoted to favourite and beaten in the Great Voltigeur.

A previous quality performance at the very highest level of competition is the best and most desired criterion to win this race, and with such performances readily identifiable the market has been a fairly accurate guide to pinpointing the winner, with seven favourites, three 2nd favourites, two 3rd favourites and two outsiders successful.

The winners, as may be expected, have only been trained by the top trainers and although English- and Irish-trained runners have been involved in gaining the prize, only J. Tree (two wins) has had more than a single success in the race.

The Great Voltigeur Stakes with its focus on select and quality 3-year-old stayers, is a race which is a fair test for selection and with results usually quite predictable, the backer who concentrates on top-class Group I form is likely to be rewarded.

88	SHERIFF'S STAR	3	0812	Lady Herries	11–4 2nd Fav.	4
87	REFERENCE POINT	3	0900	H. Cecil	1–14 Fav.	3
86	NISNAS	3	0807	P. Cole	6–1	7
85	DAMISTER	3	0811	J. Tree	7–4 Jt Fav.	4
84	RAINBOW QUEST	3	0807	J. Tree	1–1 Fav.	7
83	SEYMOUR HICKS	3	0807	J. Dunlop	11–2	5
82	ELECTRIC	3	0807	M. Stoute	7–4 2nd Fav.	7
81	GLINT OF GOLD	3	0900	I. Balding	1–1 Fav.	6
80	PRINCE BEE	3	0807	W. Hern	4–6 Fav.	5
79	NOBLE SAINT	3	0811	R. Armstrong	12–1	5
78	WHITSTEAD	3	0807	H. R. Price	3–1 Jt Fav.	8
77	ALLEGED	3	0811	M. V. O'Brien (Ire.)	5–2 2nd Fav.	7
76	HAWKBERRY	3	0807	P. Prendergast (Ire.)	4–1	7
75	PATCH	3	0900	P. Walwyn	6–4 Fav.	4

EBOR HANDICAP
0–115 Handicap   1m 6f   3 y.o. and upwards

The Ebor Handicap is a race for 3-year-olds and older horses over a distance of 1 mile 6 furlongs and is staged at York usually on the second day of the Festival Meeting. It is a race steeped in tradition, having first been run in 1843, and in 1988 was one of the richest handicaps in the British racing calendar with a first-prize money of approximately £71,000.

The race always attracts a large field of staying handicappers, 14 to 22 runners with an average of 17, and engenders a keen ante-post betting market throughout August, as connections of many of the leading fancies often have a tilt at the ring. With a closing date and publication of the weights approximately a month before, the race ideally suits the improving horse whom the handicapper has slightly underrated and who has shown recent winning form. This type of animal is the official handicapper's nightmare and can be identified among the winners, especially in the cases of KNELLER (1988), who broke the course record, and PROTECTION RACKET (1981) both of whom won the Doncaster Cup (Group III) 2¼ miles in their next race; also PRIMARY (1986), CRAZY (1984), JUPITER ISLAND (1983), and SIR MONTAGUE (1976). The latter three being among six winners who defied carrying a penalty to win this race.

Good recent form is likely to be the major criterion. Although only seven winners won their prior race, only three winners were unplaced and all winners had won at least one previous race during the season. The weights the winners have carried has covered the full range of the weight scale from the mammoth record burden of 10 st carried by SEA PIGEON (1979) down to the 8 st (including 7 lb penalty) carried by SIR MONTAGUE (1976). Five winners carried 9 st or above and eight winners between 8 st and 8 st 7lb, suggesting that higher weight is not a barrier to success, although the more moderately weighted horses over this taxing distance are likely to be slightly favoured.

Similarly, the age of the winners has varied, with 4-year-olds (seven wins) the most dominant, followed by 3-year-olds (five wins),

THE EBOR HANDICAP – The major betting handicap of the York Festival that provides often lively Ante-Post interest in the period since Goodwood. It was a race in the 1970's in which Northern trained horses held the call.

The old war horse SEA PIGEON as a 9 y.o. and yes, with John Jo O'Neil aboard, are led in, after winning the 1979 Ebor Handicap, carrying a mammoth 10 st, and notching up another Northern trained victory, this time for M. H. (Peter) Easterby.

5-year-olds (one win), and completed by the success of the grand old man SEA PIGEON who won the Ebor as a 9-year-old.

With winners coming from such a variety of sources no single race has had a particular influence on the outcome of the Ebor although the 'Sea Pigeon' Handicap (formerly Vaux Gold Tankard), run at Redcar over the same distance approximately three weeks before, has been the prior engagement of four winners. The distance of 1 mile 6 furlongs of this race demands that a horse thoroughly sees out the trip and in this aspect seven winners had tackled an equal or longer distance in their previous races.

The market has not always been a good indication of a horse's chance, with only one favourite, four 2nd favourites, two 3rd favourites and seven outsiders (with prices ranging from 9–1 to 20–1) successful. There have, however, been no really major shocks, and although this race would seem to be a very good one for the bookmakers overall, a number of winners have been far from friendless in the market, with their eventual starting price not necessarily giving an accurate reflection of their strength in the ante-post market. This applies particularly to two recent winners KNELLER (1988) and DAARKOM (1987) who were long-time ante-post favourites only to drift in the market on the day.

The difficulty of winning the Ebor Handicap is also reflected by the fact that only one trainer, G. Harwood (two wins), has won the race on more than a single occasion. The famous and less well known handlers share success almost equally.

The Ebor Handicap cannot be readily recommended as a race for selection purposes. Any careful analysis reveals that numerous probables and a number of apparent handicap 'good things' have been beaten. There are few constant factors to pinpoint the winner and the backer who takes this race as a betting proposition must do so warily. Possibly the best selection advice is to look for the older horse of proven ability who will be certain to stay the distance.

88	KNELLER	3	0801	H. Cecil	9–1 Jt 2nd Fav	9
87	DAARKOM	4	0903	A. Stewart	13–2	15
86	PRIMARY	3	0807	G. Harwood	6–1 2nd Fav.	22
85	WESTERN DANCER	4	0806	C. Horgan	20–1	19
84	CRAZY	3	0813	G. Harwood	10–1	14
83	JUPITER ISLAND	4	0900	C. Brittain	9–1	16
82	ANOTHER SAM	5	0902	R. Hannon	16–1	15
81	PROTECTION RACKET	3	0801	J. Hindley	15–2 2nd Fav.	22
80	SHAFTESBURY	4	0805	M. Stoute	12–1	16
79	SEA PIGEON	9	1000	M. H. Easterby	18–1	17
78	TOTOWAH	4	0801	M. Jarvis	20–1	22
77	MOVE OFF	4	0801	J. Calvert	9–1	14
76	SIR MONTAGUE	3	0800	H. R. Price	11–4 Fav.	15
75	DAKOTA	4	0904	S. Hall	7–1 2nd Fav.	18

GIMCRACK STAKES

Group II   6f   2 y.o. only   colts and geldings only
Level weights, with varying penalties for a winner of a Group
I, II or III race.

The Gimcrack Stakes is a Group II race for 2-year-olds only,
over a distance of 6 furlongs and is staged on the Wednesday, the
second day of the Festival Meeting at York. It is one of the leading
races for juveniles and is often regarded as an early indicator of
who will be the following season's Classic contenders. However,
like its fillies' counterpart the Lowther Stakes, the Gimcrack has
had only a slight influence on the colts' Classic, with NEBBIOLO
(1976) the only winner to capture a major Classic prize, the Two
Thousand Guineas of the following season, and BEL BOLIDE
(1980) being placed in 1981. Winners have generally disappointed
in their 3-year-old career, most certainly in terms of any Classic
pretensions. Although HORAGE (1982) was able to win a group
race over a distance of a mile, the other winners successful as
3-year-olds, MUSIC BOY (1975), and STEEL HEART (1974) found
their forte as sprinters.

The Gimcrack demands that a horse be forward in condition,
and with the likelihood that rivals will be of similar disposition,
racing experience is likely to be a vital factor in deciding this
race. Eleven winners had at least four prior races, and a winner
such as PRECOCIOUS (1983) was unbeaten in four previous races
(including two Group races); HORAGE (1982) was unbeaten in
eight previous races (including two Group prizes), FULL EXTENT
(1981) won three of his four previous races; SONNEN GOLD
(1979) had won six of his seven previous races; and MUSIC
BOY (1975) won four of his five previous races; NEBBIOLO
(1976) had won consecutively four of his last five races; whilst
TUMBLEDOWNWIND (1977) won three of his five races.

These winners between them had gained an awful lot of
racing experience in their short careers which they used to good
advantage in gaining victory. Speed is the factor which will be of
the essence here with a particular emphasis on a horse's ability to
quicken in the final furlong.

THE GIMCRACK STAKES – A 2 y.o. race for colts, over 6 furlongs, invariably won by a very fast experienced 2 y.o. whose forte will always be as a specialist sprinter.

MUSIC BOY (Johnny Seagrave) beats STAND TO REASON (Willie Carson, Quartered cap) and the Irish trained favourite GALWAY BAY (Lester Piggott) to strike a blow for a northern trained Group race winner in 1975. MUSIC BOY, now a stallion at stud, has proved himself also as a sire of fast horses.

Whilst no particular race has held any special influence on the outcome of the Gimcrack Stakes, Goodwood's Richmond Stakes (Group II, 6 furlongs, 21–22 days earlier) has had some. It produced two winners, DOULAB (1984) and BEL BOLIDE (1980), although both were only placed on the Sussex course. Negatively, another horse promoted to favourite after being placed in the Richmond Stakes was beaten in the Gimcrack. Goodwood's Molecombe Stakes (Group III, 5 furlongs) has produced two winners, PRECOCIOUS (1983) who completed the double and SHARP N' EARLY (1988) who was fourth at Goodwood. Other prior 2-year-old Group races such as the July Stakes (6 furlongs, Newmarket) and races such as the Norfolk Stakes and Coventry Stakes at Royal Ascot also sometimes play a role, without any holding a consistent influence.

Five of the recent winners of the Gimcrack were racing in Group company for the first time and successfully bridged the raising in class. In such instances winning form would be essential and it is therefore not surprising that eight horses won their previous race. Similarly, recent form is quite essential, as the development of the juvenile generation unfolds very quickly – so twelve winners ran within the previous 28 days, eight within the past 21 days. Also all but three winners, the brilliantly fast PRECOCIOUS (1983), MUSIC BOY (1975) and STALKER (1985), had won at 6 furlongs and were proven at the distance.

A feature to note on the training front is how the Gimcrack Stakes has not been confined to the top trainers, quite a number of unfamiliar names not normally associated with Group race prizes gaining the honours. Henry Cecil (two wins) is the only handler with more than a single victory.

The market has been fairly helpful in pinpointing the winners, with five favourites (three of which were odds-on), three 2nd favourites, three 3rd favourites and three outsiders successful. However, unless the market leader presents itself as an outstanding candidate for selection the backer may be better served looking at the others further down the betting for a horse with a fair amount of racing experience and proven record.

88	SHARP N' EARLY	2	0900	R. Hannon	14–1	8
87	REPRIMAND	2	0900	H. Cecil	2–7 Fav.	6
86	WIGANTHORPE	2	0900	M. W. Easterby	9–2 Jt 2nd Fav.	11
85	STALKER	2	0900	B. Walwyn	17–2	6
84	DOULAB	2	0900	H. Thomson Jones	10–1	8
83	PRECOCIOUS	2	0900	H Cecil	8–11 Fav.	6
82	HORAGE	2	0900	M. McCormack	8–13 Fav.	7
81	FULL EXTENT	2	0900	S. Norton	13–2 Jt 2nd Fav.	8
80	BEL BOLIDE	2	0900	J. Tree	11–2 Jt 2nd Fav.	9
79	SONNEN GOLD	2	0900	M. H. Easterby	5–1	7
78	STANFORD	2	0900	N. Callaghan	15–2	11
77	TUMBLEDOWNWIND	2	0900	B. Hobbs	6–5 Fav.	5
76	NEBBIOLO	2	0900	K. Prendergast (Ire.)	2–1 Jt Fav.	7
75	MUSIC BOY	2	0900	S. Wainwright	14–1	14

LOWTHER STAKES

Group II   6f   2 y.o. fillies only
Level weights, with varying penalties for a winner of a Group
I, II or III race

The Lowther Stakes is a Group II race for 2-year-old fillies, over a distance of 6 furlongs, and is staged usually on the third day of the Festival Meeting at York. It is a race that gives reliable indication of who is the fastest filly seen on a racecourse up to this moment in the season, and who may figure prominently in the remaining 2-year-old fillies races during the Autumn.

The Lowther Stakes has been won by some very speedy fillies such as AL BAHATHRI (1984), HABIBTI (1982), CIRCUS RING (1981) and DEVON DITTY (1978). However, it has not proved to be a very informative guide to the following season's Classics and ENSTONE SPARK (1977) is the only winner later to gain an English Classic victory. The winners have tended to be the most precocious fillies of their generation, which does not necessarily bode well for their longer term career. In fact six winners failed to win after their 2-year-old career. With the exception of POLONIA (1986), who later won the Prix de l'Abbaye de Longchamp (Group I, 5 furlongs, Longchamp), beating many of Europes top sprinters; AL BAHATHRI (1984), who was just about the best mile filly of her generation as a 3-year-old; HABIBTI (1982), who became a champion sprinter as a 3-year-old; and MRS PENNY (1979), who developed into a top-class stayer, the winners of the Lowther Stakes have generally disappointed afterwards.

The race attracts medium-sized fields of 5 to 13 runners, 8 on average, many of whom will be racing in Group company for the first time (only four winners previously contested Group races). Most horses will have had only a few previous races and with the exception of POLONIA (1986), DEVON DITTY (1978) and ENSTONE SPARK (1977) who had five, six and seven previous races respectively, no other winner had more than three prior races. All the winners with the exception of MISS DEMURE (1988) and KITTY HAWK (1980), who were still maidens before this race,

THE LOWTHER STAKES – A 6 furlong race for 2 y.o. fillies which quickly establishes the fastest filly seen at this stage in the season.

The brilliant DEVON DITTY (Greville Starkey) seen going to post at Newmarket prior to her first Group race win. She won the 1978 Lowther Stakes and subsequent performances led her to be acknowledged as the fastest 2 y.o. of her generation.

had won at least one previous race with eleven winners winning their prior race before the Lowther Stakes.

The winners have had widely varying previous race engagements with some subject to easy introductory races to build up their confidence and gain racing experience, while others from the outset were pitched against much sterner rivals. The only race which has been of significant influence on the Lowther Stakes is the Princess Margaret Stakes (Group III; formerly Listed race) over 6 furlongs at Ascot, 25–26 days earlier, in which six winners ran, four winning it to complete the double. However, on the negative side six other fillies were promoted to favourite, five after winning the Princess Margaret Stakes, and were beaten in the Lowther Stakes. Twelve winners had run over six furlongs and therefore were not tackling anything new or unknown.

The market has been a reliable guide to pinpointing the winner; five favourites and five 2nd favourites have been successful, with just one 3rd favourite and three outsiders (16–1, 25–1 and 33–1). When it is considered that there are often no proven form lines between basically inexperienced fillies, much trust has to be placed in reputation and assumptions. Yet the market has regularly got it right, with the market leaders dominating.

On the training front this race has been the domain of the top stables, but only H. Thomson Jones (three wins) has more than one victory.

The Lowther Stakes is a fair test of selection skill, and since its elevation to Group II status in 1981 has been quite predictable, with all but one race won by the first or second favourites. Therefore the backer should focus closely on the two market leaders and pay due regard to recent form which at this time of the season is a premium (eleven winners ran within the previous 28 days).

88	MISS DEMURE	2	0811	R. Armstrong	16–1	9
87	ELA ROMANA	2	0811	G. Wragg	2–1 2nd Fav.	5
86	POLONIA	2	0900	J. Bolger (Ire.)	5–2 2nd Fav.	9
85	KINGSCOTE	2	0811	J. Tree	5–2 Jt 2nd Fav.	7
84	AL BAHATHRI	2	0811	H. Thomson Jones	11–10 Fav.	10
83	PRICKLE	2	0811	H. Cecil	11–4 Fav.	9
82	HABIBTI	2	0811	J. Dunlop	4–1 2nd Fav.	8
81	CIRCUS RING	2	0811	M. Stoute	1–4 Fav.	8
80	KITTYHAWK	2	0808	W. Hern	10–11 Fav.	5
79	MRS PENNY	2	0900	I. Balding	11–2	7
78	DEVON DITTY	2	0900	H. Thomson Jones	3–1 2nd Fav.	11
77	ENSTONE SPARK	2	0811	R. Hannon	33–1	9
76	ICENA	2	0811	H. Thomson Jones	25–1	13
75	PATSY	2	0811	P. Walwyn	15–8 Fav.	7

WILLIAM HILL SPRINT CHAMPIONSHIP STAKES
(Formerly – up to 1975 – Nunthorpe Stakes)

Group I   5f   2 y.o. and upwards   colts, geldings and fillies
Level weights, sex allowance, WFA

The William Hill Sprint Championship is a Group I race (elevated to this status in 1984) for 2-year-olds and older horses, although juveniles rarely take part, over a distance of 5 furlongs. It is staged on a Thursday, the final day of York's three-day Festival Meeting. It stands on a par with the other two Group I sprint races, the July Cup, over 6 furlongs at Newmarket six weeks earlier, and the Vernons Sprint Cup over 6 furlongs at Haydock, 16 days later. These form a triple alliance of sprint races that will decide who is champion sprinter.

The King's Stand Stakes at Royal Ascot over 5 furlongs (now Group II but formerly Group I) was previously considered the first leg in the sprinters' triple crown, but since its demotion, it no longer holds that position. Therefore the William Hill Sprint Championship has become the second rather than the final leg of the sprint triple crown. Then it was the crowning glory, proclaiming the champion, as in the cases of NEVER SO BOLD (1985), HABIBTI (1983), SHARPO (1982), SOLINUS (1978) and LOCHNAGER (1976).

Over York's easy flat 5 furlong track, this is a race that demands blinding speed. This was ably demonstrated by the acclaimed champions, yet has also been vividly displayed by AJDAL (1987), LAST TYCOON (1986), COMMITTED (1984) and BAY EXPRESS (1975).

The William Hill Sprint Championship since its elevation to Group I status, with horses meeting at level weights (except for sex allowance and WFA), attracts only the very best sprinters. Therefore a horse will need form of the very highest class to succeed here. Newmarket's July Cup (Group I, 42 days earlier) has been the race of greatest influence, with eleven winners running in it, nine as their previous race, with six winning to complete the double. Five other horses were unsuccessfully promoted to favourite in the William Hill Sprint after their performance in

WILLIAM HILL SPRINT CHAMPIONSHIP – *A quick dash over York's flat 5 furlong track is one of the races which decide who is the champion sprinter.*

SHARPO (Willie Carson) the only horse to win the William Hill Sprint in three consecutive seasons (1982, 1981 and 1980), and now standing as a successful stallion who imparts similar speed into his offspring.

the July Cup, three of whom won it. This ably testifies to the influence the Newmarket sprint holds over this race; whilst the beaten favourites show the disappointments possible. Generally July Cup form, although over a furlong longer on a stiffer track, is upheld on the Knavesmire course. LAST TYCOON (1986), desperately unfortunate in running in the July Cup, has been the only winner to reverse form with his conqueror. The King's Stand Stakes also had nine winners run in it in one of their prior races, but only SHARPO (1981) (on the second of his consecutive victories in the William Hill Sprint) competed in it as its immediate prior race. Four winners, LAST TYCOON, NEVER SO BOLD, SOLINUS and LOCHNAGER, have been the only horses to win both. All the winners have had a fairly light programme, none having more than five prior races, and with the July Cup holding such an influence on the race, ten were comparatively fresh, having had an absence of 42 days or longer from racing.

146

The race attracts compact sized fields of 7 to 12 runners with an average of 10, that usually comprise challengers from England and Ireland and sometimes France. Thus the trainers' honours have also been shared by the three nations. English-based handlers hold sway, but only J. Tree (three wins), responsible for SHARPO's unique post-war record of victories, has had more than one success. This championship is not the exclusive domain of the top establishments and anyone fortunate enough to have in their care a top sprinter could take the prize.

The market has been a fairly reliable guide with six favourites and four 2nd favourites successful, whilst three 3rd favourites and one outsider (SHARPO (1981), 14–1, gaining its second victory) have also won. Defeated favourites have included GREEN DESERT (1986), HABIBTI (1984), MARWELL (1981), THATCHING (1979) (disqualified) and GODSWALK (1977), suggesting that the backer must be wary of just plumping for the market leader. Winners have come from each of the older age groups: 3-year-olds (six wins), 4-year-olds (five wins) and 5-year-olds (three wins), suggesting it is a matter of which generation that season holds the best sprinters, rather than this race favouring one age group.

The William Hill Sprint Championship is a race about speed, and this is an element which the backer should have no great difficulty in identifying. The form of the July Cup has proved extremely reliable and unless a candidate emerges from some other race with very imposing credentials, this is the race the backer will most profitably focus on to find the winner.

88	HANDSOME SAILOR	5	0906	B. Hills	5–2 Fav.	12
87	AJDAL	3	0902	M. Stoute	2–1 2nd Fav.	11
86	LAST TYCOON	3	0902	R. Collett (Fr.)	7–2	8
85	NEVER SO BOLD	5	0900	R. Armstrong	4–6 Fav.	7
84	COMMITTED	4	0811	D. K. Weld (Ire.)	5–1	8
83	HABIBTI	3	0807	J. Dunlop	13–8 Fav.	10
82	SHARPO	5	0900	J. Tree	1–1 Fav.	11
81	SHARPO	4	0900	J. Tree	14–1	9
80	SHARPO	3	0902	J. Tree	3–1 2nd Fav.	11
79	AHONOORA	4	0906	F. Durr	3–1 2nd Fav.	10
78	SOLINUS	3	0902	M. V. O'Brien (Ire.)	1–2 Fav.	9
77	HAVEROID	3	0902	N. Adam	10–1	8
76	LOCHNAGER	4	0906	M. W. Easterby	4–5 Fav.	11
75	BAY EXPRESS	4	0907	P. Nelson	10–3 2nd Fav.	10

WATERFORD CRYSTAL MILE

Group II 1m 3 y.o. and upwards colts, geldings and fillies
Level weights, sex allowance, WFA with a penalty for a winner
of a Group I or II race in the current season

The Waterford Crystal mile is a Group II race for 3-year-olds
and upwards over a distance of 1 mile and is staged over the
old mile course, on the Saturday of the two-day meeting at
Goodwood at the end of August. Formerly a Group III race, it
was elevated to Group II status in 1977 and since has seen a rise
in the standard of its contestants, having been won by two Two
Thousand Guineas winners TO-AGORI-MOU (1981), KNOWN FACT
(1980) and the champion miler of his generation KRIS (1979).
However, whilst being won by these notable horses, because it has
an entry condition that gives weight penalties to recent Group I
or II winners, the race often provides a suitable opportunity for
unpenalised horses to succeed at this level – seven winners have
been unpenalised horses, who previously just missed winning the
higher-grade races. It is not surprising to find eight winners who
contested a Group I race in their prior race and who appreciated
a slight easing in grade here.

Two previous races hold a significant influence on the outcome
of the Crystal Mile. The first is the Sussex Stakes, over 1 mile
at Goodwood over the same course and distance, either 24 or
31 days earlier depending on how the calendar falls. This has
served as the immediate prior race for four winners, three of
whom finished second and only KRIS (1979) won to complete
the double. However, on the negative side, five other horses,
four of whom also were second, and JAAZEIRO (1978) who won
the Sussex Stakes, were promoted to favourite in the Crystal Mile
only to be defeated. So an air of caution is required in appraising
candidates from this race.

Two other runners also competed in the Sussex Stakes without
success before subsequently running in Prix Jacques le Marios
(Group I) over 1 mile at Deauville in France 13 days earlier,
which serves as the second race of influence over the Crystal Mile.
Three winners have competed in this and the two prior Sussex

148

Stakes contestants MONTEKIN (1983) and TO-AGORI-MOU (1981) were both placed. Another race contested by two of the three Irish-trained winners has been the Desmond Stakes (Group III over 1 mile at the Curragh), which BE MY GUEST (1977) won before also winning the Waterford Crystal.

Although this Irish-sponsored race has a generous travel allowance to attract entrants and usually encourages a runner or two from across the Irish Sea, the race only attracts small-sized fields of 4 to 8 runners of good class milers, but selection usually resolves to only one or two probables. The market reflects this with five favourites, four 2nd favourites, one 3rd favourite and three outsiders (which were the only 4-year-old winners) successful.

The Waterford Crystal Mile often serves as a compensating victory for 3-year-olds who missed out at the highest level, and only three winners won their previous race. As would be expected, only the top trainers tend to succeed at this level and G. Harwood (three wins) holds the call over M. V. O'Brien (Ire.) (two wins) as the stables with more than one victory.

The Waterford Crystal Mile with its record of normally predictable results is definitely a race to be considered for selection and a close inspection of the two leaders in the market is likely to point the backer in the winning direction.

88	PRINCE RUPERT	4	0903	B. Hills	16–1	6
87	MILLIGRAM	3	0807	M. Stoute	5–2 2nd Fav.	4
86	THEN AGAIN	3	0807	L. Cumani	8–1	8
85				——— ABANDONED ———		
84	ROUSILLON	3	0806	G. Harwood	8–13 Fav.	5
83	MONTEKIN	4	0813	J. Dunlop	8–1	6
82	SANDHURST PRINCE	3	0804	G. Harwood	7–4 2nd Fav.	8
81	TO-AGORI-MOU	3	0812	G. Harwood	5–4 Fav.	6
80	KNOWN FACT	3	0812	J. Tree	5–2 2nd Fav.	6
79	KRIS	3	0812	H. Cecil	30–100 Fav.	8
78	CAPTAIN JAMES	4	0813	McGrath (Ire.)	25–1	5
77	BE MY GUEST	3	0807	M. V. O'Brien (Ire.)	6–4 Fav.	6
76	FREE STATE	3	0803	P. Walwyn	13–8 Fav.	6
75	GAY FANDANGO	3	0808	M. V. O'Brien (Ire.)	5–1 2nd Fav.	8

VERNONS SPRINT CUP
Group I   6f   3 y.o. and upwards   colts, geldings and fillies
Level weights, sex allowance, WFA

The Vernons Sprint Cup is a Group I race (upgraded from Group II in 1988) for 3-year-olds and upwards over a distance of 6 furlongs, and is staged at Haydock Park on the Saturday of the two-day meeting in early September. Until 1978 it was held on the first Saturday in November. However, since its change of date to two months earlier, the race's complexion has also changed. It is less subject to the more unpredictable elements which held sway when it was one of the final fixtures of the season. The race then was invariably run on Soft or Heavy going, so late in the season that some leading contenders had been retired to winter quarters, whilst those who did take part were feeling the effects of a long season and producing rather lacklustre performances.

Therefore the study here of the Vernons Sprint Cup has been confined to the shorter period of 1979–88 since it has been run in September. The change of the date of the fixture has meant a raising in the standard of the race with most of the leading contenders for the champion sprinter's laurels taking part. The Vernons Sprint Cup has thus become the final leg in a quartet of races – with the King's Stand Stakes (5 furlongs, Group II, Royal Ascot); July Stakes (6 furlongs, Group I, Newmarket); William Hill Sprint Championship (5 furlongs, Group I, York) – which decide who wears the sprint champion's crown.

A number of winners have emerged after this race as the top English-trained sprinter of their respective seasons: AJDAL (1987), GREEN DESERT (1986), HABIBTI (1983), MOORESTYLE (1980) and DOUBLE FORM (1979). Yet the race has also seen three other possible champions, COMMITTED (1984), SHARPO (1982) and MARWELL (1981), beaten here. The latter two were defeated by rivals INDIAN KING (1982) and RUNNETT (1981) whom they had beaten in earlier encounters. These two defeats highlight fluctuations in form that have occurred in the Vernons Sprint Cup, where only three winners (1979–88), AJDAL, HABIBTI and MOORESTYLE, have confirmed previous form with rivals. Other

VERNONS SPRINT CUP – The final race in the quartet of sprint races that decides who will be acclaimed Champion.

RUNNETT, a very fast horse suited to Haydocks 6 furlong sprint track gave trainer John Dunlop one of his two wins in the Vernons Sprint Cup in 1981.

winners either reversed the form of previous encounters or were successfully making the transition to this higher grade of competition, not previously having run against the established Group race sprinters. Not surprisingly, only three winners won their previous race, although every winner had won at least two prior races during the season. And all but the shock winners DOWSING (1988), OROJOYA (1985) and PETONG (1984) (the winner of the two toughest 6 furlong handicaps, the Wokingham Stakes and the Steward's Cup) had won at least one Group race previously during the season.

The previous race of greatest influence has been the William Hill Sprint Championship (Group I, 5 furlongs, York, 16 days

151

earlier), in which four winners (1979–88) ran. Two won it, AJDAL (1987) and HABIBTI (1983), and two, GREEN DESERT (1986) and DOUBLE FORM (1979), both finished third, yet reversed form with their York conquerors. On the other hand, four other horses promoted to favourite, three after winning at York, were beaten in the Vernons Sprint Cup.

Deauville's Prix de Maurice de Gheest (Group II, 6 furlongs, 34 days earlier) is the only other race to have more than a fleeting influence. Two horses who were second there captured the Vernon's Sprint Cup.

All the winners except DOWSING (1988) had at least five prior races during the season, with the recognised sprint championship races usually figuring prominently in their itinerary. The fluctuations in form that can occur in the Vernons Sprint Cup may be explained by it being the final race in the series. Whilst some horses may have peaked, and found this one race too many, for others it fell perfectly and caught them at their best, just as summer was on the wane. The distances and different racetracks will also have been quite varied, even for sprinters: Ascot's stiff 5 furlongs has a testing finish, compared to York's easy 5 furlongs, whilst Newmarket's 6 furlongs on the wide open heath also has a demanding finish. Haydock's 6 furlong course (until extended to be a straight 6 furlong track in 1986) had the anomaly of being the only one of the races run on a round course from a chute. This demanded that a horse broke well from the stalls and held a good position as the runners came round into the 4 furlong home straight that was slightly uphill all the way to the winning post. This variation in conditions may have been the final factor responsible for changes in form, because the races since the straight track was introduced have become more predictable.

The market has been a fairly reliable guide to finding the winner. Four favourites, two 2nd favourites, one 3rd favourite and three outsiders have been successful, although three winning favourites have been odds-on, as have the two losing ones.

As would be expected, the Vernons Cup only attracts medium-sized fields of 6 to 10 runners, with an average of 8 sprinters taking part. As befits this prestigious prize, only the top trainers win. J. Dunlop and M. Stoute (two wins each) are the only ones with more than a single success.

The Vernons Sprint Cup is a fair yet not necessarily easy race for selection, with its reversals of form in the past. However, its establishment as a Group I prize in 1988, and the installation of its straight 6 furlong course promises the race will develop into a more predictable one. The top sprint races will continue to be the deciding issue and the backer who seriously considers the form in these will usually not be far wrong in finding the winner, though with the proviso contained in the old adage 'there is no profit in the obvious'.

88	DOWSING	4	0902	J. Tree	15–2	10
87	AJDAL	3	0900	M. Stoute	8–11 Fav.	8
86	GREEN DESERT	3	0812	M. Stoute	5–4 Fav.	8
85	OROJOYA	3	0812	J. Hindley	11–1	8
84	PETONG	4	0903	M. Jarvis	11–1	9
83	HABIBTI	3	0809	J. Dunlop	8–13 Fav.	6
82	INDIAN KING	4	0903	G. Harwood	3–1 2nd Fav.	9
81	RUNNET	4	0903	J. Dunlop	6–1	6
80	MOORESTYLE	3	0812	R. Armstrong	8–13 Fav.	8
79	DOUBLE FORM	4	0908	R. Houghton	11–4 2nd Fav.	8

DONCASTER ST LEGER MEETING

The Doncaster St Leger Meeting is a four-day meeting staged on the Town Moor racecourse at Doncaster, usually in the second week of September. It begins on the Wednesday and closes on the Saturday, with the showpiece of the meeting, the final Classic of the season, the St Leger.

The meeting marks the end of Summer and the beginning of Autumn and often results of races from this meeting provide new lines of form that may influence other races in the following weeks of the season.

The four days of the Doncaster Meeting has six Group races, with the St Leger (Group I) as the highlight, followed by The Park Hill Stakes (Group II), a 1 mile 6 furlong race confined to 3-year-old fillies. There are also two Group II prizes for 2-year-olds, the Champagne Stakes over 7 furlongs, which suggests who will be the following season's classic contenders, and the Flying Childer Stakes, over 5 furlongs, which shows who are among the fastest sprinter-type 2-year-olds. Added to these are the Group III prizes of the Doncaster Cup over 2 miles 2 furlongs, and the final leg in the stayers' cup trilogy; and the May Hill Stakes over 1 mile for 2-year-old fillies, which gives an indication of the staying fillies with Group race pretensions for the following season. These Group races are interspersed over the four days with a number of competitive and popular handicaps as well as numerous stakes races.

THE DONCASTER ST LEGER MEETING – Four days of racing in early September that signals the end of summer and the first wisps of Autumn with the running of the final Classic the St. Leger.

A smiling Lester Piggott in the colours of J. O. Tobin holds a large bottle of the Sponsor's Bubbly, after winning the 1976 Champagne Stakes at Doncaster.

PARK HILL STAKES

Group II 1m 6f 127y 3 y.o. fillies only
Level weights with a penalty for a winner of a Group I or II race

The Park Hill Stakes is a Group II race for 3-year-old fillies over a distance of 1 mile 6 furlongs 127 yards, and is staged on the Wednesday, the first day of the four-day St Leger meeting at Doncaster in the second week in September. It is often called the 'Fillies' Leger' being run over the same course and distance as the final Classic, and attracts varying sized fields – from 3 to 13 runners – who will probably represent some of the best staying fillies of their generation. The Park Hill has been won by a number of good staying fillies, notably SWIFT FOOT (1982) and SHOOT A LINE (1980) who were both winners of the Irish Oaks, plus fillies such as HIGH HAWK (1983), winner of the Ribblesdale Stakes, and MAY HILL (1975), winner of the Group I Yorkshire Oaks.

From the selection viewpoint the race may fall into either of two distinct categories: either the race is dominated by an outstanding filly and results have been predictable; or no outstanding candidate has emerged and the race produces surprise results.

In the first instance, potential rivals get scared off, which results in the smaller fields. On the eight occasions when there have been less than 8 runners, the race has been won by one of the three market leaders in the betting. On the other hand, when no major candidates present themselves, the race attracts larger fields, and on the six occasions where there have been more than 8 runners outsiders have won. Of these five winning outsiders, four were tackling a Group race for the first time and had therefore made considerable improvement to gain this major Group II prize. The market, where the results have been four favourites, two 2nd favourites, two 3rd favourites and six outsiders, becomes less incomprehensible in the light of the record of the size of the fields, and is quite an informative guide.

Although when shocks have occurred the winners have appeared from an unillustrious previous race itinerary, there is one race of eminence that has had a significant influence on the outcome of the Park Hill Stakes. This is the Yorkshire Oaks (Group I, over 1½ miles, York, 22 days earlier). Six winners ran in the Yorkshire Oaks: SHOOT A LINE (1980) and MAY HILL (1975) winning it, to complete a notable double; whilst three others finished second. On the negative side two other horses promoted to favourite after their performance in the Yorkshire Oaks, SORBUS (1978) who was second, and GIVE THANKS (1983) who finished third, were beaten at Doncaster. Another race at the York Festival meeting, the Galtre Stakes (Listed race, over 1½ miles, 21 days earlier), has provided three winners: BORUSHKA (1984), who won, IDLE WATERS (1978) who was second and CASEY (1988) who was unplaced yet over this longer distance reversed form with her York conquerors. Three other winners of the Galtre Stakes were promoted to favourite in the Park Hill Stakes but found the Group II prize beyond them.

As would be expected with 3-year-old fillies seeking a top Group race prize to enhance their stud value, the Park Hill Stakes has been won exclusively by the very top trainers, especially those with a reputation for staying-type animals. L. Cumani, J. Dunlop, W. Hern, B. Hills and R. Houghton have had two wins each.

The Park Hill Stakes, alternating between opposite poles of the shock results and the predictable, must be a race the backer views with caution. However, the successful favourites and second favourites had been previously first or second in a Group I or Group II race and were promoted to prominence in the market with solid credentials. In contrast, only two of the ten beaten favourites previously contested a Group I or II race and so are likely to have had their form overrated.

As all but one winner were tackling this extended distance of 1 mile 6 furlongs 27 yards for the first time, it is a race that holds pitfalls for the unwary, but truly top-class form is likely to be upheld.

88	CASEY	3	0809	L. Cumani	14–1	9
87	TRAMPSHIP	3	0809	B. Hills	7–2	5
86	REJUVENATE	3	0809	B. Hills	8–1	12
85	I WANT TO BE	3	0900	J. Dunlop	6–5 Fav.	7
84	BORUSHKA	3	0900	R. Houghton	13–2	13
83	HIGH HAWK	3	0900	J. Dunlop	2–1 2nd Fav.	7
82	SWIFT FOOT	3	0900	W. Hern	4–6 Fav.	6
81	ALMA ATA	3	0900	L. Cumani	25–1	13
80	SHOOT A LINE	3	0900	W. Hern	1–2 Fav.	6
79	QUAY LINE	3	0900	H. Candy	3–1	5
78	IDLE WATERS	3	0900	R. Houghton	9–1	10
77	ROYAL HIVE	3	0900	H. Cecil	8–15 Fav.	3
76	AFRICAN DANCER	3	0900	H. Wragg	6–1	9
75	MAY HILL	3	0900	P. Walwyn	13–8 2nd Fav.	7

PORTLAND HANDICAP
0–115 Handicap   5f 140y   3 y.o. and upwards

The Portland Handicap is a handicap race for 3-year-olds and older horses, rated 0–115, run over a distance of 5 furlongs 140 yards, and now staged on the first day or Wednesday of the four-day St Leger Meeting at Doncaster in September. It is one of the oldest sprint handicaps (first run in 1855) and always provides a competitive betting market on the day and a mild ante-post market beforehand. It always attracts large fields of sprinters, from 11 to 23 runners, with an average of 16 to 17 for this fiercely fought prize.

It is over the unique distance of 5 furlongs 140 yards (5½ furlongs approximately) and is normally won by a very experienced sprint handicapper who is either ideally suited or most adaptable to this distance. The winners have usually been horses which have been competing throughout the season in the medium-class sprint handicaps. Eleven of the fourteen winners had at least seven previous races during the season, and those two tough sprinters DAWN'S DELIGHT (1987) (who as a 9-year-old and the oldest Portland winner this century was winning the race for a second time) and TOUCH BOY (1981), had eleven and thirteen prior races respectively and were the only ones to defy a penalty.

All the winners except WALK BY (1975), the highly weighted 3-year-old, who had even contested the One Thousand Guineas earlier in the season and then reverted to sprint distances, had won at least one prior race. SWELTER (1980) was unbeaten in her three previous races whilst FELIPE TORO (1986) had won his previous four races. The variation between these three winners gives an idea of the wide spectrum of winners of the Portland Handicap.

The weight range of the winners has similarly been wide, ranging from a bottom weight of 7 st which, with the aid of 7 lb apprentice allowance, was carried by OH SIMMIE (1979), to a highest weight of 9 st 3 lb, carried by the only once-raced and unbeaten 3-year-old ROMAN PROSE (1988). A noted feature is that ROMAN PROSE is the only winner to have beaten the 9 st barrier since WELSH ABBOT, who also broke the track record carrying

158

9 st 2 lb thirty years before in 1958. Similarly, six horses promoted to favourite but carrying above this prohibitive 9 st level were all defeated.

The record of winners reflects that none were better than Handicap class, and for most this has been the highlight of their careers, rather than a stepping-stone to greater things. Horses of all ages win the Portland Handicap, from the veteran DAWN'S DELIGHT as a 9-year-old and a 6-year-old, and other victories being shared almost equally between 3-, 4- and 5-year-olds.

In analysing the Portland Handicap, whilst many factors appear either inconsistent or contradictory, the effect of the draw would appear to be of great importance. Nine winners were in the top quarter of the draw and all the winners in the top half with the exception of ROMAN PROSE (1988) drawn 3, and FELIPE TORO (1986) who was drawn 2 when there was a flag start (and a false start that led to the eventual withdrawal of five runners). High numbers, with the stand rails to finish against, are definitely favoured to the exclusion of any horses in the bottom half.

The Portland Handicap, with winners of no more than handicap class, is definitely a race that the smaller stables can expect to win, as results testify. But only K. Ivory, handling the grand old dual winner DAWN'S DELIGHT, has had more than one success.

In such a competitive race it is not surprising that the market has been only a limited guide to finding the winner. Two favourites, one 2nd favourite, five 3rd favourites and six outsiders were successful. The reasonable consistency of the 3rd favourites shows the winners to be far from friendless in the market and the backer carefully examining that area could end up nicely rewarded.

The Portland Handicap, however, with its unique distance and obvious open nature, is not a race to recommend readily for selection, especially as it seems that the higher-weighted classier horses, with above 9 st, have invariably been unable to succeed here. It is always an exciting contest from the spectators' viewpoint and often serves as a guide to a race such as the Ayr Gold Cup, where horses prominent here often give a good account of themselves in the competitive Scottish handicap that follows approximately a week later.

88	ROMAN PROSE	3	0903	L. Cottrell	8–1	22
87	DAWN'S DELIGHT	9	0813	K. Ivory	14–1	23
86	FELIPE TORO	3	0802	M. H. Easterby	11–2 Fav.	23
85	LOCHTILLUM	6	0801	J. Doughlas-Home	14–1	17
84	DAWN'S DELIGHT	6	0708	K. Ivory	20–1	22
83	OUT OF HAND	4	0703	D. Dale	14–1	15
82	VORVADOS	5	0813	M. Haynes	6–1 2nd Fav.	14
81	TOUCH BOY	5	0811	J. Berry	16–1	21
80	SWELTER	4	0802	F. Durr	8–1	20
79	OH SIMMIE	4	0700	R. Hollinshead	10–1	21
78	GOLDHILLS PRIDE	4	0810	T. Craig	8–1	13
77	JON GEORGE	3	0712	M. W. Easterby	11–2 Fav.	12
76	HEI'LAND JAMIE	5	0713	N. Adam	20–1	11
75	WALK BY	3	0810	W. Wightman	9–1	16

THE CHAMPAGNE STAKES – A race for top 2 y.o. colts over 7 furlongs that is expected to herald a leading contender for the following season's 2,000 Guineas.

ACHIEVED, (Pat Eddery, spotted cap), wins the 1981 Champagne Stakes from the Guy Harwood-trained HAYS (Greville Starky, diamonds). His subsequent efforts as a 3 y.o. were never to match the promise of this performance.

CHAMPAGNE STAKES

Group II 7f 2 y.o.   Colts and geldings only
Level weights, with a penalty for a winner of a Pattern race

The Champagne Stakes is a Group II race for 2-year-old colts and geldings only, over a distance of 7 furlongs on the straight course at Doncaster, and is now run on Friday, the third day of the St Leger Meeting. It is one of the first end-of-season races for 2-year-olds which it is hoped will reveal leading contenders for the following season's classics. In this respect only two winners, DON'T FORGET ME (1986) and WOLLOW (1975), who won the following season's English Two Thousand Guineas, have gone on to actually capture a Classic during their 3-year-old career. WARNING (1987), while missing the first colts' Classic due to illness, did win Goodwood's Group I Sussex Stakes and was claimed to be the best miler of his 3-year-old generation. SURE BLADE (1985), however, whilst not quite aspiring to the very highest grade, did gain two Group II prizes. LEAR FAN (1983) also, although missing out in the Classic, being the same vintage generation as EL GRAN SENOR and CHIEF SINGER, did win the prestigious Group I Prix Jacques le Marois 1 mile at Deauville against the best French milers of his generation, including the French Two Thousand Guineas winner.

However, winners of the Champagne Stakes have generally failed to realise the very high expectations, and success in this Group II race has been the summit of their careers. This is something to bear in mind when bookmakers start shouting the ante-post odds on next season's first colt's Classic before the runners have hardly swept past the post. Any intrepid backer tempted to dash in for a piece of the action would do well to inspect the subsequent career of many Champagne Stakes winners. It is more likely you have witnessed a horse just capable of subsequently winning a minor Group race somewhere, as displayed by ACHIEVED (1981), FINAL STRAW (1979) and SEXTON BLAKE (1977) in their 3-year-old careers, rather than a potential champion. Other winners (with the exception of J O TOBIN (1976) who achieved success in America as a 3-year-old) were quite disappointing in their subsequent careers.

The Champagne Stakes, set late in the season, and touted as a trial for next season's Classics, consequently attracts only small fields, of 3 to 10 runners, usually classically bred. Therefore they will be quite lightly raced (only four winners had more than two prior races) and seldom will have made their racecourse debut before July, providing minimal evidence upon which to assess their abilities. The backer may have to depend on reputation and the ability of trainers to make a selection.

The market has been a constantly reliable guide, with seven favourites successful (although five were odds-on), three 2nd favourites, four 3rd favourites and no shock results in a race that can be confidently left to the very top establishments. Henry Cecil and Guy Harwood (three wins each) lead the way from Barry Hills (two wins) with the old maestro Vincent O'Brien bearing a lone flag for an Irish-trained winner.

Although the winners have come from similar backgrounds they have not trod similar paths before challenging for this prize. No prior race therefore has had a great influence on the outcome here. Goodwood's Richmond Stakes (Group II, 6 furlongs, 42–44 days earlier) has been the most prestigious race to have any influence, with both WARNING (1987) and J O TOBIN (1976) completing the double. The other Goodwood Festival race, the Lanson Champagne Stakes (Group III, 7 furlongs, 43 days earlier), has provided one winner, DON'T FORGET ME (1986), who completed the double. Yet three horses, including the subsequent top-class stayer PETOKSI (1984), promoted to favourite after success at Goodwood, were beaten here. ACHIEVED (1981), the only Irish-trained winner, won the Heinz 57 Stakes (Group I, 5 furlongs, Phoenix Park, 32 days earlier). Newcastle's Seaton Delavel (Group III, 6 furlongs; no longer in existence) also provided two winners here, whilst Newmarket's Fitzroy House Stakes (1 mile, 13-18 days earlier) saw victories for LEAR FAN (1983) and WOLLOW (1975).

Prior winning form has been essential to succeed here, and with seven horses taking on Group company for the first time, it is no wonder twelve winners won their previous race and nine maintained unbeaten records.

Whilst winners of Doncaster's Champagne Stakes have sometimes later proved disappointing, and may almost by their success be eliminated from thoughts of greater glories, a few beaten horses did well, such as PETOKSI (1984), who as a 3-year-old won the Group I King George VI and Queen Elizabeth Stakes, CREAG-EN-SNOR (1983), who won the Group I Middle Park Stakes as a 2-year-old, and SOLINUS (1977), who won the next season's July Cup (Group I) as did GENTILHOMBRE (1976).

Finding the winners of the Champagne Stakes should not be

any immensely complicated exercise. Where form has not quite clearly pointed the way, with prior winning form and sometimes unbeaten records being of prime importance, the market's view has always been a good indicator for finding the winner.

88	PRINCE OF DANCE	2	0811	N. Graham	1–2 Fav.	7
87	WARNING	2	0900	G. Harwood	1–1 Fav.	4
86	DON'T FORGET ME	2	0900	R. Hannon	6–1	9
85	SURE BLADE	2	0900	B. Hills	5–4 Fav.	5
84	YOUNG RUN WAY	2	0900	G. Harwood	5–2 2nd Fav.	6
83	LEAR FAN	2	0900	G. Harwood	1–1 Fav.	4
82	GORYTUS	2	0900	W. Hern	8–13 Fav.	5
81	ACHIEVED	2	0900	M. V. O'Brien (Ire.)	11–4 2nd Fav.	8
80	GIELGUD	2	0900	H. Cecil	11–2	10
79	FINAL STRAW	2	0900	M. Stoute	9–2	9
78	R B CHESNE	2	0900	H. Cecil	8–13 Fav.	7
77	SEXTON BLAKE	2	0900	B. Hills	5–2 2nd Fav.	6
76	J O TOBIN	2	0900	N. Murless	4–9 Fav.	6
75	WOLLOW	2	0900	H. Cecil	11–4	8

FLYING CHILDERS STAKES

Group II   5f   2 y.o. only   colts, geldings and fillies
Level weights, sex allowance with a penalty for a winner of a
Pattern race

The Flying Childers Stakes is a Group II race for 2-year-olds over a distance of 5 furlongs. It is staged on Saturday, the final day of the St Leger meeting at Doncaster. It is a race which puts the seal on deciding who are the fastest 2-year-olds over the minimum sprinters' distance, and has been won by some very speedy juveniles, SIZZLING MELODY (1986), GREEN DESERT (1985), PRINCE SABO (1984), SUPERLATIVE (1983), KAFU (1982), MARWELL (1980), ABEER (1979), DEVON DITTY (1978), MUSIC MAESTRO (1977) and HITTITE GLORY (1975). Up to 1978 the Flying Childers had Group I status but has now been demoted to Group II level, although this has since hardly affected the quality of contestants or performances.

In 1987 penalties for previous Pattern races were introduced and only time will tell whether this has a bearing on the outcome of the race.

This race is still very much the 2-year-old sprinters' championship and has therefore attracted only medium-sized fields of 5 to 10 runners, with an average of 6 or 7, of the fastest juveniles in training.

Surprisingly, winning their previous race has not been essential for success in the Flying Childers Stakes. Only five winners were successful in their prior race, but three of these were not Group races. In fact the previous race programme of the winners has been quite varied, possibly due to the fact that this race is not confined to the exclusive realm of the top stables, but open also to any handler lucky and skilful enough to train a speedy juvenile. Therefore most winners have been brought along slowly to challenge in Group company, with their speed capacity only fully appreciated as their successes give them the momentum to challenge for higher honours. M. Stoute, with three wins, holds the banner for the established yards, yet he himself has practised bringing his 2-year-olds along strictly in the company that their merits of the moment warrant, and never just tilting at windmills on the grounds of a horse's breeding.

A number of races are to be found in common on the prior agenda of some of the winners. Royal Ascot's Norfolk Stakes (Group III, 5 furlong), and Newmarket's July Stakes (Group III, 6 furlong), for the colts, and the corresponding two fillies' races on the programme of two of the three winning fillies. Other prior races include the Prix Robert Papin (Group I, 5 furlongs, Maison-Lafitte, 48 or 55 days previously), in which two winners, PRINCE SABO (1984) and SUPERLATIVE (1983), were both placed; the Lowther Stakes (then Group III, 6 furlongs, York, 24 days earlier), in which ABEER (1979) and DEVON DITTY (1978) won; and the colt's equivalent Gimcrack Stakes (Group II, 6 furlongs, York, 23 days earlier), with PETERHOF (1981) and HITTITE GLORY (1975) (the shock winners of this race), both reversing that form with rivals when reverting to 5 furlongs

This has been perhaps the key to success in the Flying Childers Stakes; horses finding their forte simply as 'flying machines' over this minimum distance, having been found wanting in the final furlong over a longer trip. In fact only four winners had won over further than 5 furlongs in any of their prior races, and pure sprinting with blistering speed in a start to finish dash was their strength.

The Flying Childers Stakes has regularly attracted both sexes as contestants and whilst colts have dominated with eleven wins, a speedy filly, if of the highest standard, has proved to be able to match them, as demonstrated by the three female winners, MARWELL (1980), ABEER (1979) and DEVON DITTY (1978).

The market has been a reliable guide in pinpointing the winner with nine favourites, one 2nd favourite, one 3rd favourite and three outsiders (9–1, 9–1 and 100–1) successful. The market dominance of the favourites has been particularly noticeable since the race was dropped to Group II status with eight favourites (5–2, 6–4, 1–1, 11–10, 7–4, 8–15, 2–1, 4–11) successful in consecutive seasons. The race has generally worked according to plan with speed being the quality a horse either possesses or doesn't, an element which is hardly likely to be concealed. Two of the three surprise results were achieved by MUSIC MAESTRO (1977) who was tackling Group race company for the first time after three consecutive wins, and HITTITE GLORY (1975) who won at the unbelievable price of 100–1, yet had already won a Group II race at Goodwood only to flop in his next race in the Gimcrack Stakes at York before returning to form here.

The Flying Childers Stakes with its normally predictable results and 'pure speed' the quality essential to all winners, is a race that is easy to define, which can be recommended for selection and only a little concentration should put the backer on the winning path on St Leger day.

88	SHUTTLECOCK CORNER	2	0811	P. Felgate	9–1	8
87	GALLIC LEAGUE	2	0811	B. Hills	5–2 Fav.	7
86	SIZZLING MELODY	2	0900	Lord John Fitzgerald	6–4 Fav.	6
85	GREEN DESERT	2	0900	M. Stoute	1–1 Fav.	8
84	PRINCE SABO	2	0900	B. Swift	11–10 Fav.	6
83	SUPERLATIVE	2	0900	W. O'Gorman	7–4 Fav.	10
82	KAFU	2	0900	G. Harwood	8–15 Fav.	5
81	PETERHOF	2	0900	M. V. O'Brien (Ire.)	2–1 Fav.	7
80	MARWELL	2	0811	M. Stoute	4–11 Fav.	6
79	ABEER	2	0811	J. Tree	5–1	6
78	DEVON DITTY	2	0811	H. Thomson Jones	2–1 2nd Fav.	7
77	MUSIC MAESTRO	2	0900	M. Stoute	9–1	8
76	MANDRAKE MAJOR	2	0900	Denys Smith	7–2 Jt Fav.	9
75	HITTITE GLORY	2	0900	A. Breasley	100–1	5

ST LEGER STAKES
Group I   1m 6f 127y   3 y.o. only   entire colts and fillies only
Level weights, sex allowance

The St Leger is a Group I race for 3-year-old entire colts and fillies only, over a distance of 1 mile 6 furlongs 127 yards, and is staged on the Saturday and final day of the four-day meeting at Doncaster in early September. It is the final classic race of the season, setting the seal on the premier Group races for the 3-year-old generation.

The St Leger is the oldest of the five Classic races and was first run in 1776, three years before the second oldest, the Oaks, but whilst its importance in turf history cannot be challenged it has now declined and is rather the poor relation of the other four races. It has less impact in the racing calendar than 'all-age' races such as the French Prix de L'Arc de Triomphe or the English Champion Stakes, and with the advent of world travel for racehorses, international races during the Autumn in America or the Far East. Therefore it has been suggested the St Leger at Doncaster be opened, like its Irish counterpart, to become an all-age contest but this would deprive it of its 3-year-old Classic status and perhaps lower it further in prestige to become just another all-age race, rather than restore its former sparkle to be the fifth jewel in the English Classic crown.

The St Leger may be the most difficult of the Classics to win, especially if credence is given to the saying 'the fittest horse wins the Guineas, the luckiest horse wins the Derby, and the best horse wins the St Leger'. In recent times very few horses have contested all three of these Classic races (most are bred and/or raced specifically at a narrow range of distances) and therefore this observation can hardly ever thoroughly be put to the test of the racecourse. The last colt to win the legendary triple crown, the great NIJINSKY (1970) was only the second winner since before the Second World War to complete the treble. No Two Thousand Guineas winner has challenged for the St Leger and the only Derby winners to do so were REFERENCE POINT (1987) who won both, and the tragically

THE ST. LEGER – A 1 mile 6 furlong race for 3 y.o. colts and fillies is the final Classic of the season and never easy to win.

OH SO SHARP (Steve Cauthen, left) wins the 1985 St. Leger and completes the third leg of the triple crown to become only the third horse and second filly to achieve this since the war. PHARDANTE (Greville Starkey, striped cap) just holds off LANFRANCO (white face) and the whip brandishing Lester Piggott for the second place.

ill-fated SHERGAR (1981), who suffered his final and only second racecourse defeat here on the Town Moor course.

In contrast, three fillies who won the English Oaks have gone on to win the St Leger, OH SO SHARP (1985) becoming only the second filly (the other was MELD (1956)) since the Second World War to win the triple crown – the One Thousand Guineas, Oaks and St Leger. Two other game and sometimes brilliant fillies, SUN PRINCESS (1983) and DUNFERMLINE (1977), did the double of the two Classics.

The St Leger does not usually attract the already proven best colts, that is horses that have figured prominently in the English or Irish Derbys, or all-age Group I races such as the King George VI and Queen Elizabeth Stakes, or the International Stakes, but more slowly maturing horses who it is considered will have staying as their forte and who are at or about to reach peak at this time of the season.

There are perhaps two keynotes to this race:

(i)   A horse must truly stay the distance, which is always a gruelling test up the long home straight on the Town Moor course;

(ii) A horse must be at its peak for this race, and not jaded from a strenuous summer racing campaign.

The former cause was most definitely the reason for the narrow defeat of one of the best horses to compete in the St Leger, ALLEGED (1977), who afterwards proceeded to demonstrate his greatness by winning the Arc de Triomphe for two consecutive seasons. In the St Leger he was outstayed by the Queen's DUNFERMLINE in an epic struggle when stamina was tested to the uttermost. This ability to see out the distance, plus courage and gameness, have been the epitome of the performance of a number of recent winners, notably MINSTER SON (1988), REFERENCE POINT (1987), OH SO SHARP (1985), SUN PRINCESS (1983), TOUCHING WOOD (1982), and particularly COMMANCHE RUN (1984), who gave Lester Piggott a record number of Classic race victories.

The other factor of major importance, whether a horse with outstanding form is still at its peak at this time in the season or has 'gone over the top', certainly appears to be responsible for the shock defeats of SHERGAR (1981) and ILE DE BOURBON (1978).

The St Leger has attracted fields varying in size from 6 to 17 runners. The larger the fields, the more open the race appears, and the smaller fields are when an outstanding horse seems to command the race. Only occasionally does an already proven top-class colt challenge for the race and usually the field is made up of horses which have either missed at the very highest level and been brought along more slowly to tackle this final Classic prize or those that had previously been found wanting in the very top races.

The winners have broadly conformed to these types, with REFERENCE POINT (1987) and OH SO SHARP (1985) being two exceptions. Eight horses began their 3-year-old campaign as maidens before gaining a Classic victory here, although the two fillies in this category also won their first Classic race along the way. The others that had previously not succeeded at the top level now grabbed their moment.

Whether vastly experienced or not, all the winners have had a fairly light season, with only the surprise French-trained winner SON OF LOVE (1979) having more than six prior races. The three

Dick Hern winners had the least, three previous races for two of them and four for SUN PRINCESS (1983). Consequently with winners gradually improving as the season progressed, yet usually not quite succeeding when they have been pitched in at the top grades, winning the previous race has not been essential for success in the St Leger. Whilst only five winners won their previous race, ten horses promoted to favourite after winning their previous race were defeated, almost suggesting this to be a liability.

The previous race of greatest significance has been the Great Voltigeur Stakes (Group II, 1½ miles, York, 24 days earlier), in which four winners ran, only REFERENCE POINT (1987) completing the double, whilst the others were placed. Negatively it has produced two winners, ELECTRIC (1982) and ALLEGED (1977), both promoted to favourite in the St Leger, who were beaten; ELECTRIC by TOUCHING WOOD, who could only finish third to it on the Knavesmire, yet reversed form over the 2 furlong longer distance at Doncaster. The International Stakes (formerly Benson Hedges Gold Cup, Group I, 1 mile 2½ furlongs, York, 25 days earlier) has produced three winners, OH SO SHARP (1985) and CROW (1976) finishing second, whilst JULIO MARINER (1978) was unplaced. Finally, the Yorkshire Oaks (Group I, 1½ miles, 25 days earlier) has provided two of the fillies, SUN PRINCESS (1983) who won and completed a notable double, whilst DUNFERMLINE (1977) could only finish third. Negatively, DIMINUENDO (1988) and UNTOLD (1986) promoted to St Leger favourite after victory in this fillies' race, found their stamina limitations fully exposed, and were defeated comprehensively in the St Leger.

The St Leger used to be considered the race where the Epsom Derby fourth would go on to win. This was in the days when such an animal was the horse that was only just beginning to run on at that stage of the race, and needed the extra 2 furlongs to bring its stamina fully into play. These days, however, such a horse is more likely to be a weakening non-stayer. Therefore only five winners who earlier contested the Derby have won the St Leger, with REFERENCE POINT the only winner of both. TOUCHING WOOD had been an honourable second but the other three, MINSTER SON, JULIO MARINER and BRUNI, failed to make the frame at the Derby.

The St Leger usually attracts an international field of runners, with regular contestants from France and sometimes Ireland. The race from the trainers' viewpoint is always won by the very top establishments. The two maestros in the art of preparing stayers, H. Cecil and W. Hern, with three wins each, lead the way from two French-trained winners.

The market over the whole period has been a strangely inconclusive guide, with five favourites and two 2nd favourites successful, whilst two 3rd favourite and five outsiders (7–1, 28–1, 20–1, 28–1 and 9–1) also won. However, four of the favourites (two of which were odds-on) have won since 1983, plus a 2nd favourite, suggesting the St Leger may be assuming a more predictable air than in the mid-1970s to early 1980s, when shock results occurred with a surprising regularity.

As the final Classic of the season the St Leger provides the backer with the last opportunity to bask in Classic glory if successfully selecting the winner, but it has not always been an easy race in which to achieve such a feat. The numerous 'good things' including four odds-on 'unbeatable' favourites DIMINUENDO (1988), SHERGAR (1981), ILE DE BOURBON (1978) and ALLEGED (1977) should warn the backer to be wary and not accept anything about this race as a foregone conclusion. The St Leger is a testing race for a horse to win, so much so that few winners have gone on to greater things, especially in the following weeks of the current season – although both SUN PRINCESS (1983) and CROW (1976) were second in The Arc de Triomphe a few weeks later in their respective seasons. REFERENCE POINT (1987) ran the worst race of his career in that event, in what was hoped would be his crowning glory.

The St Leger from the selection point of view is a race of consuming interest with a case always likely to be made out for a number of contenders. The very top-class form shown by any horse can never be lightly disregarded, but horses that may have been subject to numerous hard races at this level since the season began may now be feeling the effects, and improving, more lightly raced horses should be viewed carefully, especially if there are any stamina weaknesses in the most fancied contenders. Only two winners had proved themselves at the distance so the question of stamina has to be taken on trust. So with these thoughts in mind and with due regard to all winners except one having run within the past 28 days, nine at the York Festival Meeting, the backer is forewarned of the areas for major consideration in finding the winner of the St Leger.

88	MINSTER SON	3	0900	N. Graham	15–2		6
87	REFERENCE POINT	3	0900	H. Cecil	4–11 Fav.		7
86	MOON MADNESS	3	0900	J. Dunlop	9–2 2nd Fav.		8
85	OH SO SHARP	3	0811	H. Cecil	8–11 Fav.		6
84	COMMANCHE RUN	3	0900	L. Cumani	7–4 Fav.		11
83	SUN PRINCESS	3	0811	W. Hern	11–8 Fav.		10
82	TOUCHING WOOD	3	0900	H. Thomson Jones	7–1		15
81	CUT ABOVE	3	0900	W. Hern	28–1		7
80	LIGHT CAVALRY	3	0900	H. Cecil	3–1 2nd Fav.		7
79	SON OF LOVE	3	0900	R. Collet (Fr.)	20–1		17
78	JULIO MARINER	3	0900	C. Brittain	28–1		14
77	DUNFERMLINE	3	0811	W. Hern	10–1		13
76	CROW	3	0900	A. Penna (Fr.)	6–1 Jt Fav.		15
75	BRUNI	3	0900	H. R. Price	9–1		12

AYR GOLD CUP HANDICAP
0–115 Handicap   6f   3 y.o. and upwards

The Ayr Gold Cup Handicap is a race for 3-year-olds and upwards over a distance of 6 furlongs and staged on the Friday of the four-day meeting at Ayr in middle or late September. This competitive handicap is the highlight of this popular and entertaining meeting on the west coast of Scotland at the end of summer with the going usually riding soft.

It is always a competitive race attracting large fields, of 14 to 29 runners, with an average of 24, who represent a fair mixture of some of the better sprint handicappers in training. It has been won by a couple of horses of Group race standard rather than mere handicappers: VAIGLY GREAT (1978) who carried 9 st 6 lb as a 3-year-old to win this race, and ROMAN WARRIOR (1975), the big brave giant of a horse who carried a record 10 st to victory here. The other winners, with the exception of SPARKLING BOY (1980) who carried 9 st 2 lb as a 3-year-old, and GREEN RUBY (1986) who carried 8 st 11 lb as a 5-year old (and was the winner of the equally competitive Steward's Cup earlier in the season), were all strictly handicap class. No other horse has carried above 8 st 6 lb to victory.

This is due to the Ayr Gold Cup being an extremely competitive handicap. Seven races have been won by a margin of a neck or less, which demonstrates the efficiency of the present centralised handicapping system. Only the truly better-class winners have been able to overcome the awesome 9 st weight burden, especially on the soft ground prevalent at Ayr at this time of year. Not surprisingly therefore, seven winners have carried below 8 st, five with the help of apprentices' allowance, thus confirming the influence that weight has played in deciding the winner. Consequently seven beaten favourites carried 8 st 6 lb or higher, two of these having a winner's penalty included.

Although weight has been a considerable determining factor, all the winners had good recent form and with the exceptions of SO CAREFUL (1988) and NOT SO SILLY (1987) both of whom were unplaced in their previous race, yet won their race prior to

AYR GOLD CUP – The last really important 6 furlong sprint handicap of the season with a corresponding strong and lively betting market. A competitive race with invariably a tight finish.

The apprentice ridden NOT SO SILLY (Garry Bardwell, hooped body) leads close home from the apprentice ridden SERVE N' VOLLY (Phillip Barnard, striped body) to win the 1987 Ayr Gold Cup, with barely a length covering the first five finishers.

that with NOT SO SILLY having a penalty to carry in the Ayr Gold Cup, and ROMAN WARRIOR (1975), who was fourth in a Group II race in his previous race, all the other winners have won (five) or were placed in their prior race.

The race of greatest influence has been the Portland Handicap (5 furlongs 140 yards, Doncaster, 8 days earlier) in which five winners competed, with JON GEORGE (1977) the only one to complete the double. FAMOUS STAR (1982), SPARKLING BOY (1980) and LAST TANGO (1976) were all second, and the unplaced NOT SO SILLY (1987) reversed the Doncaster form against a previous conqueror over this longer distance. Negatively three horses promoted to favourite, all carrying a penalty after winning or being placed in the Portland Handicap, were beaten in the Ayr Gold Cup.

The reputation of the draw on Ayr's straight 6 furlong track (which has a slight fall for the first 3½ furlongs and thereafter a slight rise) is to favour the high-drawn horses in big fields except when the going is Soft. Although this theory has had support in the light of recent Ayr Gold Cup results, with low numbers (9 or under) winning on eight occasions, six of these were when the going was Good to Soft or wetter.

The higher numbers (15 plus) have also won on five occasions, four of these when the ground was Good to Soft, or Soft, making the evidence slightly inconclusive.

The age group of the winners slightly favours the younger generations, 3-year-olds with six wins, ahead of 4-year-olds with four wins and 5-year-olds with four wins.

This tough handicap is usually won by trainers noted for their handling and placing of this type of animal, and records show the names of some of the shrewdest in the business on the winners roll. M. H. (Peter) Easterby, with two wins, is the only one with more than one victory, and this is a race where northern yards can still repel the challenge of raiders from the south.

The market, as would be expected for such a competitive handicap, has only been a limited guide to pinpointing the winner. One favourite, three 2nd favourites, three 3rd favourites and seven outsiders (33–1, 25–1, 14–1, 11–1, 15–1, 40–1, 22–1) have been successful. The shortest-priced beaten favourite was ROMAN WARRIOR (1976) (3–1) trying as a 5-year-old, again under 10 st, to win the race for the second year running – showing what a tough task one of the unsuccessful market leaders had. Good recent form being a prerequisite for success in the Ayr Gold Cup, the second and third choices in the betting which have fared reasonably well demand close consideration.

As one of the more popular sprint handicaps the race attracts a competitive betting market that includes ante-post interest and provides a taunting and teasing challenge to selection. Finding the winner is unlikely to be simple, with normally a number of good probables emerging to be considered in the pre-race calculations.

The backer, unless following a really top-class horse who may have to defy a burden of weight (which the records show is possible), should always focus on good recent form (winner or second) and fitness (within the past 14 days). These have been shown to be constant factors in success here, especially on the softish going likely to be encountered. Apprentices also have been used to good effect to lighten the weight, and with the margin between victory and defeat in this race always likely to be small, any advantage to be gained could be the telling factor. The backer who gets it right here surely deserves the good-priced winner the race always provides.

88	SO CAREFUL	5	0707	J. Berry	33–1		29
87	NOT SO SILLY	3	0710	A. Bailey	12–1		29
86	GREEN RUBY	5	0811	G. Balding	25–1		29
85	CAMPS HEATH	4	0709	F. Durr	14–1		25
84	ALBE ALBERT	4	0806	M. H. Easterby	9–1	2nd Fav.	29
83	POLLYS BROTHER	5	0803	M. H. Easterby	11–1		28
82	FAMOUS STAR	3	0707	M. Albina	13–2		14
81	FIRST MOVEMENT	3	0710	G. Huffer	14–1		21
80	SPARKLING BOY	3	0902	P. Kelleway	15–1		24
79	PRIMULA BOY	4	0707	W. Bentley	40–1		22
78	VAIGLY GREAT	3	0906	M. Stoute	5–1	Fav.	24
77	JON GEORGE	3	0804	M. W. Easterby	22–1		25
76	LAST TANGO	5	0705	J. Sutcliffe	6–1	2nd Fav.	18
75	ROMAN WARRIOR	4	1000	N. Angus	8–1	2nd Fav.	23

MILL REEF STAKES

Group II 6f 2 y.o. only colts, geldings and fillies
Level weights, sex allowance with a penalty for a winner of a
Group I or II race

The Mill Reef Stakes is a Group II race for 2-year-olds over a
distance of 6 furlongs and staged at Newbury on the Saturday of
the two day meeting in the second half of September. It is one of
the important 2-year old races programmed in early autumn which
it is hoped will reveal a leading contender for the following season's
Classics. However, in this respect the Mill Reef Stakes has been
of minimal influence with no winner having gone on to capture
a Classic race. In fact most of the winners have failed to develop
as 3-year-olds on the potential shown in winning here.

Surprisingly perhaps, it has generally been left to the horses
beaten in this race to go on to better things. MISTER MAJESTIC
(1986), STALKER (1985), BASSENTHWAITE (1984), MATTABOY
(1980) and KNOWN FACT (1979) all went on, a couple of weeks
later, to win the Middle Park Stakes (Group I) over 6 furlongs
at Newmarket. KNOWN FACT was also the only horse to capture
the following season's Two Thousand Guineas – albeit on the
disqualification of the winner. Other beaten horses who showed
good form as 3-year-olds include GREEN DESERT (1985), later
winner of the July Cup (Group I) over 6 furlongs at Newmarket;
HORAGE (1982) in the St James Palace Stakes over 1 mile at Royal
Ascot; MRS PENNY (1979) who won the following season's French
Oaks (Group I) over 1½ miles at Longchamp; and YOUNG
GENERATION (1978) won the Lockinge Stakes (Group II) over 1
mile at Newbury.

The winners by comparison have tended to be rather disappoint-
ing. The 3-year-olds MAGIC OF LIFE (1987) who won the
Coronation Stakes (Group I) over 1 mile at Royal Ascot, and FOR-
EST FLOWER (1986), winner of the Irish One Thousand Guineas
(Group I) over 1 mile at the Curragh, the only two fillies to win the
Mill Reef Stakes, are notable exceptions, the others never having
won another race of this Group II status.

The Mill Reef Stakes has only attracted moderately sized fields of 4 to 12 runners – usually averaging out at 8 runners, a number of which will be aspiring to Group race level for the first time. Seven winners fill this category and therefore it is not surprising that they have highly individual programmes of previous races, where no race holds more than a fleeting influence. These have ranged from a maiden and Nursery Handicap up to a Group I race contested by FOREST FLOWER, the only winner to have won a Group race previously. An important negative factor to consider is that five winners of a Group race in their prior race and promoted to favourite in the Mill Reef Stakes were beaten.

Winning form has not been essential for success here. Only six winners gained a victory in their prior race, though of course not in group race company. Every winner had won at least one prior race, LUQMAN (1985) with four wins out of eight starts the most prolific and most experienced, with RUSSIAN BOND (1988) and LOCAL SUITOR (1984) unbeaten in their only previous race the most inexperienced.

Although predominantly won by the top trainers the race has a couple of less familiar names on the winning trainers role, but with H. Cecil and P. Welwyn (two wins each) the only trainers with more than one winner.

The record of the market leaders also reflects a lack of positive trends with five favourites, three 2nd favourites, three 3rd favourites and three outsiders (9–1, 9–1 and 20–1) winning, and success spread almost uniformly across the spectrum of the market. The market has therefore hardly been a helpful guide to pinpointing the winner and with statistical information giving so few positive indications the backer will have to rely very much on a personal assessment of form, carefully balancing the proven abilities of horses successful in maiden races against rivals with similar records yet who also may have tackled group company as well.

The Mill Reef Stakes is not a particularly easy race for selection, usually attracting contestants below the very top class, as the real high flyers amongst the two year old generation (who will be penalised for any Group I or II victories) are likely to be aimed at the more established and greater-value 2-year-old races, especially the Group I Middle Park Stakes, which is programmed not long after.

It may seem somewhat surprising therefore to find that a number of horses beaten in the Mill Reef Stakes go on to win that Newmarket race. It perhaps shows that these basically sprinter-bred types need the recent race to bring them to their peak. So unless the backer holds very strong views as to a horse's chances here, where consistent pointers are few, a non-participating role is advised – whilst placing a careful eye on beaten horses and the occasional winner who often holds the key to success in the future.

88	RUSSIAN BOND	2	0811	H. Cecil	2–5 Fav.	4
87	MAGIC OF LIFE	2	0806	J. Tree	4–1 2nd Fav.	5
86	FOREST FLOWER	2	0808	I. Blading	4–7 Fav.	9
85	LUQMAN	2	0811	P. Walwyn	20–1	9
84	LOCAL SUITOR	2	0811	W. Hern	3–1 Jt Fav.	12
83	VACARME	2	0811	H. Cecil	2–7 Fav.	7
82	SALIERI	2	0811	H. Cecil	11–4 2nd Fav.	5
81	HAYS	2	0811	G. Harwood	5–2 2nd Fav.	8
80	SWEET MONDAY	2	0811	J. Holt	9–1	7
79	LORD SEYMOUR	2	0811	M. Stoute	9–2	7
78	KING OF SPAIN	2	0811	P. Cundell	9–1	9
77	FORMIDABLE	2	0811	P. Walwyn	13–8 Fav.	6
76	ANAX	2	0811	B. Hobbs	4–1	6
75	ROYAL BOY	2	0811	M. Jarvis	5–1	8

179

HOOVER FILLIES MILE STAKES

Group II   1m   2 y.o.   fillies only
Level weights with a penalty for a winner of a Pattern race

The Hoover Fillies Mile Stakes is a Group II race (upgraded in 1986) for 2-year-old fillies over a distance of 1 mile on the round course at Ascot. It is now staged on Saturday, the final day of the three-day Festival of British Racing Meeting in late September. It is a race that is expected to provide an indication of which 2-year-old fillies will be challenging for the leading staying race honours when they become 3-year-olds.

The race has had only a minor influence on the first fillies' Classic of the following season, the One Thousand Guineas, which is run over the same distance, with just two winners OH SO SHARP (1985) and QUICK AS LIGHTNING (1979) completing the double. However, it has had considerable influence on the Epsom Oaks over 1½ miles. Two winners, DIMINUENDO (1987) (who also dead-heated in the Irish Oaks and finished third in the English One Thousand Guineas), and the previously mentioned OH SO SHARP (1984) both completed the double. Other winners ACCLIMATISE (1982), UNTOLD (1985) who finished second, and LEAP LIVELY (1980) who finished third.

Beaten fillies in this Ascot mile race cannot be dismissed either, as DUNFERMLINE (1976), CIRCUS PLUME (1983) and SCINTILATE (1978), who finished second, third and fourth respectively, all won the English Oaks of the following season, DUNFERMLINE also winning the St Leger. And another filly, VIELLE (1980) only second at Ascot, was also runner-up in the Oaks, and then, like ACCLIMATISE, went on to win the Nassau Stakes (Group II) over 1¼ miles at Goodwood, being possibly better suited to this middle distance than the Classic stayers' trip. HEIGHT OF FASHION (1981) whilst not contesting the following season's Classic, also won a noted prize in Group II, the Princess of Wales Stakes, over 1½ miles at Newmarket, the following summer. It is therefore apparent that contestants who have figured prominently in the Hoover Fillies Mile are likely to

HOOVER FILLIES MILE – An important 2 y.o. fillies race in early Autumn that provides an informative guide to the following seasons Classics.

Irish trained ICING (Christy Roche) is just pushed out to beat BEDFELLOW (Pat Eddery, spots) and the Queen's grey filly GILDING (Joe Mercer) to win Ascot's fillies mile in 1975. ICING later had a successful career as a brood mare at stud, being the dam of AL HAREB winner of the William Hill Futurity 1988.

develop into useful performers, sometimes of the very highest class, as 3-year-olds.

181

The Hoover Fillies Mile has attracted fields of 6 to 12 runners with an average of 8. These are usually very choicely bred fillies who still have aspirations for the Classics of the following season. The mile distance of this race is a stiff test for these 2-year-old fillies, who will have been previously lightly raced. Ten winners had a maximum of three prior races, with their racing careers very much directed to their second season's campaign. Therefore most have been handled tenderly, given easy introductory races to gain confidence and then raised in class as their performance warrants it. Eight winners made their first appearance in Group company in this race. Consequently ten winners won their previous race and five of these had unbeaten records. Improving fillies on a high, or else ones now able to reverse previous form with rivals (five winners did this) hold the key to winning this race.

Two races have a particular influence on the outcome here. The May Hill Stakes for 2-year-old fillies (Group III) over 1 mile at Doncaster, 14 to 16 days earlier, in which four winners ran TESSLA (1988), HEIGHT OF FASHION (1981) and FORMULATE (1978) completing the double whilst NEPULA (1983) finished second at Doncaster. However, two winners promoted to favourite after winning the May Hill were defeated here. Also Goodwood's Waterford Candelabra Stakes for 2-year-old fillies (Group III) over 7 furlongs, 34–35 days earlier, in which three winners ran. INVITED GUEST (1986) won and two others finished third. Seven winners had previously tackled a mile before, and five others were proven over 7 furlongs and so made the transition without difficulty.

The Hoover Fillies race, as would be expected of a race contested by future Classic race aspirants, has been dominated by the leading trainers with H. Cecil (four wins) the only trainer with more than a single success.

The market has been a very reliable guide to pinpointing the winner with eight favourites, four 2nd favourites, one 3rd favourite and one outsider (9–1) successful, and hardly a shock result to upset the composure of followers of the market leaders.

It is certainly an interesting race to consider for selection, with the outcome likely to have an influence on some of the leading staying and middle-distance races for fillies in the following season. In pinpointing the winner, the improving filly, perhaps especially now a long distance is being tackled, is likely to hold the key to success. If unable to identify such a candidate the backer will probably only have to glance at the market to find the answer, with twelve races won by the first or second favourite.

88	TESSLA	2	0813	H. Cecil	5–2 Fav.	8
87	DIMINUENDO	2	0813	H. Cecil	2–1 Fav.	7
86	INVITED GUEST	2	0900	R. Armstrong	8–11 Fav.	12
85	UNTOLD	2	0807	M. Stoute	6–4 Fav.	9
84	OH SO SHARP	2	0810	H. Cecil	6–5 Fav.	8
83	NEPULA	2	0809	G. Huffer	3–1 2nd Fav.	8
82	ACCLIMATISE	2	0809	B. Hobbs	3–1 2nd Fav.	8
81	HEIGHT OF FASHION	2	0902	W. Hern	15–8 Fav.	8
80	LEAP LIVELY	2	0812	I. Balding	9–2 2nd Fav.	7
79	QUICK AS LIGHTNING	2	0812	J. Dunlop	9–1	9
78	FORMULATE	2	0901	H. Cecil	5–4 Fav.	9
77	CHERRY HINTON	2	0901	H. Wragg	10–11 Fav.	8
76	MISS PINKIE	2	0901	N. Murless	5–1	8
75	ICING	2	0901	P. Prendergast (Ire.)	5–1 2nd Fav.	6

QUEEN ELIZABETH II STAKES

Group I   1m   3 y.o. and upwards   colts, geldings and fillies
Level weights, sex allowance, WFA

The Queen Elizabeth II Stakes is a Group I race (upgraded from Group II in 1987) for 3-year-olds and upwards over 1 mile round course. It is staged at Ascot and now serves as the centrepiece of the Festival of British Racing day on the Saturday of the three-day meeting in late September. If not decided in earlier contests during the summer, the Queen Elizabeth II Stakes has provided the concluding evidence of who may assume the champion miler's crown. Now elevated to Group I status on the richest day's racing in Britain, it is expected to assume the role of European Championship for milers, as the Arc is for stayers. It has always attracted the leading milers from both the current Classic generation and older horses in select sized fields of 5 to 11 runners.

It has been won by some very good horses, SHADEED (1985), TO-AGORI-MOU (1981) and KNOWN FACT (1980) who all won the Two Thousand Guineas of their respective years, plus WARNING (1988) (who missed the first colts classic through illness) and whose win here just about sealed their position as the best miler of their generation. When you add KRIS (1979), who was just defeated in the Two Thousand Guineas yet was the best miler of his year; TELEPROMPTER (1984), who later received wider international acclaim; and the only dual winner ROSE BOWL (1976 and 1975); the quality of horse which has won this race can be clearly seen.

However, whilst it has been the crowning glory for a number of winners, the race has brought shock defeat for some others. MIESQUE, the brilliant French-trained filly, and considered champion miler in Europe, was beaten by MILLIGRAM in 1987. CHIEF SINGER (1984), who had proved himself a most brilliant and adaptable horse from 6 furlongs to 1 mile, was humbled by TELEPROMPTER. KRIS (1980), as a 4-year-old, and who had taken all before him, suffered the second defeat of his career. And BOLKONSKI (1975), the Two Thousand Guineas winner, also suffered his second defeat on English soil.

From the backer's viewpoint these surprise defeats suggest a note of caution. The Queen Elizabeth II Stakes for many of these erstwhile champions came at the end of a hard season's campaign against top-class opposition, which had begun in the spring and now, by early autumn, this race could be just the back-breaking final straw. Ideally perhaps, this is a race to bring a horse back after a summer rest for an autumn campaign. In this respect four winners who returned after an absence from racing of 100 days or more showed the benefits of being fresh. Four other winners had not ran for 31 days or more. Yet seven beaten favourites (that included three odds-on shots and joint favourite) had all raced within the previous 28 days. This suggests that freshness rather than recent race fitness may be the order of the day and six winners had four previous races or less during the season.

Until elevated to Group I status in 1987, the Queen Elizabeth II Stakes had entry conditions penalising previous Group I or II winners and therefore gave an opportunity for a horse previously unsuccessful at these higher Group race levels. Six winners filled this category, three of these responsible for the only results which have gone against the two market leaders.

The prior race of most consistent influence has been the Waterford Crystal Mile (Group II) over 1 mile at Goodwood 28 days earlier, in which four winners ran, MILLIGRAM (1987), TO-AGORI-MOU (1981) and KRIS (1979) all winning it; whilst ROSE BOWL (1975) finished second before winning here. KNOWN FACT (1980) also won the Crystal Mile but had an intervening race before winning here. On the negative side, DON (1977) was promoted unsuccessfully to favourite after finishing second at Goodwood.

Whilst every winner had won at least one prior race during the season, (KRIS (1979) winning five, TELEPROMPTER (1984) and HOMING (1978) four each, TO-AGORI-MOU (1981) and KNOWN FACT (1980) three each) winning the previous race has not been essential, and only six winners achieved this.

Since being promoted to Group I grade the Queen Elizabeth II Stakes should remain strictly in the top league of trainers. There has been just one shock win, by BUZZARD'S BAY (1982), which gave encouragement to the smaller yards. G. Harwood (three wins) with R. Houghton and M. Stoute (two wins apiece) share the honours as the only trainers with more than one success.

The market would seem to hold the solution to finding the winner of the Queen Elizabeth II Stakes with six favourites and five 2nd favourites successful, plus one 3rd favourite and two outsiders. But with eight favourites beaten, and three of these odds-on – MIESQUE (1–4 Fav.), CHIEF SINGER (4–6 Fav.) and KRIS (1–2 Fav.) – the backer should eye the market leader warily.

Now elevated to the highest level in the Pattern Race scale, the Queen Elizabeth II Stakes may become subject to less shocks as horses will be unpenalised and strict merit should prevail. However, this is an early autumn contest where the improving filly is always likely to come into her own, and animals with outstanding earlier form, especially if subjected to tough races, may find this race one too many. The backer should not take short odds for any favourite and with the record of the 2nd favourite holding up equally well, this is the area to consider for value.

88	WARNING	3	0811	G. Harwood	9–4 Jt Fav.	8
87	MILLIGRAM	3	0808	M. Stoute	6–1 Jt 2nd Fav.	5
86	SURE BLADE	3	0811	B. Hills	6–5 Fav.	7
85	SHADEED	3	0900	M. Stoute	9–4 Fav.	7
84	TELEPROMPTER	4	0900	J. W. Watts	11–2 2nd Fav.	6
83	SACKFORD	3	0807	G. Harwood	11–2 2nd Fav.	9
82	BUZZARD'S BAY	4	0900	H. Collingridge	50–1	10
81	TO-AGORI-MOU	3	0900	G. Harwood	5–4 Fav.	6
80	KNOWN FACT	3	0900	J. Tree	3–1 2nd Fav.	7
79	KRIS	3	0900	H. Cecil	8–11 Fav.	7
78	HOMING	3	0807	W. Hern	9–2 2nd Fav.	11
77	TRUSTED	4	0900	J. Dunlop	20–1	7
76	ROSE BOWL	4	0904	R. Houghton	13–8 Fav.	8
75	ROSE BOWL	3	0804	R. Houghton	9–2	5

ROYAL LODGE STAKES

Group II   1m   2 y.o. only   colts and geldings
Level weights, with a penalty for a winner of a Pattern race

The Royal Lodge Stakes is a Group II race for 2-year-old colts and geldings only, over a distance of 1 mile on the round course at Ascot, and is staged as part of the Festival of British Racing on Saturday, the final day of the three-day meeting in September.

It is the first 2-year-old Group race of the season over the mile distance open to colts and geldings, and like the equivalent race confined to fillies (the Hoover Fillies Mile) is considered to provide a guide to the leading middle-distance and staying horses of the following season.

Most recently its positive value may be called into question as winners and beaten horses have afterwards proved disappointing. Yet up to the early 1980s it could be seen as a race which for many served as a stepping-stone to even better things. Winners such as ELA-MANA-MOU (1978), who later in its career won the Group I Eclipse Stakes and King George VI and Queen Elizabeth Stakes; and SHIRLEY HEIGHTS (1977), who won the English and Irish Derbys, highlight the quality of winners. HELLO GORGEOUS (1979) comes next in line as a winning Derby trialist who won the Group II Dante Stakes at York as a 3-year-old, yet was not quite good enough in the main event; while more recently BONHOMIE (1985) was successful in the Group II King Edward VII Stakes at Royal Ascot as a 3-year-old. Compared to these horses the other winners fade into insignificance, with most of them, after winning this race, sinking without trace. However, the record of beaten horses remains impressive: DUNBEATH (1982) who actually won and EMMSON (1987) who was only fourth in the Royal Lodge won the Group I William Hill Futurity Stakes over 1 mile at Doncaster 28 days later. PETOSKI (1984), beaten favourite in this Ascot race and unplaced, won the Group I King George VI and Queen Elizabeth Stakes as a 3-year-old. ROUSILLON (1983) second here, as a 4-year-old won the Group I Sussex Stakes to be crowned champion miler. Similarly RECTITATION (1980), only second in the Royal Lodge Stakes, won the next season's French Two Thousand

THE ROYAL LODGE STAKES – A mile race for 2 y.o. colts which it is expected will produce a Classic contender for the following season. Beaten horses in this race often prove superior to the winner in their later careers.

The field turns right for home in the 1980 Royal Lodge Stakes with two and a half furlongs to go. Eventual winner ROBELLING (striped cap) is hidden by BELDALE FLUTTER (Taffy Thomas, centre), winner of the Futurity Stakes later in the season. To the right RECITATION (Greville Starkey, striped cap), although only second here, won the following season's French 2,000 Guineas.

Guineas. BELDALE FLUTTER (1980), fourth in the same year, won the William Hill Futurity Stakes 28 days later and as a 3-year-old went on to capture the Group I International Stakes (then the Benson and Hedges Gold Cup) at York. TROY (1978), beaten by ELA-MANA-MOU, became undoubtedly the best defeated horse to emerge from the race, winning the English and Irish Derbys in the following season, the King George VI and Queen Elizabeth Stakes, and the International Stakes; while HAWAIIAN SOUND (1977), beaten favourite behind SHIRLEY HEIGHTS, finished second to that horse in the Derby, but won the International Stakes. Also unplaced, JULIO MARINER (1977) gained the following season's St Leger; and PAMPA PAUL (1976), another beaten favourite, won the following season's Irish Two Thousand Guineas to complete a fearsome array of subsequent Group I winners from contestants of the Royal Lodge Stakes.

The race usually attracts only medium-sized fields of 4 to 10 runners, some of whom have later proved to be of real class. Not surprisingly most horses enter this race with high aspirations for future Pattern Race success, and therefore will have been lightly raced. Eight winners had three or less previous races, their careers being directed more towards a second-season campaign. Consequently with winners normally inexperienced, yet nine of them successfully meeting Group race company at the first time of asking, winning form can be seen to be an essential commodity. Eleven winners won their previous race, six horses defended unbeaten records, and none were maidens.

With each winner having a prior race programme tailored to individual needs, only one race holding any positive influence has emerged. This is the Solario Stakes, Group III, over 7 furlongs at Sandown, 36 days earlier. Two horses have completed the double, HIGH ESTATE (1988) and SANQUIRICO (1987). However, two other winners of the Solario Stakes (before it was elevated to Group Status) were promoted to favourite and beaten in the Royal Lodge Stakes. However, negatively, the Champagne Stakes (Group II), over 7 furlongs at Doncaster, 15 days earlier, has seen three horses promoted to favourite after finishing first second or third there, yet all were beaten in the Royal Lodge Stakes. It may be that the form of this race has been overrated or else that the race over the Doncaster straight 7 furlongs bears little comparison to the stiff mile at Ascot, which will find out those lacking in stamina.

As would be expected for horses with pretensions for next season's Classics, only the very top trainers associated with this kind of material succeed here. H. Cecil (five wins) leads the way from I. Balding and G. Harwood (two wins each).

The market clearly reflects the unpredictable nature of the Royal Lodge Stakes with six favourites and one 2nd favourite successful as opposed to two 3rd favourites and five outsiders (14–1, 15–2, 25–1, 12–1 and 10–1). This shows how the pendulum can swing and warns the backer against taking a short price on any horse.

It is not an easy race for selection and the backer must guard against being too enthusiastic at the form of any challenger in this race as a number with very sound credentials have suffered reverses. The improving 2-year-old aptly suited by this strenuous mile course with its testing final furlong finish, which will find out any but the gamest and toughest battlers, is the horse to look for in this quite difficult race.

88	HIGH ESTATE	2	0813	H. Cecil	4–6 Fav.	5
87	SANQUIRICO	2	0813	H. Cecil	8–11 Fav.	10
86	BENGAL FIRE	2	0811	C. Brittain	14–1	9
85	BONHOMMIE	2	0811	H. Cecil	2–1 Fav.	7
84	REACH	2	0811	P. Cole	15–2	8
83	GOLD AND IVORY	2	0811	I. Balding	25–1	5
82	DUNBEATH	2	0811	H. Cecil	5–2 Fav.	9
81	NORWICK	2	0811	G. Harwood	12–1	9
80	ROBELLINO	2	0811	I. Balding	4–1 2nd Fav.	8
79	HELLO GORGEOUS	2	0811	H. Cecil	5–4 Fav.	4
78	ELLA-MANA-MOU	2	0811	G. Harwood	10–1	8
77	SHIRLEY HEIGHTS	2	0811	J. Dunlop	10–1	8
76	GAIRLOCH	2	0811	H. R. Price	6–1	6
75	SIR WIMBOURNE	2	0811	M. V. O'Brien (Ire.)	4–6 Fav.	6

THE NEWMARKET AUTUMN MEETINGS

There are two major meetings held on the Rowley course at Newmarket each Autumn. The first is a four-day fixture lasting from Wednesday until Saturday and scheduled for the last days of September or the first week in October. The second meeting is a shorter three-day affair from Thursday to Saturday staged exactly two weeks later.

These meetings are usually known as the Cambridgeshire and Cesarewitch meetings respectively, in accord with the two popular and long-established handicaps which mark the final day of each fixture. They also contain a number of Group races, particularly the Group I events which may decide who is the champion 2-year-old of each sex, and the glittering showpiece Group I Champion Stakes, which usually attracts an international line-up of middle-distance horses.

Also programmed in these two fixtures are the normal range of handicaps and a number of interesting maiden races for 2-year-olds.

THE NEWMARKET AUTUMN MEETINGS – Two major meetings which between them provide, besides Group I and II races, the famous Autumn Double, the Cambridgeshire and Cesarewitch Handicaps.

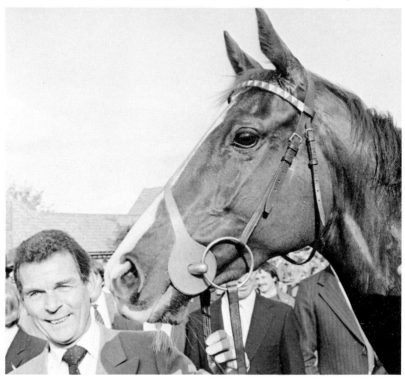

'The greatest of them all' PEBBLES, ears pricked, with trainer Clive Brittain, wonders what all the fuss is about after annihilating one of the classiest fields ever in Newmarket's 1985 Champion Stakes.

CHEVELEY PARK STAKES
Group I   6f   2 y.o.   fillies only
Level weights

The Cheveley Park Stakes is a Group I race for 2-year-old fillies over a distance of 6 furlongs and is staged on Wednesday, the first day of the four-day Cambridgeshire meeting on the Rowley course at Newmarket in the last week of September or first week in October. It is the premier race for 2 year-old fillies, and usually decides who is the best filly of her generation, with a reliable indication as to who will be the leading contenders for the fillies' Classics of the following season, and in particular the One Thousand Guineas.

Two winners, RAVINELLA (1987) and MA BICHE (1982), both French trained, went on to win the following season's English One Thousand Guineas. FOREST FLOWER (1986), the first-past-the-post winner (who was subsequently disqualified) won the Irish One Thousand Guineas of the following season; and PEBBLES (1983) (who became a champion middle distance horse later in her career) and ON THE HOUSE (1981), both only second in the Cheveley Park Stakes, won the English One Thousand Guineas the next season. Two other winners, DESIRABLE (1983) and MRS PENNY (1979), made the frame in the One Thousand Guineas, and three fillies, AL BAHATHRI (1984), FAVORIDGE (1982) and FAIR SALINIA (1977), whilst only placed here, maintained their form as 3-year-olds also to be placed in the first Classic of the next season.

These examples clearly indicate the quality of fillies competing, and the Cheveley Park Stakes is a race only won on the day by a very fast filly as exemplified by WOODSTREAM (1981), MARWELL (1980), DEVON DITTY (1978) and PATSY (1975). However, of these MARWELL was the only one really to progress as a 3-year-old, becoming champion sprinter. WOODSTREAM, although finishing second in the Irish One Thousand Guineas, in one of only two racecourse appearances as a 3-year-old, was really disappointing; as was PATSY, who was unplaced in her second-season campaign. Also DEVON DITTY, winner of seven races

THE CHEVELEY PARK STAKES – The only Group I race for 2 y.o. fillies. It is staged in early Autumn and decides who is the fastest juvenile. It is a reliable guide to the following season's 1,000 Guineas.

PATSY (Pat Eddery, black sleeves) just beats DAME FOOLISH (Alan Bond, No. 2) and the blinkered SOLAR (Geoff Baxter, No. 16) to win the 1975 Cheveley Park Stakes.

including the Cheveley Park Stakes as a 2-year-old, could win only once as a 3-year-old, although placed a few times in Group races for sprinters, and never achieved the greatness which her juvenile career promised.

Surprisingly perhaps for a race in which the main demand is pure speed, one winner, MRS PENNY (1979) was later capable of winning the French Oaks over 1¼ miles and the Prix Vermeille (Group I) over 1½ miles as a 3-year-old, as well as being placed in the King George VI and Queen Elizabeth Stakes and the English and Irish One Thousand Guineas. Similarly, FAIR SALINIA (1977) although only second in the Cheveley Park Stakes, won the English, Irish and Yorkshire Oaks (Group I) over 1½ miles during her 3-year-old campaign.

Having examined the subsequent careers of a number of winners, it is also essential to review the factors common to these winners before their success in this prestigous race.

The Cheveley Park Stakes regularly attracts good sized fields of 5 to 15 runners from the leading 2 year old fillies of England, Ireland and France. Fillies therefore come to this race with deservedly good reputations from their previous exploits which will now be thoroughly tested on Newmarket's straight open course. Previous top-class form is essential, for this is the championship race for 2-year-old fillies, and unless a filly has already proved herself in top-class company she is likely to find the sudden elevation in grade too severe.

Fillies have come to this race as two different types: those previously unbeaten with a reputation to maintain, and those who suffered a defeat or two along the way and so have a reputation to re-establish. The former category, which since 1980 has accounted for four winners, may be the trend for the future, as more recent winners have had slightly fewer prior races.

Recent winning form has been fairly crucial. Nine fillies won their previous race and only two winners, MA BICHE (1982) and MRS PENNY (1979), were out of the first two in their prior engagement (placed third and fourth respectively).

The race which holds greatest influence has been Moyglare Stud Stakes, (Group I) over 6 furlongs at the Curragh, 17–18 days previously, in which four winners ran. Three were Irish trained, PARK APPEAL (1984), WOODSTREAM (1981), who both won, and SOOKERA (1977) who was second at the Curragh. DESIRABLE (1983), the English-trained winner, also finished second at the Curragh. Negatively, two horses promoted to favourite after success at the Curragh, MINISTRELLA (1986) (who was awarded the race at a subsequent Jockey Club appeal but lost it on the day) and PETIPA (1975), were beaten in the Cheveley Park Stakes.

The other race of influence has been Flying Childer Stakes

(Group II) over 5 furlongs at Doncaster, 18 days earlier, which those two flying fillies MARWELL (1980) and DEVON DITTY (1978) both won.

As an immediate previous race the Lowther Stakes (Group II) over 6 furlongs at York, 41 days earlier, has been a disastrous influence. Of five fillies promoted to favourite in the Cheveley Park Stakes, four after winning at York, all were defeated. And only PATSY (1975) as winner of the two races holds out any hope for redemption.

The Mill Reef Stakes (Group II) over 6 furlongs at Newbury 11 days previously, also saw two winners emerge, although FOREST FLOWER's subsequent disqualification leaves this race very much in the balance.

Another factor to emerge is that nine winners ran within the previous 21 days, suggesting that recent form is essential. As autumn unfurls it may also herald a new form of line, so long absence from the racecourse must shed doubts on any filly's credentials.

As may be expected, this race has belonged exclusively to the top trainers, with B. Hills (two wins) the only English trainer with more than a single victory, although I. Balding (having trained the subsequently disqualified FOREST FLOWER) shares this distinction. The prize has been captured by three Irish trainers, J. Bolger, M. O'Brien and D. Weld sharing the successes, and twice by the French trainer Mme. C. Head.

The market has been a fairly reliable indicator in pinpointing the winner with four favourites, six 2nd favourites, one 3rd favourite and three outsiders (20–1, 12–1 and 9–1) successful. (These statistics count 2nd favourite FOREST FLOWER as the 1986 winner.) There is usually a fairly open market for this race with only one successful favourite odds-on – MARWELL (1980) – and all beaten favourites odds-against, except for DANCING TRIBE (1988).

The winner has fairly regularly come from among the two leaders in the market and a close inspection of these candidates is likely to reward the backer with success. Recent form within the last 21 days also plays an important role as older form may have been superseded. In this respect The Moyglare Stud Stakes, as the only recent Group I contest, demands the closest scrutiny should the winner or second emerge to challenge here.

88	PASS THE PEACE	2	0811	P. Cole	5–1 2nd Fav.	7
87	RAVINELLA	2	0811	Mme. C. Head (Fr.)	9–2 2nd Fav.	8
*86	MINISTRELLA	2	0811	C. Nelson	11–10 Fav.	5
85	EMBLA	2	0811	L. Cumani	20–1	14
84	PARK APPEAL	2	0811	J. Bolger (Ire.)	4–1 2nd Fav.	13
83	DESIRABLE	2	0811	B. Hills	12–1	12
82	MA BICHE	2	0811	Mme. C. Head (Fr.)	11–4 2nd Fav.	9
81	WOODSTREAM	2	0811	M. V. O'Brien (Ire.)	5–2 Jt Fav.	13
80	MARWELL	2	0811	M. Stoute	4–9 Fav.	8
79	MRS PENNY	2	0811	I. Balding	7–1	12
78	DEVON DITTY	2	0811	H. Thomson-Jones	11–8 Fav.	7
77	SOOKERA	2	0811	D. K. Weld (Ire.)	3–1 Fav.	10
76	DURTAL	2	0811	B. Hills	5–1 2nd Fav.	15
75	PATSY	2	0811	P. Walwyn	9–1	14

*86 FOREST FLOWER 2 0811 I. Balding 13–8 2nd Fav. FOREST FLOWER for betting purposes treated as the winner – disqualified after a successful legal appeal to the Jockey Club a few weeks after the race, but all bets on the day were settled with her as the winner.

MIDDLE PARK STAKES

Group I 6f 2 y.o. entire colts only
Level weights

The Middle Park Stakes is a Group I race for 2-year-old entire colts only, over a distance of 6 furlongs and is staged at Newmarket now on the Wednesday of the Cambridgeshire meeting in early Autumn. The Middle Park Stakes is the colt's equivalent of the 2-year-old fillies' race the Cheveley Park Stakes which is held earlier on the opening day. Correspondingly it attracts some of the fastest 2-year-old colts vying to be acclaimed as leading juveniles.

It is therefore of some influence as a guide to the following season's mile Classic although only one winner has gone on to complete the double with the Two Thousand Guineas – that being KNOWN FACT (1979) (who was promoted to being the winner on the disqualification of NUREYEV). However, NEBBIOLO (1976), although only second to TACHYPOUS in the Middle Park, reversed these placings the following season as a 3-year-old to capture the Two Thousand Guineas prize. MATTABOY (1980) winner of the Middle Park Stakes, was second in the Newmarket Mile Classic and YOUNG GENERATION (1978), who was only second in the Middle Park, finished third in the Guineas, as did BEL BOLIDE (1980) who was similarly placed in the two events.

While these successes highlight the positive influence of the Middle Park Stakes on the following season's mile Classic, this influence has not been constant and a number of the other winners have proved to be below the top grade. In fact winning the Middle Park Stakes has been for many of the winners the pinnacle of their career, and seven winners failed to win another race. Two recent winners CREAG-AN-SGOR (1983) and CAJUN (1981) both won the Greenham Stakes (Group III) at Newbury over 7 furlongs in their seasonal debut the following season, but after that failed to build on their success. However, RISK ME (1986), who finished second, also won the Greenham Stakes the next season before capturing two Group I prizes in France; and PERSIAN HEIGHTS (1987), who could only finish third here, won Royal Ascot's Group I St James Palace Stakes as a 3-year-old.

MIDDLE PARK STAKES – The 2 y.o. colts equivalent to the Cheveley Park Stakes. However its influence on the followings seasons 2,000 Guineas is negligible.

The 50–1 shock winner CREAG-ON-SGOR (noseband) with Steve Cauthen holds on to win 1983 Middle Park Stakes from SUPERLATIVE (Tony Ives, diamonds) and the disappointing 8–13 favourite VACARME next to the rails (Joe Mercer, white cap).

The Middle Park Stakes has attracted fields ranging in size from 5 to 13 runners, with an average of 8, and comprising some of the fastest English juveniles in training and sometimes challengers from Ireland as well. However, this is not a race which can be comfortably predicted. Results often veer towards the unexpected, and at times the incomprehensible, as horses without comparable form meet for the first time, or ones that renew rivalry reverse previous form. Therefore in this early autumn encounter winning a previous race is no criterion for success, and only seven winners did so.

The race of greatest influence has been Mill Reef Stakes (Group II) over 6 furlongs at Newbury, 14 days earlier, in which six winners competed, but only FORMIDABLE (1977) won it, and STALKER (1985), BASSENTHWAITE (1984) and KNOWN FACT (1979) reversed form with their Newbury conquerors. Negatively, three horses promoted to favourite in the Middle Park Stakes, two after winning the Mill Reef Stakes, were defeated on Newmarket's open heath. Doncaster's Flying Childer (Group II) over 5 furlongs,

199

21 days before, has seen two winners complete the double of these prestigious races: GALLIC LEAGUE (1987) and HITTITE GLORY (1975). The Gimcrack Stakes (Group III) over 6 furlongs at York, has also appeared in the itinerary of three winners and was the immediate prior race of beaten favourite BEL BOLIDE (1980) who won at York.

Only two horses, DIESIS (1982) (the most inexperienced winner, with only two prior races) and JUNIUS (1978), had not previously contested a Group race and yet successfully made the huge transition to gain a Group I prize at the first time of asking. Conversely, five beaten favourites, although also winners of their previous race, but making their debut in a Pattern race, failed to make the change in grade, confirming that experience of racing in good-class company is essential to success here.

The market has not been a very reliable guide to pinpointing the winner, with four favourites and one 2nd favourite successful and two 3rd favourites and seven outsiders (33–1, 50–1, 20–1, 8–1, 7–1, 7–1 and 9–2). So the backer must be wary of the two market leaders.

The Middle Park Stakes, as befits a race of top-grade status, is invariably won by the very top trainers. H. Cecil, J. Tree and P. Walwyn have two victories each, and M. V. O'Brien waves a solitary flag for an Irish-trained winner. However, a win each for R. Williams and C. Nelson, in the younger generation of trainers, holds out hope that this is still a race an aspiring handler can win, to break into the big league.

The Middle Park Stakes, as the first English Group I race for 2-year-old colts, is an interesting race to consider for selection especially when its implications for the following season are taken into account. However, it is a race to be approached with caution as there have been surprises fairly regularly. Recent improving form is the likely keynote as it is to most autumn racecourse encounters, where earlier good performances in the summer on sun-baked surfaces may not be repeated on the more testing conditions often encountered now. The surprise success of CREAG-AN-SGOR (1983), CAJUN (1981), KNOWN FACT (1979) and to a lesser extent BASSENTHWAITE (1984), who all defeated rivals that previously had beaten them, means that the backer cannot discount horses just because they are held on prior form, especially if the margins were small. No horse has retained an unbeaten record in winning the Middle Park Stakes, so the backer prepared to make judicious allowance for an experienced competitor and to avoid being swept along by general enthusiasm for the most fancied horses, could be rewarded with a good priced winner. However, do not take out an ante-post voucher on the winner in the following season's classic, as results warn strictly against it!

88	MON TRESOR	2	0900	R. Boss	8–1	6
87	GALLIC LEAGUE	2	0900	B. Hills	6–4 Fav.	5
86	MISTER MAJESTIC	2	0900	R. Williams	33–1	7
85	STALKER	2	0900	P. Walwyn	9–2 2nd Fav.	6
84	BASSENTHWAITE	2	0900	J. Tree	7–2	8
83	CREAG-AN-SGOR	2	0900	C. Nelson	50–1	9
82	DIESIS	2	0900	H. Cecil	10–11 Fav.	5
81	CAJUN	2	0900	H. Cecil	20–1	13
80	MATTABOY	2	0900	R. Armstrong	7–1	9
79	KNOWN FACT	2	0900	J. Tree	10–1	7
78	JUNIUS	2	0900	M. V. O'Brien (Ire.)	7–1	10
77	FORMIDABLE	2	0900	P. Walwyn	15–8 Fav.	7
76	TACHYPOUS	2	0900	B. Hobbs	5–1 Jt Fav.	11
75	HITTITE GLORY	2	0900	A. Breasley	9–2	8

SUN CHARIOT STAKES

Group II   1¼m   3.y.o and upwards   fillies only
Level weights, WFA with a penalty for a winner of a Group I or
II race since a 2 y.o.

The Sun Chariot Stakes is a Group II race for 3-year-olds and older fillies only, over a distance of 1¼ miles, and is staged on the Saturday of the Newmarket Cambridgeshire meeting in early autumn. It is the last important Group race of the season confined to fillies and often gives the opportunity to the slower developing 3-year-old filly. The entry conditions also encourage the unpenalised filly to claim a major Group race prize for the first time. The Sun Chariot Stakes therefore has an aura of unpredictability as the winning filly will often surpass all her previous performances and sweep to success here, leaving a number of proven good fillies trailing. When it is noted how top-class fillies such as VIELLE (1980), CISTUS (1978), FREEZE THE SECRET (1977) and ROUSALLKA (1975) were all promoted to favourite and beaten, and that older fillies STANERRA (1982), SAUCEBOAT (1976) and MILS BOMB (1975) also tasted defeat, it becomes obvious that selection in this race must be approached with caution. However, on the positive side the race has been won by some very good fillies, the dual winner FREE GUEST (1985 and 1984) and particularly INDIAN SKIMMER (1988), CORMORANT WOOD (1983), TIME CHARTER (1982) and SWISS MAID (1978), who epitomised the progress the improving filly can make in the autumn when two weeks later they won the final big flat race of the season (for older horses), the Champion Stakes (Group I) over the same course and distance.

The Sun Chariot Stakes attracts compact sized fields of 5 to 11 runners, with an average of 8, comprising fillies who will have already run in some of the year's most prestigious races, and also those racing in less esteemed company who now, as the season draws to a close, seek to make a successful transition to the higher echelon. Therefore the winners of the Sun Chariot are balanced between those slightly eased in class and those who have become upwardly mobile. Not surprisingly, a divergence emerges as to their previous race engagements.

Winners have also had a dissimilar number of races during the season, from the minimum of three contested by FREE GUEST (1984) to the maximum of ten by DUBOFF (1975); but with only four winners having seven or more previous races, a light programme is much more common. Only the French-trained winner RANIMER (1976) had failed to win at least one race previously during the season, whilst DUBOFF had won eight races. INFAMY (1987) and HOME ON THE RANGE (1981) had won four; FREE GUEST (1984) and SWISS MAID (1978) had won three.

The only race with more than a fleeting influence has been the Virginia Stakes (Listed race) over 1 mile 2 furlongs at Newcastle, 33–40 days earlier. Three winners, FREE GUEST (1984), CORMORANT WOOD (1983) and SWISS MAID (1978) all won there. SINGLETTA (1986) was promoted to favourite in the Sun Chariot after winning at Newcastle, but was beaten.

Only six winners won their previous race and five of these were non-group races, yet all the other winners were not necessarily competing in a Group race, so some made considerable improvement to gain this Group II prize. However, only three winners had never run in a Group race before, so it is necessary to examine all a filly's prior races to establish credentials. Only DUSTY DOLLAR (1986) had never previously run over this 1 mile 2 furlong distance, which can be very daunting on Newmarket's straight Rowley course, but her victory was gained when the race was transferred for one season to the July course, where the track for this distance is not an unrelenting straight one.

The Sun Chariot Stakes being won usually by only the most choicely bred filly, is also won only by the very top trainers and L. Cumani (three wins) leads the way from that other expert handler of fillies B. Hills, with a French- and an Irish-trained winner also in the list.

Although the race was opened to older fillies in 1974, 3-year-olds have always been numerically far superior, and have held sway except for INDIAN SKIMMER and FREE GUEST's second victory.

The market reflects the openness of the race where five favourites, three 2nd favourites, five 3rd favourites and one outsider have been successful. This shows that although there have been no shocks, actually pinpointing the winners from market moves has not been easy.

The backer will need to be very astute to interpret successfully the nuances of form. The arrival of autumn and this unique 10 furlong straight track are likely to be telling factors, and earlier season form can be superseded by the improving filly. Also, those who had run well earlier only to disappoint, perhaps over a different distance, can return to fulfil their promise now. Whether a previous contender or only now a challenger, it is the fresher fillies (seven winners had not run for at least 30 days) with a spark of improvement in them and who will relish a struggle on this large open course who may hold the key for the discerning backer.

88	INDIAN SKIMMER	4	0906	H. Cecil	40–85 Fav.	6
87	INFAMY	3	0807	L. Cumani	5–1 2nd Fav.	6
86	DUSTY DOLLAR	3	0807	W. Hern	7–2	7
85	FREE GUEST	4	0904	L. Cumani	13–8 Fav.	5
84	FREE GUEST	3	0804	L. Cumani	2–1 Fav.	8
83	CORMORANT WOOD	3	0805	B. Hills	7–2 2nd Fav.	9
82	TIME CHARTER	3	0900	H. Candy	6–1	10
81	HOME ON THE RANGE	3	0800	H. Cecil	2–1 Fav.	10
80	SNOW	3	0807	K. Prendergast (Ire.)	12–1	7
79	TOPSY	3	0807	H. Wragg	7–2 Fav.	8
78	SWISS MAID	3	0807	P. Kellaway	5–1 2nd Fav.	9
77	TRIPLE FIRST	3	0900	M. Stoute	7–1	7
76	RANIMER	3	0807	P. Head (Fr.)	9–1	10
75	DUBOFF	3	0807	B. Hills	6–1	11

CAMBRIDGESHIRE HANDICAP
0–115 Handicap   1m 1f   3 y.o. and upwards

The Cambridgeshire Handicap is for 3-year olds and upwards rated 0–115 in the handicap over a distance of 1 mile 1 furlong, and is staged at Newmarket on Saturday, the fourth and final day of the meeting. The Cambridgeshire is one of the oldest handicaps still being contested and was first run in 1839, like its marathon counterpart, The Cesarewitch, which follows two weeks later. These two races make up the popular betting duo of the Autumn Double where ante-post bets are coupled on the two events.

The Cambridgeshire is always a very competitive handicap attracting extremely large fields of 18 to 36 runners, and on average 31 to 32. It is probably the most difficult middle-distance handicap in the calendar to win, and is usually run at breakneck pace throughout, with the field split into two groups, racing against the rails on each side of the course. It takes a very tough and brave horse to win here in a handicap of weights that is usually well constructed. We must pay some homage to the accuracy of the official handicappers responsible for framing this handicap where over the seasons a three-quarter length has been the widest margin in eleven of the contests and with a neck being the widest winning margin separating the winner from the second on nine occasions.

The Cambridgeshire is won by a useful handicapper rather than a horse of any outstanding merit and represents the pinnacle of a career rather than a stepping stone to greater glories. 3-year-olds (six wins) and 4-year-olds (six wins) are the dominant age groups, broken only by that gallant dual winner BARONET (1980 and 1978) who won the race first as a 6-year-old and then as an 8-year-old.

Good horses such as the mighty TELEPROMPTER (1983), who later was to achieve international acclaim, was promoted to favourite as a 3-year-old in the Cambridgeshire yet was beaten. So were good older horses such as COMMODORE BLAKE (1982), Royal Hunt Cup winner TENDER HEART (1980) and PIPE DREAMER (1979), plus TOWN AND COUNTRY (1978) and JUMPING

THE CAMBRIDGESHIRE – A most competitive 1 mile 1 furlong handicap on Newmarket's straight Rowley course that marks the first leg of the famous Autumn double – combined bets on the Cambridgeshire and Cesarewitch.

In a typical blanket finish BARONET (Brian Rouse) holds on by the narrowest margin from DROMEFS (John Lowe, black cap) and PULSE RATE (Mark Birch, No. 7) to win the 1980 Cambridgeshire and record the first of his two victories

HILL (1976), all failing to defy weight burdens of 9 st 5 lb, 9 st, 9 st 12 lb, 10 st and 9 st 11 lb respectively. Over this unrelenting straight 9 furlong course, there is nowhere to hide and even for the better-class horse with that vital 'kick' at the business end of the race, the weight burden can find them tapped for pace inside the final furlong.

The 9 st weight mark has been quite a telling factor, with only five winners breaking the barrier. Remarkably two were 3-year-olds (both trained by Luca Cumani) – DALLAS (1986) and the ill-fated CENTURY CITY (1982), who both carried 9 st 6 lb. Dual winner BARONET carried 9 st for its first victory and 9 st 3 lb two years later. TREMBLANT (1985) at 9 st 8 lb carried the highest weight for over twenty years. A year later however, when promoted to favourite and carrying 2 lb more, TREMBLANT was defeated. Similarly, only three winners, SIN TIMON (1977), INTERMISSION (1976) and LOTTOGIFT (1975), have withstood a 7 lb winners' penalty and five beaten favourites have all been carrying one.

Whilst 9 st has proved a prohibitive mark at the higher level, lightly weighted horses carrying below 8 st have only achieved one success: SAGAMORE (1983), 7 st 8 lb. It has been the nicely handicapped horses covered in a 7 lb weight band between 8 st 1 lb and 8 st 8 lb which have fared best, with eight winners.

The paths horses have taken before winning the Cambridgeshire have been as varied as the horses themselves, and only two previous races have had more than a fleeting influence; the Swinley Forest Handicap over 1 mile at Ascot 9 days earlier, in which BARONET ran finishing first and third before gaining both his victories. Negatively two horses promoted to favourite, FEAR NAUGHT (1979), who won at Ascot, and TENDER HEART (1980) who finished second, were both beaten in the Cambridgeshire. The Courage Handicap over 1 mile 2 furlongs at Newbury 14 days earlier, which both QUINLAN TERRY (1988) and CENTURY CITY (1982) finished second before reversing form in the Cambridgeshire with their conquerors who now carried a 5 lb penalty.

The winners have split into two categories: those with six or less prior races during the season (six winners, five of them 3-year-olds); and those with seven or more previous races (seven of which were 4-year-olds or older horses). Only LEYSH (1984) who had twelve prior races as a 3-year-old, had its abilities fully exposed to the handicapper, while the other more lightly raced 3-year-old winners may have left something in the locker which the handicapper could only guess at.

Whether they have had light or heavy prior race programmes, it is interesting to find that six winners began their current campaign in the opening weeks of the season at Doncaster and therefore when winning the Cambridgeshire early in the autumn, had withstood the rigours of a long season's campaign. Toughness is definitely a quality necessary to win the first leg of the Autumn Double, with the race regularly decided in a very tight, closely fought finish. To win here a horse needs to take its racing well and still come back for more, and so it is not surprising that colts and geldings have dominated, winning all but one contest. INTERMISSION (1976) holds the lone banner for the fairer sex.

Although every winner except BRAUGHING (1981) had won at least one prior race during the season (TREMBLANT (1985) and CENTURY CITY (1982), with three wins apiece, had won most), winning the immediate prior race has not been essential for success, and only five winners have managed to do so. When it is noticed that nine beaten favourites had these winning credentials, they can be reckoned to be almost a liability.

The draw also has to be taken into account and whilst the higher numbers (or top half), with eight wins, holds the call over the lower numbers, the more important factor may be to be drawn near other leading contenders who will be strongly challenging throughout to give a horse a near rival to race against on Newmarket's wide-open track. The unique distance of the race demands a horse that is very adaptable and the majority of winners have shown some versatility in this area by being tried at a range of middle distances in their previous races.

The Cambridgeshire is not a race confined to the big stables and most famous trainers, although it takes a rare skill to win such a competitive handicap. L. Cumani and C. Benstead (responsible for dual winner BARONET) are the only handlers with more than one victory in a race that leaves the door open for new faces.

The market has been of no influence in pinpointing the winner with every favourite, 2nd favourite beaten and just one 3rd favourite successful, and the price of the thirteen winning outsiders ranges from 10–1 to 50–1.

The Cambridgeshire is most certainly a difficult race for selection and the average backer will need a fair slice of luck to be successful. However, there are certain pointers outlined here that can narrow the selection down from a mere pin-pricking exercise, and the successful backer will most certainly be rewarded with a good-priced winner.

88	QUINLAN TERRY	3	0805	Sir Mark Prescott	11–1	29
87	BALTHUS	4	0801	J. Glover	50–1	31
86	DALLAS	3	0906	L. Cumani	10–1	31
85	TREMBLANT	4	0908	R. Smyth	16–1	31
84	LEYSH	3	0807	S. Norton	33–1	34
83	SAGAMORE	4	0708	F. Durr	35–1	30
82	CENTURY CITY	3	0906	L. Cumani	20–1	29
81	BRAUGHING	4	0804	C. Brittain	50–1	28
80	BARONET	8	0903	C. Benstead	22–1	19
79	SMARTSET	4	0808	R. Houghton	33–1	24
78	BARONET	6	0900	C. Benstead	12–1	18
77	SIN TIMON	3	0803	J. Hindley	18–1	27
76	INTERMISSION	3	0806	M. Stoute	14–1	29
75	LOTTOGIFT	4	0802	D. Hanley	33–1	36

RICARD CHALLENGE STAKES

Group II   7f   3 y.o. and upwards   colts, fillies and geldings
Level weights, sex allowance, WFA with a penalty for a winner of
Group I or II race since a 2 y.o.

The Ricard Challenge Stakes is a Group II race for 3-year-olds
and upwards over 7 furlongs on the Dewhurst Stakes course (the
last 7 furlongs of the Rowley mile) at Newmarket. It is staged on
the Thursday or first day of the three-day Cesarewitch meeting in
mid-October. In a history dating back to 1878 when it was known
as 'The First Great Challenge Stakes' it was run over a distance
of 6 furlongs, until altered to its present length in 1977. Other
changes have occurred more recently.

Since 1985 it is restricted to 3-year-olds and older horses
whereas before it was an all-age event, and in 1987 it was raised to
Group II status, with the introduction of penalties for top Group
race winners. This final alteration may have a telling affect on the
character of the race. Previously it had been won by some proven
Group race winners that included real top-class performers, such
as MOORESTYLE (dual winner 1981 and 1980) and KRIS (1979),
plus some lesser lights SALIERI (1983), NOALCOHOLIC (1982)
and veteran BOLDBOY (1977), who all exploited their advantage
of weight to the maximum. Penalties may change this.

The Ricard Challenge Stakes is the only Group II race for
3-year-olds and older horses at this in-between distance of 7
furlongs, but besides attracting specialists at this trip it brings
together 6 furlong horses and milers who seek the challenge of this
compromise distance. Varying sized fields of 6 to 12 runners, have
taken part since its change in distance to 7 furlongs, the average
being 8 runners.

It has hitherto proved a happy hunting ground for previous
Group race winners running unpenalised (as the conditions
allowed until 1987) giving them a golden opportunity to wind up
the season on a winning note. Seven winners had already won a
Group race, six during their current season with two of these,
MOORESTYLE (1980) and KRIS (1979), including a Group I prize
in their haul. Entrants such as these made the selection process

210

THE RICARD CHALLENGE STAKES – The only Group II 7 furlong race for older horses and invariably won by a very good horse.

Probably the best winner, KRIS (Joe Mercer) rounds off a splendid season as champion miler to win the 1975 Challenge Stakes from the grey ABSALOM (Lester Piggott) and the blinkered PETTY PURSE (John Reid).

quite uncomplicated. Seven favourites and two 2nd favourites won, their dominance broken by only two surprise winners. (Statistics since the 1977 change to 7 furlongs.)

Winning form has been a common feature for winning the Challenge Stakes. Seven horses won their previous race, five of these being a Group race prize. Only shock winner LUCKY RING (1986) (the winner on the July Course, to where the race was transferred for one season), was not placed first or second in its previous race, nor had it won a previous race during the season. However, KRIS (1979) won six prior races during the season before successfully rounding off his autumn campaign here. MOORESTYLE (1980) won five races and BROCADE (1984), SPENCE BAY (1978) and BOLDBOY (1977) had already won three times.

Three races have had a particular influence on the outcome of the Challenge Stakes. Firstly, the Select Stakes (Group III) (formerly a Listed race) over 7 furlongs at Goodwood 17 days earlier. ASTEROID FIELD (1987) and EFISIO (1985) both won it and LUCKY RING (1986) finished fourth. Secondly, the Diadem Stakes (Group III) over 6 furlongs, at Ascot, 21 days earlier, which both SALIERI (1983) and MOORESTYLE (1981) won. Finally, the Queen Elizabeth II Stakes (now Group I but then Group II) over 1 mile at Ascot, 19 days earlier, which saw NOALCOHOLIC (1982) finish second and KRIS (1979) win to complete the double. In negative contrast, STRADAVINSKY (1978) was unsuccessfully promoted to favourite after finishing second at Ascot.

The top stables have held a strong grip on this autumn prize. H. Cecil, W. Hern and R. Armstrong (responsible for dual winner MOORESTYLE), with two wins each, head the other.

Although a horse must fully see out the 7 furlongs distance on Newmarket's unremitting track, sprinting speed is an important aspect to consider, as four winners had already won during their current season over 6 furlongs or less. Whether such past observations will hold sway in the light of the changes in the character of the race, only time will tell. However, with the elevation to Group II status the standard of entrants should be maintained or improve, and this should be reflected by the reliability of performance reflected in past results, when the Ricard Challenge Stakes could become a favourite backer's banker and a successful start to the Cesarewitch meeting.

88						
87	ASTEROID FIELD	4	0811	B. Hills	4–1 2nd Fav.	8
86	LUCKY RING	4	0900	W. Hern	20–1	12
85	EFISIO	3	0902	J. Dunlop	9–4 2nd Fav.	8
84	BROCADE	3	0813	G. Harwood	5–4 Fav.	7
83	SALIERI	3	0902	H. Cecil	13–8 Fav.	10
82	NOALCOHOLIC	5	0906	G. Pritchard-Gordon	5–2 Fav.	8
81	MOORESTYLE	4	0906	R. Armstrong	8–15 Fav.	7
80	MOORESTYLE	3	0902	R. Armstrong	2–5 Fav.	6
79	KRIS	3	0902	H. Cecil	4–9 Fav.	7
78	SPENCE BAY	3	0902	S. McGrath (Ire.)	8–1	12
77	BOLDBOY	7	0906	W. Hern	11–8 Fav.	8
*76	STAR BIRD	4	0903	P. Lallié (Fr.)	20–1	8}
*75	BE TUNEFUL	3	0813	J. Hindley	7–2 2nd Fav.	7

*The Challenge Stakes reviewed only since its change of distance to 7 furlongs 1977–88.

DEWHURST STAKES

Group I 7f 2 y.o. only entire colts and fillies
Level weights, sex allowance

The Dewhurst Stakes is a Group I race, for 2-year-old entire colts and fillies only, over a distance of 7 furlongs, and is staged at Newmarket on Friday, the second day of the three-day Cesarewitch meeting in the middle of October. It is the premier race for 2-year-olds and usually ensures that the winner will be rated the best British 2-year-old of its generation and be placed at the head of the European Free Handicap. There is also the likelihood of being promoted as winter favourite for the following spring's Two Thousand Guineas.

With such great expectations placed on the winner's head it is sad to recall that many have recently failed to fulfil their promise. HUNTINGDALE (1985), although third and fourth in the English and Irish Two Thousand Guineas of the following season, never won a race as a 3-year-old. KALA DANCER (1984), after a disappointing reappearance in the next season's Two Thousand Guineas, was shipped off to America in an attempt to salvage its reputation. DIESIS (1982) never won as a 3-year-old and was a big disappointment, although now a very successful stallion at stud. WIND AND WUTHERING (1981), although only narrowly defeated by ZINO in the Two Thousand Guineas, still failed to win as a 3-year-old. In fact all the three winners in 1978, 1979 and 1980 failed to win another race, and in the case of the two Vincent O'Brien trained and Robert Sangster owned winners STORM BIRD (1980) and MONTEVERDI (1979), considerable public controversy surrounded their demise. TRY MY BEST (1977), made favourite for the Two Thousand Guineas after winning a Group III prize, also tailed off. We have really to return to the mid-1970s to see the Dewhurst herald the rise of a new star with THE MINSTREL (1976), WOLLOW (1975) and GRUNDY (1974). However, EL GRAN SENOR (1983) with magnificent performances as a 3-year-old, winning the Two Thousand Guineas and with the narrowest of defeats in the English Derby, has helped to restore the reputation of the Dewhurst Stakes as the hallmark of future

213

THE DEWHURST STAKES – The most important 2 y.o. race of the season usually deciding who will be acclaimed the leading juvenile.

MONTEVERDI (Lester Piggott) in Robert Sangster's silks wins the 1979 Dewhurst Stakes from TYRNAVOS (Kipper Lynch, white spots) and ROMEO ROMANI (Brian Taylor, hoops). However MONTEVERDI's performances as a 3 y.o. only cast further doubts on the Dewhurst Stakes' dented reputation.

champions. More recently AJDAL (1986), although not succeeding in the Classics, found his forte to be over shorter distances and was popularly acclaimed champion sprinter as a 3-year-old. The winners of the Dewhurst Stakes therefore appear in very mixed lights, some becoming champions as 3-year-olds whilst others are flops.

However, on the afternoon of the race the air is filled with hopes and excitement as compact fields of 4 to 11 runners (average 8) come under starter's orders. There is usually an international flavour to the race, with a few runners from Ireland and sometimes France. All the aspirants are likely to have form credentials of the highest standard. HUNTINGDALE (1985) was the only maiden to win the race and broke the tradition, or perhaps we should say mandatory requirement, of every horse having won their previous race. Nine winners successfully defended unbeaten records, and whilst in some races this might seem a special feature it is quite common among challengers for the Dewhurst Stakes, for if they have had their armour already dented in defeat they are hardly likely to turn out to be future champions.

However, there is no prescribed path, or eliminating races, before horses challenge for this major prize; they are merely entered in accordance with the judgement of their trainers. Only M. V. O'Brien's name dominates the winners' trainers' role and therefore it is only races chosen for his successful candidates which have had more than a fleeting influence on the outcome of the Dewhurst Stakes. The National Stakes (Group II) over 7 furlongs at the Curragh, 49 days earlier, served as a prior race engagement for three winners and was the immediate previous race for EL GRAN SENOR (1983). Leopardstown Larkspur Stakes (Group III) over 7 furlongs, 20–27 days earlier, served as the immediate prior race of his three other winners STORM BIRD (1980), TRY MY BEST (1977) and THE MINSTREL (1976). The only English race of consequence has been the Champagne Stakes (Group II) over 7 furlongs at Doncaster, 35–37 days earlier, which PRINCE OF DANCE (1988) and WOLLOW (1975) won and the year before him GRUNDY (1974). However, on the negative side three horses, SURE BLADE (1985), GORYTUS (1982) and R.B. CHESNE (1978), all promoted to favourite in the Dewhurst Stakes after their success at Doncaster, were beaten.

It is common for horses to have had a fairly light season, being brought along most carefully for this race, and so it is not surprising that only two winners had more than three prior races. These were WIND AND WUTHERING (1981) who had seven (winning three), and STORM BIRD (1980) who had four and was unbeaten in all. Only five recent winners SCENIC (1988), AJDAL (1986), HUNTING-DALE (1985) and KALA DANCER (1984), and TROMOS (1978), had not previously contested a Group race (probably because the latter four had not seen a racecourse before September) yet still made a successful transition to the highest grade.

There are usually no strict or collateral formlines between horses from which to compare abilities, and assessment is likely to be largely based on reputation and association. However, on this often unsatisfactory basis the market has usually got it right with eight favourites successful (three of which were odds-on), and one 2nd favourite, one 3rd favourite and four outsiders.

So in considering the Dewhurst Stakes winner, recent form has been a regular feature apart from 1988 dead-heaters PRINCE OF DANCE and SCENIC, WOLLOW (1975) and the two Irish-trained runners EL GRAN SENOR (1983) and MONTEVERDI (1979) with an absence of over 30 days from their previous race. Although 2-year-old form can be subject to sweeping changes as a new formline emerges at this very highest level they will have to be most dramatic if they are to bring about reversals. Ground conditions (often responsible for shock results), are usually constant; only once has the going been worse than Good, on Newmarket's open, well-drained track. The horses are invariably proven at the distance. Eleven winners had won over 7 furlongs or further so the commonest cause for reversals in form (a change in the going or the distance) have been avoided.

Whereas winners of the Dewhurst Stakes have often been disappointing in their later careers, some beaten horses have later thrived. LAW SOCIETY (1984) was to finish second the following season in the English Derby, and subsequently won the Irish Derby. RAINBOW QUEST (1983), beaten here as a 2-year-old, won the Arc de Triomphe as a 4-year-old. TO-AGORI-MOU (1986) won the English Two Thousand Guineas. HENBIT (1979) won the following season's English Derby, and TYRNAVOS (1979) won the Irish Derby. All these give hope to beaten horses over longer distances in the future.

The Dewhurst Stakes, as would be expected for a race of its eminence, can safely be left to the top trainers. Ireland's M. V. O'Brien (five wins) leads the way from H. Cecil (two wins) and only the stables with Classic potential colts will succeed here at the very top level of the racing scale.

From the backer's viewpoint until the surprise victories of HUNTINGDALE (1985) and KALA DANCER (1984) the Dewhurst was a race that could be reliably left to the market leader. It was the race where many professional flat-racing backers made their final plunge for the season, investing heavily to provide themselves with their winter income. Setbacks, especially the controversial defeat of GORYTUS (1982) when 1–2 favourite, where many got their fingers badly burned, and before that SIMPLY GREAT (1980), may have caused a few to review their betting habits.

However, whilst the backer needs to be aware of any new trends that may be occurring, the overall record of the market leader in the Dewhurst Stakes suggests that this is the area to focus on. Any runners from the master of Ballydoyle, Vincent O'Brien, also always demands the utmost respect in this race.

88	{ PRINCE OF DANCE*	2	0900	N. Graham	6–4 Fav.	6
	{ SCENIC*	2	0900	B. Hills	33–1	
87				ABANDONED		
86	AJDAL	2	0900	M. Stoute	4–9 Fav.	5
85	HUNTINGDALE	2	0900	J. Hindley	12–1	8
84	KALA DANCER	2	0900	B. Hanbury	20–1	11
83	EL GRAN SENOR	2	0900	M. V. O'Brien (Ire.)	7–4 Fav.	10
82	DIESIS	2	0900	H. Cecil	2–1 2nd Fav.	4
81	WIND AND WUTHERING	2	0900	H. Candy	11–1	9
80	STORM BIRD	2	0900	M. V. O'Brien (Ire.)	4–5 Fav.	5
79	MONTEVERDI	2	0900	M. V. O'Brien (Ire.)	15–8 Fav.	6
78	TROMOS	2	0900	B. Hobbs	11–4	6
77	TRY MY BEST	2	0900	M. V. O'Brien (Ire.)	4–6 Fav.	7
76	THE MINSTREL	2	0900	M. V. O'Brien (Ire.)	6–5 Fav.	11
75	WOLLOW	2	0900	H. Cecil	6–4 Fav.	7

*Dead Heat

THE CHAMPION STAKES
Group I   1m 2f   3 y.o. and upwards   colts, geldings and fillies
Level weights, sex allowance, WFA

The Champion Stakes is a Group I race for 3-year-olds and older horses over a distance of 1 mile 2 furlongs on the straight Rowley course at Newmarket on Saturday, the final day of the Cesarewitch meeting in mid-October. It therefore shares the stage with the Cesarewitch as the centrefold races of the day. It is the final Group I race of the season for the older generations of horses and will be their last chance during the British season to claim a major prize.

The Champion Stakes therefore attracts competitive sized fields of 5 to 19 runners, with an average of 13, which usually has a strong international flavour with challenges from France and Ireland.

Many of the horses taking part will have contested other top British and European Group races. For any horse successful in these events the Champion Stakes will be their crowning glory, while for those that have not yet quite gained the major honours it could be their saving grace. The Champion Stakes therefore, for these horses, may well be just their final race of the season and one that now fits comfortably into their itinerary rather than as part of any long-term strategy.

However, for other competitors the Champion Stakes will always have been their long-term objective, with their programme of races completely focused towards it. This approach would seem likely to have had the greater success, as nine winners had five or less previous races during the season and thus arrived on the day cherry ripe and fresh for battle. The brilliant yet ultra-tough filly TRIPTYCH (1987 and 1986) (and the only dual winner since the great BRIGADIER GERRARD) (1971 and 1972), had seven and six previous races. SWISS MAID (1978), who was also very durable and made fantastic improvement in the late Summer and Autumn, had ten prior races, whilst PALACE MUSIC (1984) and CAIRN ROUGE (1980) had six races apiece, but these are the only winners to have had more than a fistful of previous races. Less races rather than

THE CHAMPION STAKES – The last Group I race for the older generations of horses and a race that fillies have dominated recently.

Two fillies battle it out. ROSE BOWL (Willie Carson, right) runs on well to beat the wonderful mare ALLEZ FRANCE (sheepskin noseband, Yves St. Martin) in the 1975 Champion Stakes.

more would seem the order of the day to win the Champion Stakes, and certainly not too many hard-fought ones.

The demise of really top-class horses in this race, who came to it with the highest form credentials, MTOTO (1987), PARK EXPRESS (1986), SLIP ANCHOR (1985), TOLOMEO (1983), KALAGLOW (1982), TO-AGORI-MOU (1981), MASTER WILLIE (1980), HAWAIIAN SOUND (1978), WOLLOW (1976) and ALLEZ FRANCE (1975) (the list seems endless) shows how this race can have been one too many. Horses that have already peaked during the season may find it difficult to get back to the height of fitness. Certainly they will need to be in this fiercely fought race. As well as being fresh, a horse certainly must be fighting fit, as demonstrated by nine winners who ran within the previous 21 days.

These indications show the Champion Stakes to be suited to the still-improving horse rather than one which has already reached the heights and now has to do it all over again. Therefore it favours the still-improving filly who at this time of the season will be at her peak and gain maximum advantage from her few pounds' sex allowance. This viewpoint is supported by the nine fillies or mares to have won, INDIAN SKIMMER (1988), TRIPTYCH (1987 and 1986), PEBBLES (1985), CORMORANT WOOD (1983), TIME CHARTER (1982), CAIRN ROUGE (1980), SWISS MAID (1978), FLYING WATER (1977) and ROSE BOWL (1975). These records fall in line with some other important contests in the autumn which have also been captured by the fairer sex.

With improving form rather than proven form the main criterion, winning the previous race has not been a major factor in winning here. Seven horses did fulfil that obligation, six of these in a Group II or Group III race and only PEBBLES (1985) in a Group I race. The races that have held greatest influence have been the Prix de L'Arc de Triomphe (Group I), over 1½ miles at Longchamp, 13 days previously, in which TRIPTYCH (1987 and 1986) finished third on both occasions before winning the Champion Stakes, and in which NORTHERN BABY (1979) was unplaced. ALLEZ FRANCE (1979) was also unplaced but nevertheless promoted to favourite in the Champion Stakes and beaten. Newmarket's own Sun Chariot Stakes (Group II) over 1¼ miles, 14 days earlier, has also proved to be of particular influence. Four fillies, INDIAN SKIMMER (1988), CORMORANT WOOD (1983), TIME CHARTER (1982) and SWISS MAID (1978), completed the double, but FREE GUEST (1984), promoted to favourite after winning the Sun Chariot, failed in this main event. Ascot's Queen Elizabeth Stakes (Group I, then Group II), over 1 mile, 21 days earlier, has seen ROSE BOWL complete the double, while TO-AGORI-MOU (1981), promoted to favourite after winning at Ascot, failed in this, his first and final attempt over 10 furlongs.

The surprising feature of the Champion Stakes is its course and distance – a unique straight 10 furlongs on Newmarket's wide-open heathland. It is a track where there is no place to hide, especially for horses comfortably used to running around bends on other courses. And for a miler attempting the extra 2 furlongs it is a distance most likely to find them out. Although the pace will be hot from the outset, front runners are unlikely to succeed, and it is the horse with a devastating turn of foot as they run down into the dip before the uphill climb in the final furlong who holds the key. It is not surprising therefore to see former course, and distance, winners figure prominently on the winners' role. Eight winners, INDIAN SKIMMER, TRIPTYCH, PEBBLES, CORMORANT WOOD, TIME CHARTER, SWISS MAID, FLYING WATER and ROSE BOWL, had all previously shown their liking for Newmarket's open track. In contrast, two French-trained horses, PALACE MUSIC and VAYRAAN, making their first appearance on English soil, adapted instantly to win here at the first time of asking. In respect of the distance ROSE BOWL was the only winner untried and unproven over 1¼ miles.

The international flavour of runners has been faithfully re-flected on the winners' role. Seven races have been won by French- or Irish-trained horses. Patrick Biancone (Fr.) leads the French challenge with three winners, heading those other notable internationally known handlers F. Boutin, F. Mathet and A. Penna.

The market has been a most unhelpful guide to pinpointing the winner. Only two favourite and two 2nd favourites have been successful, and four 3rd favourites and six outsiders have dominated the race, though the price of the outsiders, at fairly uncommon multiples (9–1, 9–1, 9–1, 18–1, 18–1 and 22–1) perhaps shows that they were not quite friendless in the market. The names of the beaten favourites, which reads like racing's hall of fame, must also warn the backer to proceed with caution here, and certainly not to take short odds for any horse.

An improving horse, especially a filly, would seem to hold the key. A contestant specifically laid out for the race is likely to hold an advantage over those that bear the scars of hard-fought previous races during the season. The international flavour of winners demands the backer be 'au fait' with foreign form, and in this regard, if successful, will most certainly be rewarded with a good-priced winner, as this is an area not familiar to most pundits. However, the Champion Stakes is a race that has held a number of surprises and the backer should bet with caution.

88	INDIAN SKIMMER	4	0900	H. Cecil	8–15 Fav.	5
87	TRIPTYCH	5	0900	P. Biancone (Fr.)	6–5 Fav	11
86	TRIPTYCH	4	0900	P. Biancone (Fr.)	4–1	11
85	PEBBLES	4	0900	C. Brittain	9–2	10
84	PALACE MUSIC	3	0810	P. Biancone (Fr.)	18–1	15
83	CORMORANT WOOD	3	0807	B. Hills	18–1	19
82	TIME CHARTER	3	0807	H. Candy	9–2 2nd Fav.	14
81	VAYRAAN	3	0810	F. Mathet (Fr.)	15–2 2nd Fav.	16
80	CAIRN ROUGE	3	0807	M. Cunningham (Ire.)	6–1	13
79	NORTHERN BABY	3	0810	F. Boutin (Fr.)	9–1	14
78	SWISS MAID	3	0807	P. Kellaway	9–1	10
77	FLYING WATER	4	0900	A. Penna (Fr.)	9–1	8
76	VITIGES	3	0811	P. Walwyn	22–1	19
75	ROSE BOWL	3	0807	R. Houghton	11–2	9

CESAREWITCH HANDICAP
0–115 Handicap   2m 2f   3 y.o. and upwards

The Cesarewitch Handicap is a race for 3-year-olds and older horses over the marathon stayers' distance of 2 miles 2 furlongs, and is staged on the Saturday, the third and final day of the three-day meeting at Newmarket in the middle of October. Like its counterpart the Cambridgeshire, the Cesarewitch is one of the oldest remaining handicaps (established 1839) and makes up the second leg of the popular Autumn Double (bets coupled on the two events).

It is a race across the wide expanse of Newmarket Heath, encompassing parts of the two courses, the start being way down on the part shared with the July course with horses racing for a straight mile before sweeping round right-handed on to the Rowley course proper, and racing up the daunting 10 furlong straight, where green turf will seem forever in front of them. It is a severe test of a horse's courage and stamina. There is no place to hide on this track and a horse without supreme fighting qualities or with any weakness is unlikely to last out the trip. The essence of deciding this race is a horse that can stay the distance yet have a 'turn of foot' in the final 2 furlongs to outspeed the mere dour one-paced plodders.

Having illustrated the nature of the Cesarewitch, the first element in deciding the winner is to determine a horse's staying qualities. In this respect ten winners had won, either during the current season or earlier, over 2 miles or more, basically confirming their proven stamina.

Over a long distance the next factor to consider is the weight carried. The longer the distance of a race, the more telling the weight burden becomes. Therefore it is not surprising to note that ten winners carried 8 st 6 lb or less and six of these below 8 st. Only four winners defied a penalty; JOHN CHERRY (1976) and ASSURED (1977) defied 6 lb penalties, whilst NOMADIC WAY (1988) and MOUNTAIN LODGE (1982) carried 4 lb extra.

Although weight is an important factor only one winner, SIR MICHAEL (1979), was apprentice ridden to claim the few

THE CESAREWITCH – The second leg of the Autumn double and last important handicap. A 2¼ mile marathon stretched out across Newmarket's unrelenting wide open courses.

SHANTALLAH (sheepskin noseband) and Brian Taylor quicken inside the final furlong after 2¼ miles to beat the game blinkered JOHN CHERRY (Lester Piggott) who was trying to concede 8 lb to this classy 3 y.o. in the 1975 Cesarewitch Handicap.

extra pounds. Yet he, like five other winners, surprisingly carried overweight. The trainers preferred to employ an experienced jockey with a good judgement of pace, plus the strength to ride out the horse in a finish, where in six races the winning margin was three-quarters of a length or less.

The weight factor has certainly defeated many good horses. Seven beaten favourites, including joint favourite ZERO WATT (1988) and BUCKLEY (1987), both carried 9 st 10 lb (a Group race winner), VALUABLE WITNESS (1984), 9 st, NEARLY A HAND (1979), 9 st 5 lb, and JOHN CHERRY (1975), 9 st 4 lb, all carried 8 st 7 lb or above, whilst two others were beaten by penalties.

Winners have come from all age groups, 3-year-olds (six wins), 4- and 5-year-olds (four wins apiece), but the strength and endurance necessary to win are more likely to be found among the more mature and developed older horses. Two of the winning 3-year-olds were quite exceptional. CENTURION (1978) defied 9 st 8 lb to win, and SHANTALLAH (1975), who had run in the

Irish St Leger as its previous race, were well above the average winner.

The Cesarewitch, as a competitive staying handicap has attracted 11 to 30 runners, with usually more than 20 horses in the race, and covering the full range of the handicap. The winners, with the exception of SHANTALLAH (1975) (who had won Chester's Chester Vase, Group III, 1½ miles, earlier in the season on the flat) turned out to be no better than handicappers. However, TOM SHARP (1984), BAJAN SUNSHINE (1983) and of course JOHN CHERRY (1976) developed into very useful National Hunt performers.

Winning form at certain times has been essential to win the Cesarewitch with nine winners winning their previous race, yet from 1984 all the winners were unplaced in their previous races.

A number of races have held an influence on the outcome of this marathon Handicap. The Gordon Carter Handicap, over 2 miles at Ascot, 23 days earlier, has been the previous race of two winners, PRIVATE AUDITION (1987) and ORANGE HILL (1986), both of whom were unplaced and reversed form with rivals over this longer distance. Negatively, four horses, promoted to favourite after winning, or finishing second at Ascot, were beaten on Newmarket's open heath. Haydock's Tom Caxton Homebrew Daily Mirror Apprentice Championship Handicap over 2 miles 28 yards, 14 days earlier, has provided two winners, KAYUDEE (1985) and TOM SHARP (1984), both of whom were unplaced and having only their second race of the season, and simply being brought to fitness for their Cesarewitch victory. Ayr's September Festival meeting also had two races that produced the Cesarewitch winner: the Eglington and Winter Memorial Handicap over 2 miles 1 furlong 90 yards, 22–31 days earlier, saw MOUNTAIN LODGE (1982) and ASSURED (1977) complete the double: whilst the Sam Hall Stakes, over 1 mile 7 furlongs, 29 days earlier, also provided two winners, HALSBURY (1981) and CENTURION (1978) who were also to complete the double.

Recent form has been a common feature, with all but three winners having run within the past 29 days, nine of these within the past 28 days.

The trainers who have won the Cesarewitch have varied as much as the horses, with names normally on the winners' scroll of group races, like J. Tree (the only trainer with more than one victory), J. Dunlop, P. Walwyn, I. Balding and the Wragg stable, alongside the lesser known stables gaining their moment of public glory.

The market has been a limited source of information for pinpointing the winner. Three favourites and four 2nd favourites were successful, counteracted by one 3rd favourite and six outsiders whose price ranged from 10–1 to 50–1. Whilst winning outsiders with prior winning form were understandable, and although at good prices were far from friendless in the market, some recent winners at 20–1, 40–1 and 50–1 were much less comprehensible and had the bookmakers with any commitments from the first leg of the Autumn Double laughing with glee.

The Cesarewitch, which really is the final great handicap of the season (although the November Handicap at Doncaster has still to be run), is always an intriguing affair. It must always bring out a sense of admiration for the winner who triumphs over this testing course and distance. Results, while not easy to predict, have usually remained within the bounds of reason and the backer wishing to tilt at the ring should follow a horse with recent winning form, that is proven at a staying distance, and not burdened with too much weight.

88	NOMADIC WAY	3	0709	B. Hills	6–1 Jt Fav.	24
87	PRIVATE AUDITION	5	0709	M. Tompkins	50–1	28
86	ORANGE HILL	4	0709	J. Tree	20–1	25
85	KAYUDEE	5	0801	J. Fitzgerald	7–1 2nd Fav.	21
84	TOM SHARP	4	0705	W. Wharton	40–1	26
83	BAJAN SUNSHINE	4	0808	R. Simpson	7–1 Jt Fav.	28
82	MOUNTAIN LODGE	3	0710	J. Dunlop	9–1 2nd Fav.	28
81	HALSBURY	3	0804	P. Walwyn	14–1	30
80	POPSI'S JOY	5	0806	M. Haynes	10–1 2nd Fav.	27
79	SIR MICHAEL	3	0708	G. Huffer	10–1	11
78	CENTURION	3	0908	I. Balding	9–2 Fav.	17
77	ASSURED	4	0804	H. Candy	10–1	11
76	JOHN CHERRY	5	0913	J. Tree	13–2 2nd Fav.	14
75	SHANTALLAH	3	0810	H. Wragg	7–1	17

WILLIAM HILL FUTURITY STAKES

(Formerly Observer Gold Cup, 1965–75; Timeform Gold Cup, 1962–64)
Group I   1m   2 y.o.   entire colts and fillies
Level weights and sex allowance

The William Hill Futurity Stakes is a Group I race, for 2-year-old entire colts and fillies only, over a distance of 1 mile, and is staged on the round course at Doncaster on the Saturday of the two-day meeting at the end of October. It is the final Group race of the season for the 2-year-old generation of horses and therefore the last opportunity for a juvenile to establish itself as a potentially top-class stayer of the future. It is a race with a short history, having been founded only in 1962 (when it was the Timeform Gold Cup) and in recent seasons has not attracted quite the quality of performer and winners it did in its initial years. Consequently it has lost its edge in being considered a consistent guide to the future.

REFERENCE POINT (1986) was a noted exception, later capturing two Classics the following season, plus the King George VI and Queen Elizabeth Stakes. However, other winners have hardly lived up to the standard set by RIBOCCO (1966), VAGUELY NOBLE (1967) and HIGH TOP (1971) who were to win Group I prizes as 3-year-olds. BELDALE FLUTTER (1980) has been the only other winner later to capture a European Group I prize, when winning the International Stakes (formerly the Benson and Hedges Gold Cup).

Other winners of the Futurity Stakes have either proved of no account as 3-year-olds or were in the instances of LANFRANCO (1984) and HELLO GORGEOUS (1979) merely able to capture a Group II prize as 3-year-olds, whilst COUNT PAHLEN (1981) won a Group III race. The two Guy Harwood trained winners were eventually shipped off to the United States, the land of their birth, where they were able to recapture their winning ways, although BAKHAROF (1985) won a Group II race as 3-year-old and ALPHABATIM (1983) won a Group III Classic trial.

It has been, occasionally, beaten horses who have subsequently

THE WILLIAM HILL FUTURITY – The final group race of the season which, it is hoped, will acclaim a future staying champion amongst the juveniles.

Henry Cecil trained TAKE YOUR PLACE (G. Dettori, hooped body) holds the challenge of EARTH SPIRIT (Yves St. Martin) to win the 1975 Futurity. Like other winners this was its crowning glory rather than a stepping stone to further heights.

rescued the William Hill Futurity Stakes' reputation as a race for top-class horses of the future. SALSE (1987) as a 3-year-old won the Prix de la Foret Longchamp (Group I) 7 furlongs, plus four other group races. MENDEZ (1983) as a 3-year-old won the Prix du Moulin du Longchamp (Group I) 1 mile, RECITATION (1980) won the French Two Thousand Guineas (Group I) 1 mile, the legendary SHERGAR (1980) was actually beaten here as a 2-year-old, and suffered his only other defeat in the St Leger on the Town Moor, after winning the English and Irish Derbys and King George VI and Queen Elizabeth Stakes. JULIO MARINER (1977) won the following season's St Leger, HAWAIIAN SOUND (1977) won the International Stakes after finishing second in the Derby, and ILE DE BOURBON (1977) won the King George VI and Queen Elizabeth Stakes.

The Futurity has attracted variable sized fields of 6 to 13, with an average of 9 runners, including a smattering of French- or Irish-trained horses to give this final Group race an international flavour. The winners divide into seven which had raced in Group company before, and seven which had not. This gives rise to questioning the real value of the Futurity's Group I status, as so many winners were easily able to make a smooth transition to this highest grade. Nine winners won their previous race, and as seven of these were horses that had never previously run in Group race company, this was essential. Therefore many winners have taken varied paths before contesting the Futurity.

Only one race has a constant influence. The Royal Lodge Stakes (Group II) over 1 mile, at Ascot, 28 days earlier, has provided four winners. DUNBEATH (1982) and HELLO GORGEOUS (1979) completed the double, whilst EMMSON (1987) and BELDALE FLUT-TER (1980) both finished fourth there and reversed form with an Ascot rival. Negatively, ROBELLINO (1980) and LYPHARDS WISH (1978) were both promoted to favourite after finishing first and third respectively in the Royal Lodge Stakes, only to be beaten in the Futurity.

A horse will need to see out every yard of this mile distance on this testing galloping course at Doncaster, which for this autumn contest has had going that has varied from Firm to Soft. In the latter instance this places a great emphasis on stamina. It is therefore not surprising to find that thirteen winners had won previously over 7 furlongs or 1 mile and were therefore almost proven to stay the trip.

Eleven winners had run within the past 28 days, and only three of the winners (all prepared by that master handler H. Cecil, which included LANFRANCO (1984) who had not run for 84 days, which is normally a seriously long absence for a 2-year-old) had less than quite recent form.

The Futurity Stakes, as would be expected for a Group I prize, is only won by the very top trainers. H. Cecil (five wins) heads the list from G. Harwood and P. Walwyn (two wins each). Yet it should be noted that Henry Cecil has also provided four beaten favourites. Two French-trained horses have been promoted to favourite and beaten, suggesting that an air of caution should be applied to French runners.

The market has been very inconclusive in pinpointing the winner. Three favourites and three 2nd favourites have won, whilst four 3rd favourites and three outsiders have also been successful, without there being really too many shock results. However, this has offered no consistent guidance and the backer might do well to forget the market. REFERENCE POINT (1986) was considered Henry Cecil's second string on the day and started as third favourite.

It is often a tricky race, with horses quite frequently successfully bridging the gap between non-Group and a Group I race at the first time of asking. Recent form and proof of a 2-year-old seeing out the mile are the only consistent pointers. Also, non-Group horses need to have won their previous race, but prior Group race performers are sometimes now subject to changes in form, reflecting the inconclusive nature of this race.

88	AL HAREB	2	0900	N. Graham	10–3 2nd Fav.	8
87	EMMSON	2	0900	W. Hern	7–1	6
86	REFERENCE POINT	2	0900	H. Cecil	4–1	10
85	BAKHAROF	2	0900	G. Harwood	2–1 Fav.	9
84	LANFRANCO	2	0900	H. Cecil	10–9	10
83	ALPHABATIM	2	0900	G. Harwood	9–2 2nd Fav.	9
82	DUNBEATH	2	0900	H. Cecil	4–7 Fav.	8
81	COUNT PAHLEN	2	0900	B. Hobbs	25–1	13
80	BELDALE FLUTTER	2	0900	M. Jarvis	14–1	7
79	HELLO GORGEOUS	2	0900	H. Cecil	11–8 Fav.	7
78	SANDY CREEK	2	0900	C. Collins (Ire.)	15–1	11
77	DACTYLOGRAPHER	2	0900	P. Walwyn	10–3 2nd Fav.	12
76	SPORTING YANKEE	2	0900	P. Walwyn	9–2	6
75	TAKE YOUR PLACE	2	0900	H. Cecil	4–1 2nd Fav.	11

WILLIAM HILL NOVEMBER HANDICAP

0–115 Handicap   1½m   3 y.o. and upwards

The William Hill November Handicap is a race for 3-year-olds and upwards rated 0–115 in the Handicap over a distance of 1½ miles and is staged on the final Saturday of the Flat racing season at Doncaster in early November. The Flat racing season therefore ends with a fixture in the same setting where it had opened some eight months previously, on the Town Moor course at Doncaster. The present William Hill November Handicap has replaced the famous old Manchester November Handicap, which was transferred to this Yorkshire course on the closure of Manchester's racecourse.

The November Handicap provides a very competitive stayers' handicap to sign off the season, attracting 9 to 25 runners, with an average of 18, all of whom will be seeking a valuable prize before being confined to winter quarters (unless competing as a dual-purpose horse in a National Hunt campaign). It is therefore never an easy race to win and is correspondingly quite a difficult race to predict the outcome.

It is a handicap and has been won by horses of basically handicap class. The best winners have been that very tough and consistent horse LA FONTAINE (1981), plus SWINGIT GUNNER (1987), ASIR (1983) and PATH OF PEACE (1980) who became very talented hurdlers, and one of the two winning fillies of this period GALE BRIDGE (1976).

As the race belongs in the domain of basically handicap-class horses it has been won by horses also not too harshly treated by the handicapper. Only one winner DOUBLE SHUFFLE (1982) who dead-heated, carried 9 st, and all the other winners carried weight below this prohibitive mark. Eleven winners carried 8 st 7 lb or less, and only two horses, SWINGIT GUNNER (1987) and MORSE CODE (1979) were able to defy a 4 lb penalty for winning their previous race. Also five horses promoted to favourite but carrying a penalty were beaten. These examples show the role that weight has played in this end-of-season contest.

Doncaster's wide galloping track, with its flat 4½ furlong

run-in from the turn into the straight, can be a severe test, especially at this time of year when the going gets on the softish side. Seven meetings had the going ranging from Good to Soft, to Heavy. It is in these conditions particularly that weight can become a most awesome burden.

The November Handicap is most suited to the improving horse whom the Handicapper even at this last moment in the season still has not quite got to grips with. Therefore it is the 3-year-olds, the youngest generation and those subject to most improvement, which have the call over the rest, winning eight times; 4-year-olds won five times, 5-year-olds and 6-year-olds once each (fifteen winners of thirteen races because of a dead heat). Yet the 6-year-old SWINGIT GUNNER most aptly fitted the category of an improving horse, still being a maiden on the flat at the start of his 6-year-old season, and not winning his first race until August 8th, some three months before, yet winning twice more since! However, the official Handicapper usually has a firm grip on the older horses, who by this stage of their careers are seldom able to conjure any sudden improvement.

Winning the previous race is definitely not a prerequisite for success in the November Handicap, with only two winners having also won their prior race. However, every winner had won at least one race during the season, except for YOUNG BENZ (1988) and the Irish-trained winner ONWARD TAROO (1975). EASTERN SPRING (1978) won four races, and six other horses won three races each.

No previous race has had more than a fleeting influence on producing the winner, although only two winners were unplaced in their prior race – the very tough LA FONTAINE (1981), who had 19 prior races during the season, and TURKOMAN (1982), the other horse who dead-heated. Between the extremes of 19 previous races of LA FONTAINE and only two of ASIR (1983) sit the other winners, with no pattern emerging. Eight had eight or more previous races and seven had six or less.

Similarly, there is a divergence in the time since winners last ran. Three ran within the past 7 days whilst two had not run for 61 days or more. The winner of the November Handicap is a fine balance between a fresh yet fit horse, and one razor-sharp from racing but who might have just gone over the top. The race invariably develops into a slogging finish over the last couple of furlongs.

Although not considered the greatest prize in racing, the November Handicap is regularly won by the recognised top trainers, many of whom must enjoy the challenge of this very competitive prize. Only J. Dunlop (two wins), who has made the long journey from Arundel in Sussex, has more than one success in the race, but most of his major rivals have also won.

The market has been practically of no help whatever in finding the winner. Only one favourite and two 2nd favourites have been successful, whilst three 3rd favourites and nine outsiders have won.

Coming at the end of a long season the William Hill November Handicap has served as a good friend to the bookmakers. It is a typical handicap race in that weight will be a very telling factor among horses below top class, yet it is also a race where a horse will need the added sparkle of an extra turn of foot inside the final furlong to win rather than being a one-paced stayer. A challenger nearly always emerges in the closing stages out of the pack to defeat a horse with such limitations.

The backer will need to be most skilful or very lucky to come out winning here. Therefore the prudent move will be to turn attention to the National Hunt season which now is about to gain momentum.

88	YOUNG BENZ	4	0804	M. H. Easterby	12–1		22
87	SWINGIT GUNNER	6	0811	C. Tinkler	9–1		25
86	BEIJING	3	0804	P. Cole	16–1		25
85	BOLD REX	3	0807	J. Dunlop	20–1		24
84	ABU KADRU	3	0812	M. Stoute	25–1		23
83	ASIR	3	0807	G. Harwood	10–1 2nd Fav.		25
82	DOUBLE SHUFFLE*	3	0900	G. Pritchard-Gordon	12–1		17
	TURKOMAN*	3	0807	D. Sasse	20–1		17
81	LA FONTAINE	4	0807	C. Brittain	16–1		20
80	PATH OF PEACE	4	0805	C. Thornton	14–1		22
79	MORSE CODE	4	0803	J. Dunlop	11–2 Fav.		14
78	EASTERN SPRING	4	0710	L. Cumani	17–2		21
77	SAILCLOTH	3	0707	W. Hastings-Bass	13–2 2nd Fav.		20
76	GALE BRIDGE	3	0812	H. R. Price	10–1		14
75	ONWARD TAROO	5	0805	P. Prendergast (Ire.)	5–1		9

*Dead heat

INDEX

The numerals in **bold** type refer to main entries
The numerals in *italic* type refer to picture captions